GW00801641

THE LEFT IN FRANCE

THE LEFT IN FRANCE

Neill Nugent
Senior Lecturer in Politics at Manchester Polytechnic

and

David Lowe
Member of the cabinet of Pieter Dankert,
President of the European Parliament

MACMILLAN PRESS
LONDON

© Neill Nugent and David Lowe 1982

All rights reserved. No part of this publication may be
reproduced or transmitted, in any form or by any means,
without permission

First edition 1982
Reprinted 1983

Published by
THE MACMILLAN PRESS LTD
London and Basingstoke
Companies and representatives
throughout the world

ISBN 0 333 24135 5 (hardcover)
0 333 35445 1 (paperback)

Printed in Hong Kong

Contents

Preface   vii

Acknowledgements   ix

List of Abbreviations   x

PART I   *THE HISTORICAL INHERITANCE*

1   What is the Left?   3

2   The Development of the Modern Political Parties of the
    Left   16

PART II   *THE PARTIES OF THE LEFT*

3   The Socialist Party   47

4   The Communist Party   94

5   The Left in the Fifth Republic: the Struggle for Unity   147

6   The Alternative Left   179

PART III   *THE INFLUENCE OF THE LEFT*

7   The Left in the Political System   195

8   The Left at Local Level   199

9   The Trade Unions and the Left   212

Postscript: The Left and the Assumption of Power   236

Appendixes

1   Parliamentary Election Results in the Fifth Republic,

    1958-78   252

2 Presidential Election Results in the Fifth Republic   253
3 European Election Results 1979   254
4 Parliamentary Election Results, June 1981   254
5 The Background of Voters in March 1978   255
6 Extracts from Declaration Made by PS
   and PCF, 23 June 1981   256

Notes and References   258
Select Bibliography   270
Index   272

Preface

After being in permanent opposition since the Fifth Republic was established in 1958 the French Left returned to office in 1981. Moreover it did so in a spectacular manner. François Mitterrand became, in May, the first candidate of the Left ever to be elected to the presidency by universal suffrage. In June, in the legislative elections which Mitterrand called, the Socialists won an overall parliamentary majority for the first time in their history. The Left as a whole gained more parliamentary seats than it had won even at the times of the Popular Front or the Liberation. The elections of 1981 were, in short, truly historic.

The major purpose of our book is to provide a comprehensive study of the Left in France. The book falls into three parts. In the first we define and discuss the historical inheritance of the contemporary Left. In the second the political parties of the modern Left are analysed. Finally, in the third part we show that despite its long absence from national office the Left in the Fifth Republic has nonetheless exercised considerable influence in modern France. Even now that it is in government the power of the Left at local level and in the trade union movement should not be overlooked.

It should be explained that this book was initially completed in mid-1980. Proofs arrived, inconveniently for us, shortly after Mitterrand's election. After discussions with Macmillan Press it was agreed to update the text where that seemed necessary and to add an extensive Postscript which would look in some detail at the circumstances of the 1981 upheaval. These two tasks obviously necessitated considerable changes being made to the proofs and we would particularly like to thank Tim Farmiloe and Tim Fox of Macmillan for enabling us to make them.

Many officials and representatives of Left-wing parties and groups assisted us in our research and to them we give our thanks. The unsung heroes of academic research – the librarians – have, as always, played their part and to them we also owe many debts. Neill Nugent would like to thank the Nuffield Foundation (Small Grants Scheme) for providing financial assistance to visit France and David Lowe thanks the Politics Department of Lancaster University for giving similar help. For reading and offering valuable comments on drafts of the manuscript we are grateful to John Frears, Peter Marsh and Vincent Wright. Finally our thanks go to Maureen Nugent for typing and retyping the manuscript.

July 1981   NEILL NUGENT
                                                DAVID LOWE

Acknowledgements

The author and publishers wish to thank the following who have kindly given permission for the use of copyright material:

Presses de la Fondation Nationale des Sciences Politiques for two charts from *Revue Française de Science Politique,* no. 5, October 1978, and no. 6, December 1978;

C. Hurst and Co. (Publishers) for the table from J. R. Frears and J. L. Parodi, *War Will Not Take Place;*

Le Nouvel Observateur for the chart from their issue of 23 April 1978;

Vincent Wright for the table from his book *The Government and Politics of France.*

Every effort has been made to trace all the copyright holders but if any have been inadvertently overlooked the publishers will be pleased to make the necessary arrangement at the first opportunity.

List of Abbreviations

ANECR	Association nationale des élus communistes et républicaines
BCEN	Banque commerciale pour l'Europe du Nord
CD	Centre Démocrate
CDP	Centre Dèmocratie et Progrès
CERES	Centre d'Etudes de Recherches et d'Education Socialiste
CFDT	Confédération Française Démocratique du Travail
CFTC	Confédération Française des Travailleurs Chrétiens
CGC	Confédération Générale des Cadres
CGT	Confederation Générale du Travail
CGTU	Confédération Générale du Travail Unitaire
CIR	Convention des Institutions Républicaines
EEC	European Economic Community
FA	Front Autogestionnaire
FEN	Fédération de l'Education Nationale
FGDS	Fédération de la Gauche Démocrate et Socialiste
FNESR	Fédération nationale des élus socialistes et républicaines
FO	Force Ouvrière
GEARS	Groupe d'Etude et d'Action Radical-Socialiste
IFOP	Institut Français d'Opinion Publique
ISER	Institut Socialiste d'Etudes et de Recherche
JCR	Jeunesse Communiste Révolutionnaire
LCR	Ligue Communiste Révolutionnaire
LO	Lutte Ouvrière
MJCF	Mouvement de la jeunesse communiste de France
MRG	Mouvement des Radicaux de Gauche
MRP	Mouvement Républicain Populaire
PCE	Partido Communista de España
PCF	Parti Communiste Français
PCI	Partito Communista Italiano
PCMLF	Parti Communiste Marxiste-Léniniste de France
PCR	Parti Communiste Révolutionnaire (Marxiste-Léniniste)
PDM	Progrès et Démocratie Moderne

PS	Parti Socialiste
PSA	Parti Socialiste Autonome
PSU	Parti Socialiste Unifié
RFSP	Revue Française de Science Politique
RI	Républicains Indépendants
RPR	Rassemblement pour la Republique
SFIO	Section Française de l'Internationale Ouvrière
SMC	State Monopoly Capitalism
SPD	Sozialdemokratische Partei Deutschlands
UCRG	Union des Clubs pour le Renouveau de la Gauche
UDF	Union pour la Démocratie Française
UDSR	Union Démocratique et Socialiste de la Résistance
UEC	Union des Etudiants Communistes
UGCS	Union des Groupes et Clubs Socialistes
UGS	Union de la Gauche Socialiste
UGSD	Union de la Gauche Socialiste et Démocratique
UJCML	Union des Jeunesses Communistes Marxistes-Léninistes
UNEF	Union Nationale des Etudiants Français
UNR	Union pour la Nouvelle République

Part I The Historical Inheritance

1 What is the Left?

HISTORICAL PERSPECTIVES

French political history since 1789 is, at first sight, highly complex, with upheaval and lack of continuity its most prominent features.

The very constitutional framework itself has been a constant source of controversy. Since the Revolution of 1789 there have been three monarchical systems, two Empires, five Republics and the Vichy State. Of these only one, the Third Republic, has (to date) lasted for more than twenty-five years. As a result constitutions have traditionally been seen, not as the fundamental framework of the political system, but as devices and weapons, to be used, or changed, by political forces as and when circumstances have dictated. Even today it is uncertain whether the constitutional arrangements can survive the ultimate test of a clash between President and Parliament.

On the governmental level, too, instability has been a central characteristic. Throughout the eighty-two years of the Third and Fourth Republics governments found it extremely difficult to maintain the confidence of Parliament. From the end of the First World War in particular the occupancy of office became highly precarious and the average turnover of governments fell to no more than six months. During the brief twelve-year life span of the Fourth Republic alone (1946-58) there were no fewer than seventeen changes of Prime Minister (as compared with only three in Britain).

Political institutions are not alone in having fallen victim to this highly volatile state of affairs. Political forces, too, have displayed chronic upheaval and change, as parties, movements and groups have formed, disbanded, merged, divided and been resurrected in an almost bewildering series of developments. The lack of continuity has been especially apparent at the parliamentary level where, since democracy began to establish itself in the 1870s, there have usually been at least six parties with a substantial representation. Comparison of any two periods more than twenty years apart reveals major transformations to have taken place.

3

Despite this apparent flux most historians have nonetheless sought to identify some measure of permanence. Behind the transience and immediacy of particular forces, movements and events they have looked for an ordered development of some kind. In the extreme the whole picture of change has been queried. With the suggestion that the 'political game' has rarely had repercussions beyond the political elites, it has been claimed that continuity is the true feature of French history since 1789. Uninterrupted organisational centralism, constant state intervention, no major disruption in the distribution of socio-economic resources, the unchanging nature of élites and the Left only occasionally in power, are all presented as supporting evidence.

But whilst few would deny that this view has its merits, most historians and political analysts would see it as overstating its case. They would argue that the nature of politics has changed in many important respects as the economic, social and international environments in which politics is conducted have developed and been transformed. There are many obvious examples of such political change. The role of the state has been consolidated and its responsibilities have increased through ever-expanding bureaucratic channels. The Republic has been established. The influence and status of the Church has been reduced. There is a much wider and more formal participation in political life as the franchise has been extended and as initially tentative steps towards organisation have been confirmed.

To explain this mixture of permanence and change and the frequent recurrence of familiar themes in the political debate various explanatory concepts have been developed. Many of these have centred around an interpretation of French history as an evolving competition between streams of political thought and consciousness. A largely immobile social structure, until the Second World War at least, is seen as having provided an ideal basis for the propagation and perpetuation of customs, attitudes and beliefs which could survive, albeit through different institutional manifestations. Though only vaguely and tenuously held, especially by the masses, such thoughts, attitudes and emotions have, it is argued, provided ways of perceiving, comprehending and responding to the political world. Continuous, but unfolding and developing, they have endured over time.

So, 'traditions' have been identified and described. Traditions of revolution and reaction, for example; or, the most frequently used typology, traditions of monarchism/traditionalism, republicanism, and bonapartism. In a similar way 'political families' such as liberalism, socialism and radicalism have been located. More elusively the idea of 'political temperaments' has been developed, in particular by electoral geographers who have pointed to a consistency over time in voting patterns in many areas of France. Thus François Goguel, in a classic study, suggested that the essential conflict in French politics was between two such temperaments: that of 'movement' and that of 'established order'.[1]

Associated with this type of classification and categorisation is the most common 'thematic' approach of all, which is to see the many disparate elements of political life as being basically divided between Left and Right. To these is often added the convenient Centre.

At the crudest level a strictly dualist view of events is presented, with doubters being referred to the periodic clearing of the Centre ground and the movement to the poles of Left and Right when crises have occurred. Among the most frequently cited examples are the Revolution of 1848, the Siege and Commune of 1870-1, the Dreyfus Affair at the turn of the century, and the threat of fascism in the mid 1930s. It is more usual, however, particularly of late, as the fluidity and complexity of French history has come to be more fully appreciated, for qualifications to be inserted into the discussion. These more sophisticated approaches lay greater emphases on the innumerable shades and nuances between the two poles. So, studies have shown wide bodies of popular opinion to have been interested simply in preserving the status quo. As a result the supposed polarisation in crises has been brought into question. Whilst not everyone would go as far as Douglas Johnson, he undoubtedly reflects much of modern historiography when he states, 'one is led to the conclusion that the motor of French political life is not so much an oscillation between Left and Right, as a small, almost insignificant movement between Left-centre and Right-centre'.[2]

But whichever view is accepted, the 'crude' or the 'sophisticated', the terms Left and Right are in France, as elsewhere, part of the universal language of history and politics. They provide a convenient shorthand for the categorisation and identification of ideologies, groups and individuals. They allow seemingly complex phenomena to be slotted into a readily available explanatory framework. In so doing, however, they create the risk that reality will be distorted in the interests of simplicity. 'Left', 'Right' and 'Centre', as with any general classificatory system, can hide as much as they reveal. When used loosely and out of context, they can even serve as barriers to clarification and understanding.

The problem of accurately identifying what is 'Left' and what is 'Right' may be illustrated by brief reference to three different periods of modern French history.

In the years before the First World War the Left was generally understood to be made up of three principal elements:

(1) *Radicals.* Formally constituted into a political party in 1901, though on a very decentralised basis, the Radicals were characterised principally by their commitment to the Republican form of government, their virulent anti-clericalism, and their defence of private property and public order.

(2) *Socialists.* The united Socialist Party which was founded in 1905, the *Section Française de l'Internationale Ouvrière* (SFIO), although Republican and anti-clerical, sought in addition a programme of far-reaching social reforms which were totally alien to Radicalism. Furthermore, the Party's founding Charter stated that, whilst the SFIO would press for immediate reforms to improve the condition of the working class, 'It is not a party of reform, but a party of class struggle and of revolution'.

(3) *Revolutionary Syndicalists.* Beyond the parties revolutionary syndicalism was a potent force in the trade union movement, especially in the largest union, the *Confédération Générale du Travail* (CGT). It displayed a deep antagonism to 'the bourgeois State' and all those, socialists included, who sought to change it from within. At the heart of its belief system lay a commitment to direct action as the mechanism to transform the political, social and economic order.

In the 1950s the Left again was thought to consist of three main forces:

(1) *Radicals.* The mixture was similar to fifty years earlier except that the claim to be 'of the Left' was now much more dubious. On the many occasions the Party had participated in office it had shown itself to be financially, economically and socially conservative. More than ever, to quote the frequently made observation, Radicals had their 'hearts on the Left and their pocket books on the Right'.

(2) *Socialists.* Still divided from Radicalism on social and economic questions the SFIO was increasingly a party of contradictions. It continued to proclaim itself Marxist – attempts to

get rid of this 'weighty baggage' failed in 1946 – yet it was manifestly reformist in practice. Increasingly situating itself in relation to other parties, rather than to any policy direction, much of its time was taken up ensuring that the third element of the Left was isolated and excluded from power.

(3) *Communists.* The PCF was rigidly Stalinist and slavishly pro-Soviet. Its organisation, ideology and strategy all reflected a Moscow-directed view of the world that made it quite unlike any other French party. The SFIO leader, Guy Mollet, described it as 'not to the Left but to the East' of the Socialists, and there were many in the 1950s who shared this view.

Today, at the beginning of the 1980s, there are still three main strands but once again they have changed in nature:

(1) *Socialists.* The *Parti Socialiste* (PS), which was constructed on the base of the old SFIO between 1969-71, still retains some of the characteristics of its predecessor but it has also introduced new themes and strains into reformist socialism. Professions of faith to Marx, for example, are still heard but these are less pronounced and are tempered by the attractions of new concepts and ideas. Because the Party has continued the old SFIO habit of harbouring seemingly contradictory currents, internal ideological debate remains a constant feature. Since the mid-1970s the main division has increasingly been between those (to put it at its simplest) who place their faith in the benefits of direct state intervention and those who seek to solve France's problems by less statist and more individualist/co-operativist policies.

(2) *Communists.* From the early 1960s a slow 'liberalisation' began to take place in the ideology and strategy of the PCF. By the mid-1970s this hitherto most Stalinist of parties was, though with reservations, openly attaching itself to *'la voie démocratique'*. After 1977-8, however, there was a reversal of this policy, signified by virulent attacks on the PS and strong support for the USSR. It is apparent that the PCF remains a highly distinct party, both in its general political orientation and in its still rigidly hierarchical, some would say Stalinist, organisational structure.

(3) *The 'Alternative' Left.* Difficult to generalise about because of its diverse ideological elements, the 'Alternative' Left owes much to

the upheavals of May 1968 which boosted both its morale and its support. Its philosophical foundations are many and disparate, though the roots lie in what can loosely be described as 'dissident' marxism, and in some cases, freudian psychology. From Situationists to Stalinists and from Trotskyists to Maoists the extreme Left has grown to the extent that it is now a significant factor in the political calculations of its much larger Left-wing relations.

Because such lack of unity is observable at virtually every period of modern French history the very usefulness of the term 'Left' and, by implication 'Right', is called into question. Should the terms, as has frequently been suggested, be dispensed with altogether? This seems to be impractical given their constant use by historians, political scientists, commentators and political actors alike. In any case it is undesirable, since it would be to assume that indeed they are of little use. Whilst this may be true of countries which display consensus politics, it is hardly so of France where the political struggle over the last twenty years or so has *increasingly* bi-polarised: between a divided Left and a divided Right.

It is also of interest and relevance to note that in France there appears to be a much greater self-perception of the Left-Right distinction than in, say, Britain, Germany or the United States. In a major study carried out between 1964 and 1966 almost 90 per cent of the electorate were able to identify a position for themselves on a given Left-Right spectrum:

Extreme Left	Left	Centre	Right	Extreme Right	Don't Know
16	19	31	17	7	10

Well over half the respondents therefore saw themselves as being on the Left or on the Right. This compares markedly with the Butler and Stokes study of Britain, carried out at much the same time. When they asked their respondents if they ever thought of themselves as personally being to the Left, Centre or Right in politics only 25 per cent said they did so.[3] The French study also came up with a greater congruence between self-identity in Left-Right terms and 'consistency' in political beliefs.

It is reasonable, therefore, to persist with the terms Left and Right. But in so doing two sets of questions must be answered.

IDENTIFICATION OF THE LEFT

The first of these is, what criteria, if any, justify the use of the label 'Left' to describe such diverse elements as those noted above? Does not the very use of a common term for such heterogeneous groups and ideas distort reality? Does not 'Left' simply become an artificial construct, imposed by historians to facilitate their explanatory task?

It is, after all, difficult to extract *any* programmatic or ideological unifying elements from the periods outlined above. The task becomes even more problematical when all of contemporary French history is examined. Many of the supposed perennial and distinctive features of the Left prove to be no such thing at all. They may *usually* have been associated with the Left, but not always and not always exclusively. Let us consider the most obvious examples:

Pacifism and anti-militarism. It was the Left which was the staunchest advocate of 'revolutionary wars' in the 1790s; it was the Left who wished to continue the war with Germany in 1871; and it was the Left, at least until the late 1880s, who most openly thirsted for *revanche*. This position was reversed around the turn of the century but it did not prevent most of the Left from quickly rallying to the nation's cause in 1914 and 1939, or there being a strongly pacifist Right in the 1930s.

Internationalism. In spite of the attractions of 'international brotherhood' or the Marxist dictum of 'workers of the world unite' it has been evident from revolutionary Jacobinism, through staunch republicanism to contemporary communism that certain elements of the Left have remained strongly nationalistic.

Anti-colonialism. It was during a period of republican dominance that the French Empire was extended and consolidated. Three-quarters of a century later, during the 1940s and 1950s, communists and socialists were equivocal in their attitudes towards decolonisation.

Anti-clericalism. Many of the 'liberal Right' were by no means sympathetic to the Church prior to 1848. Furthermore, there is a long tradition which goes back into the first half of the nineteenth century of Christian Democracy and Christian Socialism. In any event, since the church-school question was effectively settled in 1959, clericalism has progressively declined as a source of political division.

Democracy and popular sovereignty. These closely related concepts have been much valued by the Left but their meaning has been interpreted in very different ways. Liberal democrats, syndicalists and communists, for example, have all articulated distinct ideas as to where power should lie, how it should be exercised, and what constitutes genuine participation and democratic control. Furthermore, for Bonapartists and Gaullists popular sovereignty has been a strong belief.

Liberty and Freedom. Again, these are concepts which none on the Left have denied, but that has not prevented authoritarians from competing with individualists or state interventionists with anarchists. For years the PCF drew a sharp distinction between 'bourgeois' liberty and 'true' liberty, the latter being possible only via fundamental economic reforms. Even today the PCF, and even more so the extreme Left, have a view which differs markedly from that of most Social Democrats. They, in their turn, talk of 'freedom' and 'liberty' in a way which is often barely distinguishable from much of the Centre-Right.

Equality. This is the closest to a clearly distinguishing characteristic but again it is not wholly satisfactory. Like the other possible criteria it has been interpreted in different ways. For early liberals it meant a limited and circumscribed civil equality; for mid-nineteenth-century republicans it meant the political equality of one man one vote; for twentieth-century communists it has meant a full-blooded social and economic equality. Moreover, there have been periods when the egalitarianism of the Centre-Left has been barely distinguishable from that of the Centre-Right. For example, in the latter part of the Third Republic, it is difficult to identify any hard and fast differences on the question of equality between the Radicals and the parties immediately to their Right. Had the Radicals therefore, it might be argued, not already made the transition to the Right? In many important policy senses they clearly had, but they were still generally *seen* as being part of the Left, they still preferred to contest elections as part of the Left, and they still periodically entered governments which were balanced to the Left.

In addition to this lack of unambiguous criteria there are other factors which make a definitive historical identification of the Left difficult.

Firstly, the terms Left and Right were themselves only irregularly used until the latter part of the nineteenth century. This is despite the fact that they actually originated in France: during the Revolution when Deputies in the Assembly seated themselves to the right or left of the president according to their views on the powers that should be given to the monarch. Admittedly it was somewhat later – 1815 according to René Rémond – when the division between Left and Right was 'consciously understood',[4] but even then the labels were usually avoided. Well into the Third Republic many politicians still resisted being so categorised. They preferred to be seen simply as 'Moderates', 'Monarchists', or 'Republicans'. Moreover, even when the terms did generally begin to enter the language of politics often they were adopted more as a result of political and electoral calculation than as a consistent, let alone rigorous, standard of description. Around the turn of the century in particular many conservative groups embraced the 'Left' label because it was thought to be electorally advantageous. For similar reasons they scrambled to occupy the seats on the left in the Chamber.

Secondly, politics are in constant transition and over time the whole spectrum has moved to the Left in the sense that many erstwhile Left-wing causes and demands have been fulfilled, e.g. the establishment of the Republic, restrictions on the influence and power of the Church, and extensions in the social and economic responsibilities of the State. Accordingly, parties which at one time may have been on the Left have found themselves transformed to the Right as their goals have been achieved, as they have remained faithful to their original principles and as new challenges to the status quo have emerged. Zeldin cites a particularly graphic case in point: ' "Progressist" in 1885 meant advanced, but in 1898 it meant moderate and by 1906 it was positively right wing and even clerical'.[5]

Thirdly, parties and individuals may be 'Left' on one issue and 'Right' on another. The Radicals, as has already been noted, increasingly fell into this category. The early *Mouvement Républicain Populaire* (MRP) – the Christian Democratic Party formed in 1944 – could be said to qualify too since it was at one and the same time strongly pro-Catholic yet favourably disposed to progressive socio-economic reforms. Cleavages, whether they are issues, causes, loyalties or attitudes can thus cut across any attempted Left/Right distinction and seriously undermine its coherence. There are even important splits which, though they may be related to the Left/Right division electorally, are important in their own, non-ideological, right: the geographical loyalties and tensions of North/South, urban/rural, Paris/provinces.

A definitive identification of the Left is not therefore possible.

There are no issues or causes which have been its central and sole preserve though several, such as republicanism, anti-clericalism, egalitarianism, the championing of the exploited and the oppressed, have usually been part of its armour. Nor are there any general orientations or sentiments which can be indisputably attached to it. Whilst it may normally have represented 'progressive movement' or, as André Siegfried argued, *'l'esprit de 1789'*[6] or even, as David Caute suggests, 'popular sovereignty'[7] such descriptions are in themselves too vague and elusive to be of much practical value. They demand specification and in so doing they impose the requirement of qualification.

Themes and issues are not unwavering or timeless but are relative to particular eras. There can therefore be no one satisfactory definition of the Left. The common point, or points, of reference which justify the use of the label have constantly changed. The Left can only be what has traditionally been understood as the Left. Its defining characteristics can only be those attributed to it in the historical contexts in which political debate and struggle have been located.

LEFT OR LEFTS?

This brings us to our second question. Is it more accurate to speak of the French Left or the French Left*s*?

From what we have seen so far it would appear to be more logical and more consistent, though perhaps also more confusing, to talk of the Left*s*. Fundamental and bitter divisions between those political elements which have been seen as making up the Left have been the norm rather than the exception. If reference simply is made to the present day there are, as we have seen, *at least* three quite different Left tendencies.[8] They may be very tentatively bracketed together – around their common opposition to the Right and perhaps also around a very general commitment to 'progressive social change' – but that cannot hide their deep-seated divisions. Between the PCF's authoritarian communism, the PS's democratic socialism and the extreme Left's many varied strains, there are quite different and often conflicting perspectives on virtually all the important issues of the day.

But it must also be remembered that the warring factions of the Left have periodically come together to fight common battles: to establish the Republic, to defend it against its enemies, to pave the way for social reforms, and less heroically, simply to win elections. Unfortunately the diverse names they have adopted on such occasions hardly help to clarify the issue of Left or Lefts. In the present century the major alliances have labelled themselves *Bloc des Gauches, Cartel des Gauches, Front Populaire, Front Républicain* and *Union de la Gauche.*

Clearly a case can be argued either way and in the last analysis it is obviously a matter of preference which formulation is adopted. Of crucial significance, however, beyond the semantics, is the need to recognise the diversity which has always characterised the Left. At a minimum the existence of different strains must be acknowledged. At a maximum quite different phenomena may be identified.

METHODS OF ANALYSIS

Recognition of the plurality of the Left does not, of course, lead to a ready classification of its elements. A variety of approaches and perspectives are possible. This may be illustrated by reference to three recent French studies of the history of the Left.

Georges Lefranc in his book *Les Gauches en France*[9] takes a thematic approach, one that is analagous to that of René Rémond in his classic study of the French Right. According to Lefranc different Lefts have emerged and these have adapted and developed over time in parallel with changes in their political, social and economic environments. They are seen as living entities; being born, becoming active and growing old. Four main Lefts are identified:

(1) *The liberal and parliamentary Left.* The main embodiment of the Left until the establishment of the Third Republic, it opposed the Ancien Régime and championed individual freedom and parliamentary supremacy. During the 1880s it was pushed towards the Centre by –

(2) *The democratic and anti-clerical Left.* Devoted to the establishment of universal suffrage and the secular school, much of its programme was enacted by 1905. Thereafter the Radical party – the principal embodiment of this Left – was never quite sure whether it should be the right-wing of the Left or the left-wing of the Right.

(3) *The socialist Left.* Developing as a mass movement only in the last quarter of the nineteenth century, socialism was distinguished

from the first two Lefts by its belief in the limitations of political action to improve man's condition. Whilst equally firmly attached to individual liberty and political democracy socialists have also wanted some measure of *social* equality and *social* justice.

(4) *The communist Left.*   From 1920 a new type of socialism has competed with traditional forms: one that is highly statist and openly based on 'the cult of the Soviet model'.

Jean Touchard in *La gauche en France depuis 1900*[10] rejects the thematic or developmental approach adopted by Lefranc. He does so on the grounds that the essential relativism of the term 'Left' makes any attempt to follow single streams – such as radicalism, liberalism and socialism – virtually impossible. In his view, the Left of 1900 was quite different from the Left of 1930 or 1960 and each can *only* be understood in its own socio-economic and historical context. So, to take a specific example, the Left in the 1930s is analysed almost exclusively in its own terms. There is little reference to precursors or historical influences. It is portrayed as sharing a number of common chords, such as similar views on social hierarchies, the clerical question and international relations, but as being principally charac-terised by a three-way division into radicalism, socialism and communism.

Jean Defrasne draws on both approaches, the 'thematic' and the 'periodic' in his more modest study *La Gauche en France de 1789 à nos jours.*[11] Like Lefranc he identifies developing Lefts whose roots can be traced back to the Revolution. The categories however are different:

(1) *The liberal Left.*   Its starting position, in 1789, was the need for the rule of law, the separation of powers, and the extension of liberty and civil equality. Originally, these latter concepts were given a highly circumscribed interpretation, but over time developed and fed their way into radicalism and socialism.

(2) *The authoritarian Left.*   Associated originally with Jacobinism and dictatorship 'to save the nation' in 1792-4, communism is seen as its main twentieth-century embodiment.

(3) *The revolutionary Left.*   Central to the Revolution and the subsequent development of the Left it declined, as a significant political force, between the two World Wars.

Unlike Lefranc, Defrasne does not 'follow through' his Lefts in any rigorous way. Rather he bases the substantive part of his analysis around what he sees to be the four main eras of the Left: the birth of the Left (1789-1815); the romantic Left (1815-71); the divided Left (1871-1936); the Left in search of unity (1936-to date). The thematic and chronological approaches are thus, if not wedded together, both used.

The approaches of Lefranc, Touchard and Defrasne do not, of course, by any means exhaust the possible modes of analysis or identification. The richness of the history of the Left is such that it lends itself to many permutations, both of 'streams' and 'eras'. Only recently Michel Rocard, a prominent figure in the PS, has made much of what he calls the two political cultures in the French Left:

> The most typical, which for a long time was dominant, is jacobin, centralising, statist, nationalist and protectionist... . The other [which he traces back to Proudhon and which he claims to represent] is decentralising, it is regionalist it refuses arbitrary domination, whether it is that of the bosses or the State. It is liberalising, whether it is a question of a dependent majorities, like women, or of minorities who are poorly integrated into the social system such as the young, immigrants or the handicapped. This culture is suspicious of rules and administration, it prefers the custom and experimentation of social groups.[12]

Many other categorisations are possible.

Naturally objections can always be made to interpretative accounts of complex and changing phenomena. So, in the case of the Left, it might be argued that some approaches, such as those of Lefranc and, more so, Rocard, overstate continuities while others, like that of Touchard, underestimate them. It is best, therefore, to view the different perspectives, not in terms of which is right and which is wrong, but in terms of their varying degrees of usefulness. Laying emphasis as they do on different aspects of the Left they may all with benefit be born in mind, as we turn now to look at the history of the Left in a more specific way.

2 The Development of the Modern Political Parties of the Left

The division of history into periods and eras is an important but, inevitably, somewhat arbitrary process. Depending on the foci of concern and the level of sophistication required an almost infinite variety of possibilities exists for any extended period of time. It seems reasonable, given that our concern here is limited to providing merely a general account of major developments, to divide our analysis into two broad periods: from the beginning of the Third Republic until 1920; from 1920 to the collapse of the Fourth Republic. This framework could, of course, be extended in many ways but it does allow us to mark *the* most important turning points. Although embryonic parties of the Left existed as far back as the post-1789 Revolutionary period, it was only in the early years of the Third Republic that they began to become established. Their evolution and formation until immediately after the First World War was thereafter gradual and steady. However the shock waves which emanated from the Russian Revolution had a cataclysmic effect and resulted, in 1920, in the rupture – between communists and socialists – that has plagued the Left ever since. Consequently, 1920 witnessed the beginning of a new era, an era that can be extended to the end of the Fourth Republic when constitutional and institutional changes helped to produce another transformational effect on the political parties of the Left.

THE LEFT IN 1871

The Left at the beginning of the Third Republic was weak and divided.

On the parliamentary level it performed disastrously in the February 1871 general election: well over half the seats were won by monarchists. Although there was an element of artificiality about this, the monarchist vote being primarily a vote *against* the republicans' policy to continue the war with the Prussians rather than a vote *for* a monarchist Restoration, the fact remains that of the 650 or so new members only around 150 were republicans. (Estimates of exact figures vary). Moreover they came in many shades and shared little beyond a common desire to establish the Republic. The most moderate were essentially liberal pragmatists. For them the Republic was the regime most capable of offering a measure of freedom while still preserving social order. It was also, given the passions associated with monarchism and the recent demise of Bonapartism, the regime most likely to divide Frenchmen least. The more radical elements, many of whom were loosely grouped around Léon Gambetta and his 1869 Belleville Manifesto, looked forward to some measure of substantive change in the political sphere. In particular they hoped for the establishment of a genuinely democratic, libertarian and more open republic where greater opportunities would be available for all and the influence of the Church would be reduced.

Beyond these groupings – or, more accurately, sentiments, for they were hardly organised – were an array of socialist, anarchist and assorted revolutionary sects and small organisations. Drawing their inspiration from a number of sources – Blanqui, Fourier, Proudhon, Saint-Simon and others – they had been closely involved in the Paris Commune of March-May 1871 and had paid a high price for that. Many of their leaders and members were killed in the street fighting and during the subsequent reprisals. Those who survived were either sent into exile or forced underground, able to continue political activity in only a conspiratorial manner.

The dominating 'political' wing of the Left was thus overshadowed in Parliament by the reactionary Right and moreover was internally divided between two competing strands. The minority 'socialist/ revolutionary' wing, which included a vast array of different tendencies, was reduced to little more than an exiled, quasi-legal, rump.

1871-1920

There were two main developments on the Left during this period.

1. The Movement of the Political Left

The political Left progressively moved towards the Right in the sense
that it became less interested in pioneering reforms and more
concerned with preserving the *status quo* it itself had created. This
process took place in stages as the various elements successively
moved across.

During the early 1870s moderate republicanism was increasingly
seen as the best guarantee of stability and prosperity. With the
Republican movement dominated by such 'safe' figures as Ferry,
Simon, Favre and Grèvy it was possible for conservative bourgeois
and peasant elements to rally to both the compromise constitution of
1875 – which was monarchist in spirit but republican in name — and
Republican candidates at the polls. Accordingly, by 1879,
Republicans had taken control of all three major national institutions:
the Chamber of Deputies, the Senate and the Presidency. For the most
moderate of Republicans, particularly those who had only recently
been converted from liberal monarchism, this was progress enough.
For most, however, further reform was necessary if the principles of
1789 were to be achieved. As a result, between 1879 and 1885,
Republicans, including most of Gambetta's Radicals, combined to
enact a range of legislation which extended individual and collective
freedom: from the recognition of divorce to the full legalisation of
trade unions. Above all, there was a major expansion of public
education and the role of the Church therein was severely curtailed.
By the mid-1880s, for the majority of Republicans, further wholesale
reform was both unattractive and unnecessary. Jules Ferry himself,
the leader of the moderate Republicans – or Opportunists as they
came to be called – could proclaim in 1885, 'the peril lies to the Left'.

With socialism still in its infancy this enemy to the Left comprised
mainly Radicals. Now led by Georges Clemenceau they had resisted
the increasing accommodation between the *Gambettistes* and the
moderates in the late 1870s, and in the 1881 elections had confronted
the Opportunists in many constituencies. Though by no means a
coherent group they enjoyed a measure of identity by virtue of their
advocacy of further 'democratic' and 'progressive' political reforms:
abolition of the Senate and the consequent complete supremacy of the
lower Chamber, separation of Church and State, and greater local
autonomy were among their more prominent demands. There were
even suggestions, especially from those who described themselves as
Radical-Socialists, that interventionist economic measures, including

the introduction of a progressive income tax, were desirable. On the whole, however, such 'social' demands were not advocated with any zeal and were usually very much secondary to the proposals for further political reform.

But the Radicals in their turn were to become more cautious and conservative. An important turning point in this process, as indeed it was in some ways for French politics as a whole, came with the scandal of the Dreyfus Affair in the last few years of the century.

During the late 1880s and throughout the 1890s there had been signs of a possible re-adjustment taking place between Left and Right. The Opportunists, after losing their majority in the 1885 elections and initially courting the Left, increasingly looked to their Right for allies. This was because, as we have seen, they were broadly content with the system they had established since the beginning of the Third Republic. At the same time moderate Catholics, encouraged by a comparatively liberal papacy, were beginning – under the movement that came to be known as the *Ralliement* – to reconcile themselves to the Republic. There was, thus, the foundation, all the more as socialism in the 1890s extended its base, of an increasing understanding between moderates on all sides. There seemed a chance that the age-old clerical issue, the very touchstone of political conflict, might, given understanding on both sides, be resolved. There was, after all, much to be gained. For Catholics there was the opportunity of re-integration into the body politic. For Republicans, who had already drawn much of the teeth of the clerical issue, there was the prospect of widening the 'moderate' base and also of having the use, in the form of the Church, of a useful prop to the social order.

By the 1890s these early signs of accommodation, if not reconciliation, were causing problems for the Radicals. As what was to become the familiar twentieth-century pattern of centrist coalition governments developed, they had to choose between siding with 'bourgeois preservation' or 'socialist advance'. In making their choice they went, as ever, in different directions: some supported socialist 'minimal' reforms, others watered down their Jacobin and egalitarian pretensions and thought about compromise.

The Dreyfus Affair, for a while at least, released the Radicals from their dilemma by restoring to the political agenda hostilities and antagonisms that apparently had been fading. The army's clumsy and secretive attempt to falsely incriminate Dreyfus, a Jewish officer, of espionage, coupled with the general sympathy their efforts received from the Catholic Church, resulted in a *cause célèbre*. Republicans once again thought they saw the old alliance of sword and cassock and in some quarters the very regime itself was thought to be endangered. Following previous crises in 1877 (the *seize mai* dissolution) and 1887-8 (the Boulanger Affair), the Dreyfus case came to be viewed by many as the third great assault by the forces of reaction against the Republic in just over twenty years. Even those Republicans who did not take such an alarmist view had their attention drawn to the still very powerful positions of church and army.

Among the consequences of the Affair was the suspension of that tendency for governments to be increasingly of the Centre-Right. With the constitutional and clerical issues again stirred the Opportunists split: one section linked up with the *Ralliés* and the Right; the other, which was strongly anti-clerical, created, with the Radicals and the 'ministerial' Socialists, the *Bloc des Gauches* which, in 1899, formed a Government of National Defence. This unholy coalition, welded together on an essentially negative basis, proceeded, particularly during the Combes administration of 1902-5, to a purging of the army and a major assault on the Church. The programme culminated in the Separation of Church and State in 1905.

The Dreyfus Affair had a two-fold effect on the political Left.

Its most immediate consequence was to bring it back into prominence, to re-emphasise its internal bonds and to increase its strength enormously. The Radicals were the principal beneficiaries. They dominated both the Waldeck-Rousseau and Combes governments and in the 1902 elections emerged, for the first time, as the largest grouping in the Chamber. A working relationship with the 'social-economic' Left was forged around a programme based on defence of the Republic and virulent anti-clericalism and until 1905 the Left provided stable government for the nation.

In the longer term, the Affair hastened the movement of the Radicals from their position on the Left to a more ambiguous role in the Centre. Even before the Affair they had been uncertain and divided as to their exact direction, a fact which was exemplified in the tortuous title they chose when they formally constituted themselves as a political party in 1901: *Parti républicain radical et radical-socialiste*. Their lack of cohesion was further illustrated by the very loose, decentralised structure of the new party and by its inability, and even unwillingness, to attempt discipline. It had been formed for little more than reasons of electoral convenience and even then, on occasions when it seemed advantageous, Deputies would drop their Radical label and simply call themselves Republicans. By 1905, thanks to the wave of anti-clericalism which followed the Dreyfus Affair, they had enacted most of their legislative goals. They desired no further wholesale reforms. They still clung to republican, libertarian and anti-clerical ideals, but their main desire increasingly was to consolidate and defend the existing political and economic system.

Other factors, too, pushed the Radicals towards the shifting ground of Centre and Centre-Right government coalitions which was to become their most frequent home until the Fifth Republic. Firstly, the rise of socialism posed a threat which was increasingly seen to be more immediate and dangerous than the dying flames of reactionary monarchism. At their Nancy Conference in 1907 the Radicals had formally declared themselves as being 'resolutely attached to the principle of individual property'. When this appeared to be challenged the few unfulfilled points of their programme were easily postponed. Secondly, and partly as a result of their hostility towards socialism, the Radicals' membership and electorate became increasingly conservative. The Party's combination of economic moderation and political/constitutional vigilance proved attractive to many middle-class and peasant anti-clericals. In addition, electoral success itself led to an influx of moderates, non-doctrinaires and power seekers who used the weak organisation to construct their own arrangements, often with conservatives of various kinds, at local level. Thirdly, and in large part because of the developments just noted, socialism succeeded in pushing the Radicals from their remaining urban bases. More than ever the Party thus became dependent on the small town and rural bourgeoisie and peasantry.

From 1905 the political Left, which the Radicals now dominated, was thus increasingly willing to co-operate with the Centre and the Right. It could still rally to 'Leftist' causes – many Radicals, for example, supported anti-militarism and pacifism in the years before the outbreak of war – but their commitment to orthodox economic policies inevitably meant that any alliance or arrangement with the developing socialist Left was, at the very least, subject to extreme strain. Radicalism was, as many historians have said, increasingly as much a state of mind as a political party. It saw itself as the defender of the 'little man', the protector against the ever encroaching state, and the watchdog of the Republican constitution. The lack of a clear identity is encapsulated by the events of 1914-19: in 1914 the strands which had assumed a common banner in 1901 eventually managed to form a single parliamentary group; they, then, almost unanimously supported the Republic in its hour of need and participated in government throughout the war; but in 1919, when elections to a new chamber were held, Radicals went in quite different directions: some preferred to be part of the great right-wing *Bloc National* coalition which swept to power; others either fought alone or in harness with socialists.

2.   The Emergence of the Socialist Left

Three problems faced the development of socialism in France in 1871.

Firstly, the socialist heritage, notwithstanding its rich revolutionary and intellectual traditions, was weak. There had been at various times friendly and mutual-aid societies, co-operatives and even, from the mid-1860s, embryonic trade unions, but these had been only barely tolerated and had quite failed to exercise anything other than a marginal influence over the masses. On those rare occasions when the working class had sought to bring its power to bear it had been mercilessly crushed. At the beginning of the Third Republic the socialist movement consisted of little more than small bands of Utopian and bourgeois romantics who were making little impact on, indeed who were largely isolated from, the working class. Moreover, they did not offer any common framework of ideas but ranged from Proudhonian anarchism, anti-Statist federalism, to Blanquist insurrectionism and dreams of the dictatorship of the proletariat.

Secondly, the Commune had seen the elimination, if not in the actual street fighting of May then in the subsequent executions and exiles, of the best part of a generation of Socialist leaders. Thiers said the Republic would be conservative or it would not be at all and his sentiment was put to work in the restrictions that were often placed on socialist activities, many of them continuing even after an amnesty was granted to the Communards in 1880.

Thirdly, the economic structure was not favourable to the development of socialism. Although accurate figures on the composition of the work force in the nineteenth century do not exist, it is clear that the industrial sector, and hence the proletariat, barely expanded at all from the beginning of the Third Republic until the outbreak of war in 1914. According to Dupeux, for example, the proportion of the working population engaged in industry increased from only 29.0% in 1866 to 30.6% in 1906; this compares with 49.8% who were engaged in agriculture, fisheries and forestry in 1866 and 47.7% in 1906. Furthermore, the bulk of the industrial labour force were still employed in small, isolated and often highly paternalistic establishments: in 1906 half worked in establishments with between one and five employees, only one tenth in establishments with over one hundred employees.[1] The working class were as much artisans as industrial proletariat and as such they hardly provided fertile ground for the development of class and socialist consciousness.

Not that the problems should be overstated. Socialism did develop over the period as is seen in its increasing representation in Parliament: five Deputies in 1885, 20 in 1899, 50 in 1893, 75 in 1906 and 125 – the second largest group – in 1914. A major reason for this advance is that it was able to attract support from many different quarters. French society was (and is) highly complex and sections and classes were not undifferentiated. While industrial concentration in some areas, notably the *départements* of the Nord and the Pas-de-Calais, did assist the Socialist emergence, in others, especially where there was a strong Catholic tradition, it had only a slight effect. By the same token the peasantry, usually thought of as a bastion of individualism, anti-collectivism and, hence, conservatism, provided, especially in the south and parts of the centre, considerable Socialist support. As much as, if not more than, the other classes the peasantry, far from being homogeneous, displayed a veritable mosaic of different patterns and forms arising from distinct local and personal allegiances, political traditions, clerical influences and economic relationships. The many differing forms of land exploitation alone – share-cropping, tenant farming, landless labouring, private small ownership etc. – all affected political behaviour in different ways.[2]

But though Socialists increased their representation in the Chamber of Deputies the full potential of socialism itself was not realised. There are three principal reasons for this and each is still a source of weakness today. Two of these we shall consider in Chapter 9: the inability of the trade union movement to mobilise more than a minority of the workforce, and the divisions between that movement and the socialist political parties. The third reason is the divisions between the socialist parties themselves.

As socialists began to pick up the pieces in the late 1870s and establish formal political groupings in the 1880s the age-old differences, which had divided the earlier generations of intellectuals, reappeared; revolution/reform, statism/voluntarism, force/persuasion, centralisation/localism. The general breach which opened up in most European socialist movements in the latter part of the nineteenth century – between reformists and revolutionaries (or minimalists and maximalists as some would prefer) – was complicated in France by sub-divisions. By the early 1890s, when numerical strength was increasing rapidly, there were five major groups:

(1) *Guesdists.* Of Marxist inspiration they had little faith in universal suffrage. Great stress was put on class antagonisms and the need for wholesale social and economic restructuring, with collectivisation as the central goal. The necessity of organisation was also emphasised and Guesde's *Parti Ouvrier Français,* which was formed in 1887, was the first party in France to develop, in any systematic way, a structure and a programme.

(2) *Blanquists.* The main insurrectionary strand of the socialist movement, they sought to build an essentially conspiratorial group, which would prepare itself for the revolution that would pave the way to the construction of an egalitarian society.

(3) *Possibilistes.* Led by Paul Brousse, they believed genuine reforms could be achieved within the parliamentary democratic system. Attention should, however, be switched away from the supposed benefits of centralist intervention to the role of the local political units and the opportunities for municipal socialism.

(4) *Allemanistes.* Jean Allemane and his followers were a breakaway group from the Possibilistes. They thought the Party was becoming too electoralist and too elitist. Greater weight should be given to the workers themselves, through their unions and industrial sanctions.

(5) *Independents.* Though not formally organised until 1898, and then only very loosely, they were the largest Socialist group in Parliament. Embracing a range of predominantly reformists and minimalists they were to provide a training ground for three future 'centrist' Prime Ministers; Millerand, Briand and Viviani.

Despite these divisions, movements towards unification began in the 1890s. The Guesdists and the Independents increasingly came to dominate and though there were considerable differences between them common ground did appear as the Guesdists, if not becoming reformist, began to enter elections and recognise the validity of pursuing a minimum programme of improved wages, better working conditions, collectivisations, etc. A series of meetings were held between 1899-1901 but they failed, foundering on the question of ministerialism which had been provoked by the entry of the Independent Millerand into the Waldeck-Rousseau government. In consequence, by 1901, two main parties existed; the Guesdist-dominated *Parti Socialiste de France* and the Independents' (who were now led by Jean Jaurès) *Parti Socialiste Français*.

These parties did not exist independently for very long. At the 1904 Amsterdam Congress of the Second Socialist International, which was dominated by the German Sozialdemokratische Partei Deutschlands (SPD) and the fundamental debates about reform and revolution which were being conducted within it, a motion was passed demanding the unification of the French parties. Moreover, the terms on which this should take place were specified. Having adopted the SPD's own 1903 Dresden Resolution, which had reasserted a commitment to class war and revolutionary struggle, the French were obliged to proceed on the basis of an orthodox Marxist position.

This was clearly a defeat for Jaurès. Though he was no orthodox reformist – his career in many ways was devoted to an attempt to synthesise reform and revolution – he did believe in the value of governmental participation, from which he was now obliged to withdraw, and he did oppose the dogma and rigidity which he now had imposed upon him. As he often said of himself, he sought the ideal but recognised the real. Nonetheless, in the cause of unity and perhaps too because the value of the *Bloc des gauches* was nearing its end, he and most of his followers bowed to the will of the Congress, even though they were the majority current in France. Accordingly, in 1905, the *Section Française de l'Internationale Ouvrière* was formed.

Guesde's victory, as it turned out, was less than total. His influence declined as Jaurès, through his forceful rhetoric and firm humanitarian beliefs, increasingly became the most influential member of the Party. There was no formal departure from the terms of the 1905 merger – the Party's language remained Marxist and its posture continued to be aggressively oppositionist – but there was a perceptible change in style and mood. According to Robert Wohl, a new consensus, based on a commitment to parliamentary action and Republican defence was created: 'The shared assumption was that if the SFIO preserved its own political purity, it could not help but fall heir to the bourgeois legacy...the striking thing about this party was the breadth of its centre and the weakness of its extremes'.[3]

So it can be seen that, despite tensions, there was some prospect of the 1905 merger being gradually consolidated. The reformist/

revolutionary split became less sharp and in 1914, when the hoped-for international workers solidarity failed to materialise, virtually the whole Party rallied to the *union sacrée*.[4] Guesde, of all people, entered the Government of National Defence as one of the SFIO's two representatives.

The pre-war division did not, therefore, make the post-war schism inevitable. It did, however, provide an important background, perhaps even a predisposition, to another rift in the Party which led more directly to the events of 1920. This turned on attitudes to the war and opened up as disillusionment with both the course and protracted nature of hostilities spread. Opposition to participation in office and the continued prosecution of the war built up to such an extent that in 1917 the SFIO withdrew from government and only narrowly agreed to vote for the war credits. This movement to the left, which was accompanied by a large turnover in membership and entry of revolutionary syndicalists paved the way for the bitter disputes which were to culminate at Tours in 1920.

1920-1958

1. Tours

The SFIO Congress at Tours in 1920 marks a watershed in the development of the French Left, for it was there that the Communist Party was born when three-quarters of the delegates present voted to affiliate to the recently established Third International. In so doing they created the split which has plagued French socialism ever since. A reformist wing (though Socialist leaders would rarely have described themselves as such) has vied and competed with a Moscow-orientated communist wing. As with so many quarrels originating in the family, bitterness and hostility has usually characterised their exchanges. With competition covering much of the same ground – for the socialist mantle and the working class electorate – there has only rarely been room for accommodation and never any for a real reconciliation.

But the 1920 rupture did not *in itself* condemn French socialism to its subsequent division or preclude the emergence of a strong and united party such as was developing in Britain. There are two reasons for this.

Firstly, there was nothing inevitable about subsequent Communist success. Though historians are frequently prone to explain the PCF's growth in terms of a propitious French political tradition – revolutionary propensities, hostility towards authority, affinity for 'anti-government' parties etc. – the PCF, in fact, rapidly *declined* in the first few years and by the early 1930s seemed well on the way to becoming merely an awkward, but not especially important, Soviet outpost. It was the quite specific events of the mid-1930s and then again of the Second World War which made the PCF one of the major parties of France.

Secondly, it seems that many of the delegates who supported affiliation to the Third International did not fully appreciate the implications of their action despite the fact that the issues were well publicised in the months preceding the Congress. In the preliminary skirmishing one side, pointing to the failures of the SFIO and the strengths of communism, had argued that the exploited working class had nothing to lose. The other – mainly made up of the SFIO 'old guard' led by Paul Faure and Léon Blum – had disputed this and had emphasised the danger of becoming a mere Moscow appendage. They claimed that the twenty-one conditions laid down by Moscow as the basis of entry into Comintern were wholly alien to the French socialist tradition of toleration, decentralisation and accommodation. Among the more objectionable and potentially divisive conditions, they argued, were the demand for a complete break with social democracy and parliamentarianism, the requirement to infiltrate the trade union movement, and the need to reorganise the party along democratic centralist lines.

But a simple polarisation of views along these lines did not occur, and at Tours itself there were many different motives behind the vote for the affiliation motion. In the mood of disillusionment which pervaded the socialist movement in 1919-20 and amidst a widespread feeling that the SFIO had betrayed its roots, the majority seem to have merely wanted a more vigorous, militant and ideologically pure party. The Bolshevik model appeared to offer just that, and success too. In Annie Kriegel's words 'They yearned to preserve their own traditions while capturing some of the dynamism of the Russian Revolution.[5] As for the 'twenty-one conditions' laid down by Comintern it was generally assumed, given the long reformist tradition in France, that they would not, or could not, be rigidly applied.

Bolshevisation, and the total break with the SFIO it brought about, was thus far from inevitable in the early stages of the PCF's existence. It was only after a fierce struggle, which was not finally resolved until the early 1930s, that it was achieved and the three-fold nature of the party political Left, which was to endure into the 1960s became clear; SFIO, PCF and, still clinging tenuously to its leftist roots, Radicals. Each was to experience fluctuating fortunes and to suffer periodic breakaways, but their joint overall dominance was not to be seriously challenged.

Doubt has already been cast on the importance of tradition in explaining the foundation and subsequent development of the PCF. Certainly there were favourable pre-dispositions, such as the pre-war Jaurès/Guesde division, the syndicalist taste for revolution and the apparent willingness of some areas of France to vote as Republican or as Left as they could. But it was the particular configuration of events and circumstances immediately prior to Tours which provided the triggering factors behind the establishment of the *Section française de l'Internationale Communiste,* as the Communists originally called themselves.

In the first place, the war, 'which will be over by Christmas' had lasted for four years and had inflicted untold suffering and misery. The 'brotherhood' of the Second International had proved totally ineffective as the working class of each nation had rallied to the flag, truly believing they were the aggrieved and not the aggressor. Small wonder that voices of dissension were increasingly heard in Socialist ranks. If the line of division was different to the dispute which had characterised the pre-war years it became no less bitter.

Secondly, there was a great change in the composition of the SFIO during and immediately after the war. As compared with 72,000 members in 1914 there were nearly 180,000 in September 1920. Although the importance of this should not be exaggerated, as the new members were by no means all at one in supporting affiliation to Comintern, their entry inevitably created flux in the Party and resulted in an erosion of many loyalties. (In fact no discernible voting pattern at Tours is apparent, there having been strong support to affiliate from both large industrial and smaller rural federations.)

Thirdly, the end of the war saw the emergence of a number of social grievances: demobilisation was slow and many wartime controls remained; wages did not keep pace with inflation; the government acceded to only one of a long list of 'minimum demands drawn up by the CGT in December 1918. Even after this one 'concession', which introduced the eight-hour day, was passed many employers refused to implement it.

Fourthly, the morale of the established socialist forces was at a low ebb. Although the SFIO had increased its vote in the 1919 elections the electoral system had worked against it and the number of its Deputies had fallen from 103 to 68. At the same time the *Bloc National* had been elected to government with a huge parliamentary majority. The weakness of the union movement had similarly been exposed. Strikes in 1919-1920, which at one time had threatened to develop into a general strike, had petered out, some thought because of over-cautious SFIO and CGT leadership.

Fifthly and finally, a genuine alternative was now on offer in the form of the new star which had risen in the East. The memory of October 1917 was still vivid, glorious and all the more attractive since it was the one clear success in a generally dispirited socialist world. The two SFIO leaders, L.O. Frossard and M. Cachin, who were dispatched to Russia in January 1920 to study the new system at close quarters, returned with glowing reports and a strong recommendation to affiliate.

2. The Communist Party

The PCF was born out of the SFIO. A majority of Socialist delegates had voted to create it and the new leadership took with them the bulk of the SFIO membership and the Party newspaper *L'Humanité*. In consequence communism in France did not appear as quite the foreign import it did elsewhere. But nor was it quite as strong as it may have seemed. People had joined for many different reasons and it was thus prone from the very outset to factionalism. In addition, many of the leaders of the SFIO, at both national and local level, and a majority of the Deputies (55 out of 68) remained hostile and refused to affiliate. They were soon using their influence to rebuild SFIO dominance.

The pre-1958 history of the PCF can be divided into six phases.[6]

(1) *Factionalism and Struggle 1920-3.*   The party formed at Tours was made up of competing elements. In the months following the Congress debates raged on many issues but particularly over Comintern, which almost immediately had put pressure on the leaders to institutionalise the twenty-one conditions. At the 1921 Marseilles Congress many delegates openly expressed their hostility to this unwanted interference. Dissatisfaction increased even further when Comintern adopted, and insisted constituent parties should practise, a united front policy. In essence this required communist parties to extend their influence into the working class and build up a solid wall

of resistance against the bourgeoisie. The tactic could be pursued either from above (with socialist leaders) or below (with workers against the socialist leaders). Either way, and Comintern increasingly expressed a preference for the latter, it was a hostile gesture towards the SFIO since it was really designed, as many communist leaders admitted, to undermine socialist support and build up communism.

For many French Communists this tactic brought to the surface Moscow's real intent: to control the Party. For others, who wished to remain loyal, it simply made little sense since the PCF was already France's largest working-class party. As a result, despite strong protestations from Trotsky and others, the strategy was not immediately implemented. But constant pressure paid off in the end. With dissatisfaction provoking many resignations, including that of the first General Secretary, Frossard, and with expulsions removing other 'recalcitrants', the united front was eventually accepted. It formed the basis of the 1924 election campaign when the Party called itself the *Bloc ouvrier et paysan*. Fighting in most places on its own it gained only 9.5 per cent of the votes and 26 seats.

(2) *Bolshevisation and Party Isolation (1924-34)*. Though preliminary moves began in 1923, Bolshevisation as an organisational ideal was formally launched by Comintern at its fifth Congress in July 1924. The intent was to create in each country, including France, a unified, centralised revolutionary party which would owe complete allegiance to the Soviet Union and which, by virtue of its structure, discipline and fervour would be ready to assume power whenever the occasion demanded. There were, as Kriegel says, three main components.[7] Firstly, the transformation of party structures so as to emphasise factory cells as the basic unit. Secondly, the consolidation of power in the upper echelons of parties and the elimination of autonomy at the lower levels. Thirdly, the creation of disciplined and united party leaderships supported by loyal networks of officials.

By the early 1930s, though not without causing dissension, these three principles were firmly embodied in the PCF's structure. If factory cells had not been as successful as anticipated other means had been found to 'proletarianise' the apparatus and thus flush out the more critical, questioning and independent middle class. And again, if Maurice Thorez, who had emerged as leader, was not the ideal choice (some Comintern officials apparently regarded him as lacking in initiative and political courage) he was at least completely loyal. The Party founded at Tours had thus been totally destroyed and a new one had been built in its shell.

As Bolshevisation proceeded the united front policy became more militant and developed into one based on 'class against class'. The Socialists, because they 'duped' the workers through reformism, were now the main enemy: 'social fascists' as the Communists came to call them. All remaining vestiges of co-operation disappeared as uncompromising dogmatism became the hallmark of the party.

Not surprisingly, as Moscow's influence became more apparent, as purges continued, as demands on members grew, and as the two ballot electoral system exercised its usual influence on isolated parties, the PCF declined, to be replaced by the SFIO as once again the largest party of the Left. From 109,000 members in 1921 the PCF fell to 28,000 in 1933. Its electoral and parliamentary strength also declined, though not so dramatically: from the 9.5 per cent and 26 seats of 1924, to 8.4 per cent and 12 seats in 1932. Moscow and its supporters inside the PCF may not have been too concerned about this since electoralist/reformist elements had been removed and a disciplined, compliant party had been created. But the PCF, if trends had continued, would soon have been little more than a marginal sect.

(3) *Popular Front (1934-39)*.   In the spring of 1934 the PCF began to change course and adopted a more conciliatory attitude towards both the SFIO and Radicals. It began to champion the cause of an anti-fascist republican front amongst the 'democratic' parties and it offered its 'outstretched hand' to its 'Catholic brothers'.

Internal pressures for such a change in direction had been building up in the PCF for some time, though those who had advocated it too loudly or too early, such as the powerful politbureau member Jacques Doriot, had been expelled or forced to resign. The structural reorganisation and strategic isolation since the mid-1920s had been, at best, only a partial success. A potential vanguard of the masses had undeniably been created but the revolution itself seemed further away than ever as capitalism in France, despite its problems, showed no signs of collapse, and as social democracy, far from being checked, continued to flourish. To this background of general unease was added the immediate and urgent problem of fascism. The Nazi assumption to power in Germany in 1933 and the extreme Right-wing inspired riots of 6 February 1934 in Paris (which many thought had been an attempted coup) highlighted the threat, especially when the Left was divided.

The enthusiasm of many Communists (though by no means all leaders) for the more open strategy is thus understandable. But the decisive initiative for change came not from Paris but from Moscow.

As Albert Vassart, the PCF delegate to Comintern from April 1934 to April 1935, was later to state, the abrupt change in the PCF position in 1934 'can be understood only by taking into account the requirements of USSR foreign policy at that time'.[8] These requirements were headed by the need for closer links with the democracies. Stalin feared Germany might be able to live in peace with all countries except the Soviet Union. Accordingly more 'reasonable', 'co-operative' and 'patriotic' communist parties were needed in the West so as to improve the image.

In a series of stages the Left parties built the Popular Front coalition which was victorious in the April/May 1936 elections. Though this government was not to last – not least because of suspicions arising from the PCF's sudden about-turn and its decision to remain out of office – the episode as a whole was of great importance for the PCF in that it brought about its partial re-integration into the political system. The patriotic and accommodating image it presented found considerable favour amongst the masses and both the membership and electorate of the hitherto declining Party mushroomed: from 30,000 members in 1934 to 340,000 in 1937; from 8.4 per cent of the vote and 12 seats in 1932 to 15.3 per cent and 72 seats.

(4) *The Nazi Soviet Pact (1939-41).* The Nazi Soviet non-aggression pact of August 1939 and the PCF' remarkably rapid acceptance of it has since been a source of embarrassment.[9] The Popular Front strategy had, after all, arisen directly from the supposed fascist menace. From being the most anti-Munich of all the French parties, it now denounced the war of the 'imperialists', and from demanding a policy of 'no capitulation to Hitler' it suddenly insisted on peace. No wonder this most sudden of all the about-turns in the Party's history provoked mass resignations from the top-most level downwards, (twenty-one of the seventy-two deputies resigned). Loyalties were never more strained as the slavish devotion to Moscow's self-interested will was ruthlessly exposed.

The confusion and disorganisation occasioned by the pact was exacerbated by the banning of the Party, a police campaign against its activists and the arrest and imprisonment of thousands of its members. With the Party being virtually leaderless and with activity, of necessity, being underground, no co-ordinated action was possible. In any event no one was quite sure what appropriate action would be or even who was the enemy: presumably not Germany, but then the Soviet Union was not at war with Britain or Vichy either. It is little surprise that the Nazi invasion of the Soviet Union in June 1941 was received almost as a form of liberation by members who were still active.

(5) *Resistance and Post-War Government (1941-7)*. Whatever their problems prior to June 1941 Communists were to play a major role in the Resistance movement for the rest of the war. Through their heroism, organisational skills and propaganda they came to dominate or deeply penetrate many of the individual Resistance groups. If they never achieved the total control they worked for, they did succeed, through the many networks of the Resistance movement, in establishing a very strong position by the Liberation. Whether the leaders ever seriously considered using this strength as a springboard for revolution is still a matter of debate amongst historians. (See Chapter 4). The fact is however, that, for the most part, the leadership willingly acquiesced in post-war reconstruction and exhorted members to do likewise.

This self-effacing and moderating policy was continued in the immediate post-war period when, for the very first time in its history, the PCF entered government. Along with its two partners in office – the SFIO and the newly established Christian Democratic *Mouvement Républicain Populaire* – it reaped the gains of the Resistance record. In two of the three elections held in 1945-6 it polled more votes than any other party and in all three it gained between 26 and 28 per cent. Its membership also mushroomed to around 800,000 by the spring of 1947.

But pressures for the end of tripartism, as this period was known, soon built up. Despite the PCF helping to push through important social reforms and despite Thorez expending considerable energy encouraging workers to maximise production and minimise militancy, the SFIO and MRP remained uneasy. Apart from obvious ideological differences they suspected the PCF of wanting to use government as a springboard for extending its influence throughout the 'bourgeois' State. Their position became even more difficult as the division of Europe into two hostile blocs became ever more apparent and as America, just as in Italy, Belgium, and elsewhere, made anti-communism a condition of the economic aid that was proposed through the Marshall Plan. For its part the PCF had become increasingly embarrassed at supporting policies that, in its heart, it opposed. Furthermore, the increasing signs, in the spring of 1947, of a developing strike movement, appeared to pose a threat to the newly established position it had won amongst the working class and the trade union movement at the end of the war. Accordingly, in May 1947, the PCF did not support a motion of confidence on government economic policy and, as a consequence, was dismissed by the Socialist Prime Minister, Paul Ramadier.

(6) *Isolation (1947-62).*   At first Party leaders assumed they were leaving office for only a short period and they continued to describe the PCF as a 'party of government'. From the autumn of 1947, however, under instruction from the recently established Cominform, a new wave of 'revolutionary activity' began as the Party returned once more to total opposition. Over the next fifteen years, apart from short, half-hearted interludes, the PCF showed little desire to leave its, largely self-imposed, exile. Continually emphasising its distinctiveness, it showed its most Stalinist face and more than lived up, though perhaps not quite in the way that was intended, to Thorez's proud boast of 1950, 'We are not a party like the others'.

The Party's rigid and inflexible brand of communism showed itself in a number of ways. Domestically, the return to dogmatism resulted in the erstwhile Socialist partners again being consigned to the role of 'class traitors' and to the newly-won power in the CGT being used to encourage 'political' as well as 'economic' strikes. Ideologically the keynote was sterility, the only significant development occurring in the mid-1950s when the 'impoverishment' campaign was launched, wherein it was claimed, against all the evidence, that the working class was becoming increasingly poorer in absolute terms. In its general orientation the party was always mindful of, and obedient to, Soviet policy, whether this involved assisting the Moscow inspired Peace Campaign, as it did from 1948-52, or giving unblinking support to the 1956 invasion of Hungary. The only unease with the Soviet Union stemmed not from objections to dogmatism but rather to the 'liberalisation' programme announced in 1956. Having virtually deified Stalin the PCF tried to brush aside the logic of the secret speech 'attributed to Comrade Khrushchev'. As for the possibility of 'peaceful roads to socialism', which the PCI seized upon so eagerly, there was only the barest interest.

Somewhat surprisingly, in view of this slavish acceptance of Soviet dominance and the apparent contentment with the political ghetto, the PCF vote, which had peaked at 28 per cent in November 1946, held up at 26 per cent in both 1951 and 1956. Other loyalties however, which were more sorely tested, were often found wanting: membership fell to around 300,000 by 1955 and readership of the press declined from an estimated 2,770,000 copies of daily communist newspapers sold in 1947 to 800,000 in 1955.[10] Progress was also limited in other areas and the Party did not succeed in penetrating, to the extent that had seemed possible just after the Liberation, the many advisory and decision-making bodies that exist at all levels in France. Most disappointing of all, from the PCF's viewpoint, the CGT proved not to be quite the potent weapon that had been anticipated.

The PCF balance sheet in 1958 was therefore a mixed one. Its electorate and membership both made it the largest of all French parties. Its strength was further underlined by the considerable, though not excessive, influence it exercised in local councils, trade unions, boards of nationalised industries etc. But where was the Party going? The events of the Popular Front and the Liberation suggested, whatever might still be claimed, that it would never attempt a classic revolutionary seizure of power. Yet it languished in its political ghetto, unwilling seriously to enter the parliamentary game other than on conditions that were quite impossible for potential allies to contemplate. Furthermore, the characteristics which the Party had maintained and emphasised amidst its many twists and turns – in particular its unquestioning pro-Sovietism and its rigid internal discipline – were so alien to other parties that it was difficult to see on what basis the PCF could re-enter the political mainstream. It seemed to be condemned to continued isolation.

3. The Socialist Party

The SFIO quickly recovered from the schism which had left it in a minority at Tours. Some support was permanently lost, notably in urban and industrial areas, and the Party's newspaper *L'Humanité* was taken over by the Communists, but there were compensations which soon proved to be major sources of strength. Many of the more experienced and influential leaders retained their allegiance to *la vieille maison*. A number of powerful positions in different parts of the country were maintained such as in the Nord (notably in Lille), the Gironde, and the Bouches-du-Rhône. Above all, most of the parliamentary group remained firmly loyal. To this base many 'deserters' soon returned, disillusioned with Bolshevisation or removed by the 'cleansing purges' in the PCF. In addition new support was gradually added, often at the Radicals' expense, as the split made the SFIO more reliable in the eyes of the rural and anti-clerical petit bourgeoisie and sections of the urban middle class. As a result the number of SFIO Deputies grew, from 54 in 1920, to 101 in 1924, 100 in 1928, 132 in 1932 and, to make it the largest party in France, 141 in 1936. Membership, which had initially slumped to 30,000 in 1920, also recovered to reach 110,000 in 1928 and a pre-war peak of 250,000 during the Popular Front.

At Tours the opponents of affiliation to Comintern had advanced four main objections.[11] Firstly, they rejected the proposed methods of capturing and exercising political power. In particular they were not prepared to accept the idea of the dictatorship of the proletariat and the implications therein for individual liberty. Secondly, they did not want to be part of a closely integrated, Moscow-dominated, communist movement. Thirdly, they did not favour the proposed organisational structure based on the Leninist principles of democratic centralism. Fourthly, they disagreed with the intention of changing the relationships between the socialist political party and the trade union movement whereby the latter would become subservient to the former.

Fearing the consequences of Bolshevik discipline and control the SFIO put its faith into freedom and democracy. It emphasised its opposition to narrow dogmatism and firmly asserted its attachment to organisational flexibility and trade union autonomy. At the same time, however, it was reluctant to dispense with the Marxism which was such a part of its heritage. Class struggle was to remain at the heart of its formal analysis of French society and the revolutionary transformation of that society was still to be its final goal. The strain, which had been present in the SFIO since its foundation, between revolutionary pretensions and potential reformist practice, was thus maintained in the post-Tours era.

Though never far from the surface this strain was largely held in check until after the Second World War. Ironically, given the affirmations to internal democracy in 1920, a major reason for it holding together was that its structure became increasingly oligarchic. A dyarchy emerged at the top, with Léon Blum the leading parliamentary spokesman and Paul Faure in charge of the party organisation. Other posts of responsibility were dominated by long-serving officials appointed almost on a seniority basis. There was always a running current of ideological debate, the importance of which ebbed and flowed with the tide of events. There were even break-aways. But there were no major ruptures and a balancing act between developing reformism and latent fundamentalism was maintained. So, in 1924 and 1932 the Party's electoral situation led it into electoral agreements with the Radicals. But it did not follow its partner into government and it reserved its right to withdraw support when the Radicals pursued conservative economic policies. Even when the Socialists did eventually enter government, to head the Popular Front in 1936, they could claim that the circumstances were such that no denial of their underlying revolutionary beliefs was implied. Quite apart from the necessity of resisting fascism they could point to many radical proposals in their programme. And in any event had Marxism not long recognised the compatibility of holding both minimum and maximum positions?

But the logic of the SFIO's ideology, support, and strategic situation inevitably moved it, whatever the official pretence, towards a *de facto* reformism. Because of this, Blum and the General Secretary Daniel Mayer attempted, immediately after the war, to divest the Party of its increasingly anachronistic Marxism. Hoping to build on the spirit of co-operation which had come out of the Resistance – in which they had been actively involved (and which helped to make up for the fact that in 1940 three quarters of the SFIO Deputies were amongst those who had voted plenary powers to Pétain) – they sought to construct a British style Labour Party: a party which could transcend the bitterness of the age-old clerical issue; a party which, by virtue of both its idealism and moderation could attract reformers from all political and religious backgrounds; a party which would thus come to the very centre of the political stage.

But they failed, and Mayer, amidst accusations of betrayal of the Socialist heritage, was removed from his post at the 1946 Congress by the 'purist' Guy Mollet: in Philip Williams' words 'The rank and file remained attached to the old doctrines, the old prejudices and the old faces'.[12] The opportunity for rejuvenating the non-Communist Left was therefore lost. The SFIO and the Catholic MRP did continue to work together in government after the removal of the PCF in May 1947 – and in so doing they raised some hopes of a permanent 'Third Force' – but gradually the two drifted apart as the MRP, pushed by a conservative electorate and pulled by the re-emergence of the church schools question, increasingly co-operated with Conservatives and Gaullists.

The collapse of Tripartism (SFIO, MRP and PCF) and then of the Third Force (SFIO, MRP plus smaller parties) ended any lingering hopes that the Socialists might become the fulcrum of a stable, progressively reforming coalition. Thereafter they could enter government only with parties to their Right. However the balance of forces during the Fourth Republic was such that they constantly felt the need to do precisely that, for in each parliament around 200 of the approximately 600 Deputies (both figures wavered) seemed intent on disrupting the system or even actually bringing it down. Before the 1951 elections these were principally Communists, but afterwards they were supplemented by a vituperative extreme Right, made up initially of Gaullists and after 1956 of Poujadists. Governments could only be formed therefore from amongst the 400 or so who were prepared to work within the system. This put the Socialists in a pivotal position since they made up about one quarter of these 'available Deputies': 105 Socialists were elected to the 1946 Chamber, 107 in 1951 and 99 in 1956. It was a position not dissimilar to that held by the Radicals in the latter part of the Third Republic; governments could always be formed without their active support but it was a precarious business and such governments would always have an uncertain future.

The Party was, therefore, continually in a dilemma. Should it take office so as to defend parliamentary democracy and with the hope that it could persuade its assorted Radical/MRP/Conservative allies to pass social reforms? Or should it concentrate on retaining its ideological zeal and defending its electorate from Communist advances by remaining in the safe haven of opposition? The conflict was never satisfactorily resolved. Despite bringing down six governments in the 1946-51 parliament the Party continued to return to similarly composed Cabinets where the balance lay increasingly to the Right. After 1951, stimulated by electoral losses, it withdrew from office altogether, although it did give some support to the Mendès-France government in 1954. After the elections of 1956 it returned to office with Mollet as Prime Minister, but after initially succeeding in passing some important social reforms the old problems set in and the Socialists were again imprisoned by parties to their Right.

Like the system which it defended, the SFIO from the late 1940s thus became increasingly *immobiliste*. The gap between rhetoric and practice developed into a chasm as caution and uncertainty became the Party's principal features. The phrases which were included in the Party's 1946 Declaration of Principles – 'abolish the capitalist property system', a party of 'class struggle', 'essentially a revolutionary party' – increasingly bore no relationship to reality. With internal policy divisions, such as those over the European Defence Community and Suez, exacerbating the situation further, initiatives became more and more infrequent.

This inability to generate new ideas was paralleled by, and partly occasioned by, a stagnation in support and influence. Like the PCF and MRP the SFIO had benefitted, though not so spectacularly, from a creditable Resistance record. But from gaining 23 per cent of the vote in 1945 there was a gradual slide: to 21 per cent in June 1946, 18 per cent the following November, 15 per cent in 1951 and again in 1956. This decline was largely a result of waning support amongst the working class. Inevitably this resulted in an increasingly conservative electorate. Membership fell even more sharply. From a post-war peak of 350,000 in 1946 it settled down in the 1950s to around 110,000, almost half of whom by the end of the Fourth Republic were local councillors.

The low membership (which still placed the SFIO, amongst all parties, second only to the PCF) and the deep entrenchment in local government emphasised how firmly the Socialists were embedded in the French tradition. Other related features also made it a typically French – rather than socialist – party. Tactically it was unable, and was not even especially willing, to build up its outside influence in the trade unions or in community, social and civic associations. Its organisation, despite a nominally hierarchical and democratic structure was, in practice, like the parties of the Centre and the Right, highly decentralised and *notabiliste*. Many federations were dominated by a few key individuals and in some cases were virtually personal fiefs. Outside the major federations – the Nord, Pas-de-Calais, Seine Saint-Denis, and Bouches-du-Rhône were the largest – there were often hardly any Party activities at all other than at election times. Moreover, during the election campaigns there was, whatever was negotiated in Paris, considerable local autonomy and flexibility. Manoeuvering as adroitly as the most seasoned opportunists, local organisations frequently went in quite different directions, depending on whether circumstances dictated an alliance with or against Communists, Christian Democrats, Radicals or even Conservatives.

The SFIO in 1958 was thus in a weak position to face the challenges that were to come. Like most other French parties it was more concerned to hang on to its assets – in local government and in Parliament – rather than, by new initiatives, seek to expand them. Being tainted with the faults of the increasingly discredited Fourth Republic it was inevitably exposed to attack from the new force, Gaullism, which was soon to re-emerge on the political scene. While it may after the war have participated in government for honourable reasons the suspicion was that its motives were now essentially opportunistic. The seeming lack of purpose and direction were no more clearly demonstrated than in Mollet's sixteen-month premiership which was best remembered for the Suez fiasco and the rapid escalation of the bitter and bloody war in Algeria.

The events of 1958 themselves showed the problems only too clearly. In March the Party's National Council divided over the question of continued participation in the Gaullist government (2754 votes were cast in favour, 1157 against). In June the Parliamentary group split over de Gaulle's investiture as Prime Minister (42 'for', 49 'against'). In September the National Congress could not agree on whether to support the new Constitution (2786 'yes' votes, 1176 'no' votes). Following the Congress a number of members, including prominent and long-standing figures such as Daniel Mayer, Edouard Depreux, André Philip and Alan Savary left the party. The hesitations, divisions and final decisions of 1958 were, for them, the culmination of a disillusionment which in some cases went back many years and which had been sharpened by Suez and Algeria. Many became involved in the formation of a new party, the *Parti Socialiste Autonome* (PSA).

The SFIO at the end of the Fourth Republic was thus in a state of confusion, division, and upheaval.

4. The Radical Party

The history of the Radicals is less turbulent than that of the PCF and SFIO, since the trends and features which were apparent before 1914 continued not only after the First World War but into the Fourth and even the Fifth Republics.

The most notable of these was its ability to straddle the political spectrum. On the whole, because of both tradition and electoral advantage, it preferred to contest elections as part of a loose, non-communist, Left-wing alliance. In government, because of its orthodox, liberal economic views, it felt more comfortable with Centrist or Rightist partners. As a result it frequently began a parliament as part of a victorious Left coalition and ended that same parliament firmly implanted in a Right-wing government.

This 'flexibility' was only possible because of the continued lack of any coherent or restricting ideological identity. The Radical label was increasingly used simply for reasons of electoral convenience. Power itself became the principal binding force as, at both local and national levels, the Party was able to offer considerable opportunities for political advancement without demanding anything other than vague attachments to elusive concepts. This was no more clearly demonstrated than in the Fourth Republic when Radicals were represented in every government from January 1947. Eleven of the Republic's twenty-eight Prime Ministers came from the Party. In local government, other than in the large towns, Radical influence was equally strong. It is a remarkable fact, to foreign eyes at least, that in the last years of the Fourth Republic, when Party membership had fallen to around 30,000, there were still over 40,000 municipal councillors who had been elected on the Radical label.

But as well as being a strength, in that it provided disproportionate opportunities for manoeuvre and power, the flexibility, not to say vacuousness of Radicalism, was also a weakness; in two senses.

Firstly, it inevitably contributed to, although it was also a reflection of, organisational weakness. There was barely even the semblance of a structured apparatus. Power lay very much in the hands of local committees, most of which were presided over, and dominated by, well known local figures. With electoral success being the prime goal and with the Party being increasingly pinned back into small towns and rural areas, especially in the south-west, this lack of hierarchical restraint, coupled with the absence of restrictive ideological baggage, allowed for a veritable myriad of local arrangements to develop. In some areas Radicals would appear as reformers and partners of the 'progressive social forces' but in others they would be allies of the Conservatives in campaigns to defend the Republic against Socialist or Communist change. When, in the Fifth Republic, politics became less local and more national this extreme decentralisation was to prove a great handicap.

Secondly, the ideological width of radicalism, coupled with its weak structure, inevitably meant that many different strains jostled uneasily together. The lack of discipline and absence of sanctions had the advantage that the different elements could go their different ways and still share the same umbrella, but it also undermined the ability of the Party to act together coherently. In the inter-war period this was most dramatically seen during the Popular Front when interests pulled in quite different directions. One section of the Party rallied to traditional Radical symbols and supported the then Party leader, Daladier, in his policy of republican defence. The more conservative sections, however, not wishing to be associated with the 'socialistic' elements of the Popular Front programme, openly resisted this strategy and eventually had their day when they were able to use their power in the Senate to bring the Blum government down.

After the Second World War division was more apparent than ever. A major reason for this was that although there was a partial recovery from the handicaps which had faced the Party at the end of the war – association with the little lamented Third Republic, an indifferent Resistance record coupled with taints of Vichyism, an unfavourable electoral system – it never quite regained its central parliamentary positions. In the 1945-6 elections it averaged, with allies, 11 per cent of the vote and gained between 53 and 70 seats; in 1951 it won 10 per cent and 95 seats; in 1956 it won 15 per cent and 94 seats. This, coupled with disillusionment at the continual 'drifting', brought about a reaction in the mid-1950s and a campaign, led by Pierre Mendès-France, for a more disciplined party grouped around a progressive programme. Almost inevitably this demand for reform was opposed by many of the old guard and led to heated debates and deep antagonisms. Initially Mendès-France's campaign enjoyed some success. He became Prime Minister and, for a while, was able to attract support from both the PCF and the SFIO. The excitements he generated were a major reason for the increase in the Radical vote in 1956. In the longer term, however, because of the deep opposition he faced in sections of his own Party, and perhaps too because he was not as radical or as determined as had at first been thought, his campaign's principal effect was to bring to the surface the many festering divisions amongst Radicals. Between 1955-8 there were three significant break-away groups and, though none was to make a lasting impact in its own right, much young lifeblood was lost to the Party.

Like the SFIO the Radicals were, therefore, in a state of some disarray, and not a little disillusion, when the Fourth Republic collapsed.

THE LEFT IN 1958

From the first appearance of political parties in the 1870s the Left was mainly characterised by divisions. As a result, and despite the fact that it frequently commanded a numerical majority amongst the electorate, the Left was normally also characterised by political weakness, especially at governmental level.

There had been numerous attempts to overcome the differences, suspicions and hostilities. The most ambitious of these were the attempts at organic unity, but since the temporary unity forged in

1905 none had come to fruition. Negotiations between the SFIO and the PCF at the times of the Popular Front and the Liberation hardly got off the ground and had largely been initiated for reasons internal to the PCF. In government, and most notably during the Popular Front and Tripartism, there had been a different form of co-operation but then too the divisions had been such that they could not long be fudged. In the first case, the 'right of the Left' (the Radicals) had withdrawn support because of the socialism of the government. In the second case, the 'left of the Left' (the PCF) provoked their own dismissal because they were concerned at their association with moderation. Less ambitiously various other truncated forms of co-operation had been attempted. Many of these had taken the form of electoral arrangements between Radicals and Socialists. Once again, however, they usually proved to be ephemeral, rarely lasting much beyond the immediacy of winning seats.

There was no reason to think in 1958 that this situation would change. The three principal Lefts – Radicals, Socialists and Communists – were divided on many important issues and some of these were of a fundamental nature. On the very question of the new Constitution they each went their different ways; the PCF firmly opposed it, the SFIO was almost evenly divided, and the Radicals were broadly in favour of it.

Not only were the divisions, at least between the PCF and the others, as potent as ever but the Left was also weaker than it had been for a generation. From 1945 it had gained an overall majority of votes in every one of the five national contests held, (including for the Constituent Assemblies). But in October 1958 it won a total of only 43 per cent in the elections held for the first Assembly of the new Fifth Republic. Many of its votes went to the resurgent Gaullists.

The political prospects of the Left, as the Fifth Republic dawned, were thus decidedly gloomy.

Part II The Parties of the Left

3 The Socialist Party

INTRODUCTION: PERSISTING PROBLEMS

In France the political party which has most openly borne the colours of socialism has always been a party of contradictions. In spite of the resuscitation and rejuvenation which it has experienced since 1969 it continues to face many of the dilemmas and divisions which have plagued it since its foundation in 1905.

On the whole individuals have joined, influenced and led the Socialist Party because they have believed in its ambitions for a more just and humane society where man can live freely and without exploitation. Such ideals, however, which are also those of the international socialist movement, are vague and tenuous. As a result they are able to act as a uniting bond only at the most general level. Fundamental questions remain, notably on the structural nature of the projected socialist society and the means by which that society is to be brought about.

In the early years the main line of division within the SFIO was over the basic issue of reform or revolution. As we saw in Chapter 2 this question was quickly resolved in favour of the former. From having originally envisaged the total collectivisation of society and from having been totally opposed to the established order of the 'bourgeois state' the Party after Tours – in practice if not always in theory – came to moderate its perceptions and policies. In particular, it accepted parliamentary institutions as the legitimate organs for the democratic expression of the will of the people and as the channels through which reform should be pursued.

This commitment to parliamentary reformism has since meant that to achieve national power the Party has normally been obliged to seek alliances with other political groupings. For even if the Socialists have usually been capable of obtaining a significant proportion of seats in Parliament they never approached until 1981 an overall majority. The fact that the Party has usually had a choice, either to its Left or its Right, when thinking about alliances, and furthermore has had to

47

decide on what terms agreements are permissible, has been a persisting source of tension.

Underlying the choice of alliance strategies have been different views concerning the role of the State, the position of the Party within the State, and the nature and extent of the reforms that the Party should pursue. To cite just one example, a sharp internal division developed between 1930 and 1934 over the possibility of 'using the bourgeois State' in order to bring about its decline. Blum and his supporters advocated a 'Popular Front' strategy which would be confined to parties of the Left. To this was contrasted the so-called 'neo-socialist' approach of Déat and others who proposed the association of the SFIO with bourgeois parties in an attempt to push the development of capitalism in a socialistic direction. Central to the difference between the two sides was the neo-socialist's view that the *ownership* of the forces of production was less important than its *control*. A similar debate continues in the Socialist Party today with the 'Left-wing' CERES grouping giving collectivisation a high priority, while the more 'moderate' Rocard supporters look upon many collectivist proposals as 'redundant and archaic statism'.

Such recurring divisions have inevitably undermined the political effectiveness of the Socialists. Until recently other features have also been a source of weakness. Firstly, in spite of brave rhetoric from its leaders, the Party, particularly after the Second World War, increasingly became identified with ossified local power bases in which it did little to pursue clearly defined objectives beyond seeking advantageous local electoral agreements. Secondly, the Party's decentralised organisational structure, while allowing for almost unlimited local electoral flexibility, greatly contributed to a lack of coherence at the national level. Thirdly, when the Party did hold office, whether in national or local government, it often felt compelled to bow to pressure from the Left or the Right. As a result it failed to fulfil the hopes and wishes of many of its militants and much of its highly disparate electorate.

As we proceed now to examine the development of the Socialists in the Fifth Republic we shall see that the major resuscitation and rejuvenation which the Party experienced after 1969 enabled it partially to overcome some of its persisting problems. But at the heart of the Party there lay, right up to the 1981 elections, a seemingly inherent agonising over both its conception of socialism and its preferred political strategy. Divisions on these questions became particularly pronounced following the defeat in the 1978 legislative elections as the frustrations of unfulfilled electoral expectations and the continuance of what had already been a long period of parliamentary opposition had their effect. Having adopted a Left-wing strategy and accompanying radical policies in the early 1970s, and then finding in the late 1970s that these were in some ways contributing to the opposition role, dissenting voices began to question the direction which the Party was taking. The persisting tendencies of factionalism and internal struggle came once more to the fore. However, the tactical skills of the Party leadership under François Mitterrand, greatly aided by divisions in the governing Majority coalition and also by the increasingly intransigent policies that were pursued by the PCF, allowed the Socialists to surmount their internal difficulties. In 1981, for the first time in French history, a Socialist was elected to the presidency by universal suffrage. This was quickly followed by the most spectacular parliamentary election victory any single party of the Left has ever achieved.

THE DEVELOPMENT OF THE SOCIALIST PARTY IN THE FIFTH REPUBLIC

1.   Coming to terms with the Constitution: 1958-62

Though the SFIO began life in the new regime as a divided and much discredited force Mollet believed the Party could become the vanguard of the new regime. Placing much faith in the newly introduced two ballot electoral system he anticipated a rise in Socialist strength. This would place the Party in a position where it could mould the institutions designated in the ambiguous 1958 Constitution in such a way that they would fit in with Socialist interests.

It soon became clear that this intention to become the vanguard, or pivot, of the Fifth Republic would not succeed. For one thing it was also the aim of the newly-established Gaullist party, the *Union pour la Nouvelle République (UNR)*, and it quickly established itself in the central position by virtue of its great success in the 1958 elections. A second and more fundamental problem facing the SFIO concerned de Gaulle himself who began to act in a way which contravened the Socialist's conception of the new Republic. They had been willing to accept a parliamentary regime with a strengthened executive because they believed it to be the only way of reasserting the authority of the State at a time of crisis. It soon became apparent to them however that de Gaulle wished to be as independent as possible of parliamentary constraints.

So, for Mollet and the SFIO, coming to terms with the constitution demanded an initial recognition of their near impotence in terms of influencing government policy. It also forced them to re-evaluate the fact that they had endorsed, by majority vote, a regime which they now distrusted. For Mollet, who was particularly associated with that endorsement, there was little choice but to go on to the attack if he was to hold the Party together and preserve his position as leader.

One might be forgiven for thinking that de Gaulle engaged in collusion in assisting Mollet in his quest for a new strategy. In August 1962 it was announced that a referendum would be held to amend the Constitution, in order that the President might henceforth be elected by universal suffrage. This *de facto* expansion of presidential authority met with the predictable anger of the SFIO and on 5 October, along with the MRP, the PCF and the Radicals they voted a motion of censure on the government of Georges Pompidou. This, together with their implacable opposition in the referendum campaign, confirmed their complete break with Gaullism. When the pro-Gaullist parties achieved a landslide victory in the subsequent November elections it was clear that the Socialists would need a new strategy if they were to compete effectively for political office.

2.   Options for a new direction 1962-9

From 1962 two strategies began to emerge and to compete with one another in the SFIO. Though conflicting in important respects they shared three important characteristics. Firstly, they were closely associated with the political careers of their main protagonists. Secondly, they were both dependent on reversing the decline in Party support and re-activating the many areas where activity had virtually ceased. Thirdly, since there were now few parliamentary constituencies where the Socialists could win by themselves, they were both also dependent on forging links with other political parties.

The first strategy was championed by Mollet and was based on the dual aim of preserving Party autonomy while at the same time creating some sort of Left-wing alliance in which the PCF would have a role to play. The reasoning behind his choice was essentially pragmatic and opportunistic, though his habitual indulgence in Marxist rhetoric and references to the 'lessons of history' were used to give public credence to the decision. But 'fundamental opportunism' had always been his most prominent characteristic even if it was masked by a certain doctrinal rigidity, a fervent anti-communism, and an absolute faith in the class struggle. The control he had exercised over the Party machine since 1946 had allowed him to place his followers in positions of responsibility and this had considerably facilitated his ability to change direction when it was tactically desirable. Not only that, control at the centre had also enabled him to prevent a coherent opposition from establishing itself within the central Party organisation. Whenever any attempt was made to do this, Mollet was sure to hear of it and to act so as to divert it.

Antagonism towards Mollet partly explains the attraction which many Socialists saw in the second strategy, which was espoused by the mayor of Marseilles and leader of the powerful Bouches-du-Rhône federation, Gaston Defferre. In essence Defferre proposed the creation of a new Third Force, stretching between the Gaullists on the Right and the Communists on the Left. The 1965 presidential elections, he believed, offered the opportunity for its creation. For whereas Mollet condemned the 'progression towards presidentialism' in no uncertain terms and initially wanted little to do with the election at all, Defferre had a more open approach to this new aspect of the regime and saw it as providing possibilities for the rejuvenation of the Socialists within the context of a re-animated Centre.

The details of the unfolding of the two strategies are discussed in Chapter 5, when we look at the development and transformation of the whole nature of Left-wing unity in the Fifth Republic. For the present, it may be said that together the two strategies raised questions which went to the very heart of the future role and nature of Socialism. Against Mollet's preference for a Party placed firmly on the Left Defferre was proposing and was attempting to launch a presidential campaign around a Centrist course which challenged deep-rooted assumptions of many Socialist leaders and members. Among the more controversial aspects of his strategy were proposals that certain long-standing differences with competitors, notably over the clerical issue, ought to be buried, that a stiff dose of anti-Communism was desirable, and that in the long term (though this was more muted) the Socialists might merge their identity into a new political grouping with the Radicals, the MRP and other smaller Centre and Centre-Left groupings.

When Defferre's campaign collapsed in June 1965 amidst divisions, jealousies and suspicions, the SFIO moved to the Leftist approach advocated by Mollet. There were two aspects to this. The first involved increased collaboration with the rest of the non-Communist Left. In the autumn of 1965 with the Radicals – who were now a rapidly declining political force – and some of the recently emerged political clubs (see below) they supported the presidential campaign of François Mitterrand, an ex-Centre-Left minister from the Fourth Republic and now a prominent figure in the club movement. The occasion of his candidature was taken to consolidate collaboration and a new body was established, which the SFIO dominated but over which Mitterrand presided, to co-ordinate and some hoped ultimately unite the non-Communist Left: the *Fédération de la Gauche Démocrate et Socialiste.* The second aspect saw the SFIO, through the FGDS, build up contacts with the PCF. This led to formal electoral agreements between the Communist and non-Communist Lefts for the 1967 and 1968 parliamentary elections.

During the mid-1960s there were two significant additions to the forces of the non-Communist Left which had important implications for the development of Socialism.

Firstly, there had emerged in the late 1950s and early 1960s a number of political clubs which drew most of their support from sections of the Centre-Left. Originally primarily motivated by a 'non-partisan' concern to rectify the general cynicism and disillusionment with politics which had accompanied the end of the Fourth Republic, many clubs from 1962-3 began to move in a more explicitly political direction within the Left, though they were by no means all at one in their specific motivations or sympathies. Some, for example, including the influential *Club Jean Moulin,* supported Defferre's presidential campaign, while others were either unsympathetic to his policies or preferred to retain their independent and essentially pedagogic character. Most of those clubs which did become more openly political were, however, in accord on a basic minimum: that the non-Communist Left urgently needed regeneration.[1]

The most influential organisation to come out of the club movement was the *Convention des Institutions Républicaines (CIR).*[2] It was created in June 1964 and emerged from a series of symposia amongst club members around the theme of 'the renovation of the Left and the appropriate practical activity to take in the present political circumstances'. Initially it served principally as a meeting place for sympathisers to the Left-wing cause who felt unable, usually for policy or organisational reasons, to associate themselves with the Socialists or Radicals. Soon however the CIR was moving in a much more explicitly political direction and by 1967 was, to all intents and purposes, acting as a political party itself. A principal reason for this vas that it was increasingly a vehicle for the political ambitions of Mitterrand. Another factor though, and this also affected other groups of political clubs such as the *Union des Clubs pour la Renouveau de la Gauche* (UCRG) led by Alain Savary and Pierre Bérégovoy, and the *Union des Groupes et Clubs Socialistes* (UGCS) directed by Jean Poperen, was that influence could more effectively be brought to bear from *inside* the Left. Accordingly many clubs became associated with the FGDS. Later (mainly from 1969) they found their way into the Socialist Party where they soon became influential.

The second important addition to the non-Communist Left was the *Centre d'Etudes de Recherches et d'Education Socialiste* (CERES). The originators, sometimes referred to as the *'chefs historiques'*, were Jean-Pierre Chevènement, Didier Motchane and Pierre Guidoni, all of whom graduated from the prestigious *Ecole Nationale d'Administration* in Paris, and Georges Sarre who worked for the Paris postal service and was a union organiser. CERES made the decision to join the SFIO and to try to change it from within. In this way they were notably different in their strategy from the other clubs and activist groups. It was their intention to ally themselves to what they perceived to be the mainstream of socialism in France, although they recognised from the outset what they called the 'social-mediocrity' which pervaded the SFIO. They felt it was important, if their 'revivified' Marxist approach was to have any real impact, to work within an existing party rather than attempt to make a *tabula rasa* of the past. In making this decision CERES became the only significant group to join the SFIO during what was a general period of decline.[3]

The upheavals which occurred in the spring of 1968 (and which have been extensively described elsewhere[4]) occurred at a time when the various elements of the non-Communist Left were apparently closer than they had been since the period of the Popular Front. Yet despite expectations within the FGDS that it would be possible to capitalise on the disorders of the popular revolt the 'events' ultimately served to emphasise its weakness. Internal divisions were brought to a head and the fragility of a Left-wing movement lacking a firm organisational base, a mass support, or a strong influence in the trade union movement was clearly shown. In November 1968 the FGDS was dissolved and the SFIO seemed once more to be without a viable strategy.

3.   Renovation and Rejuvenation 1969-77

The failure of the FGDS in no way diminished the need for a more
united non-Communist Left. It had shown, however, that if unity was
to be sustained it would probably have to be more narrowly based.
Accordingly when the SFIO National Council met in December 1968 it
decided that the Party should make way for a 'resolutely socialist
movement', and that to facilitate the task Mollet should stand down
as General Secretary. Discussions with the CIR and other clubs, which
had already informally begun, were made official, and steps were
taken to draft outline proposals for the formation of a new party.
Suspicion of SFIO domination led to some delay in the establishment
of local registration bodies which were given the task of recruiting
members, but by April 1969 the new party had attained an embryonic
existence at sub-national level and at national level a co-ordinating
committee was established on which all potential participants were
represented.

But the presidential election which followed de Gaulle's referendum
defeat and subsequent resignation at the end of April, ruined these
plans as prospective candidates began tactical manoeuvring for the
right to represent the new party. A campaign in favour of Mitterrand
orchestrated by the CIR was quickly pre-empted by a declaration of
intent by Defferre, but this in its turn was opposed by Mollet. Rival
political ambitions and jealousies thus brought the unification process
to a virtual halt. The Alfortville Congress in early May, which was to
have founded the new party, was characterised by divisiveness and
bitterness rather than the hoped-for harmony. A decision was taken in
principle to establish a new Socialist Party but this had little
significance since most of the potential 'newcomers' from the Clubs
did not attend. Angry at Defferre's attempt to establish a *fait
accompli,* and not wishing to be associated with a process which was
seemingly bringing about yet another SFIO-led Third Force option,
the CIR met separately at Saint-Gratien. There they decided they
could not support a party – the 'ex-SFIO' as some called it – which,
according to Mitterrand was 'a hundred years old before it was born'.

Defferre's candidature was accepted by the Alfortville Congress but
only half-heartedly. This, along with the general malaise and seeming
purposelessness of the Party was reflected in the presidential election
itself where he obtained a derisory five per cent of the vote. It was thus
more essential than ever that when the Socialists met again in July, at
Issy-les-Moulineaux, – this time with a much better representation

from the Clubs, though not the CIR – that a firm and coherent base be established on which the socialist current could be resurrected. Inevitably divisions were again apparent around the old problems: representation of groups and *tendances* on decision-making bodies; relations with the PCF and with the Centrists; who should be allowed into the Party and on what terms; and, of course, the long-standing personal rivalries.[5] Eventually, after much informal discussion and tactical manoeuvring a number of decisions were taken. The UCRG joined the Party, as did the section of the UGCS led by Jean Poperen. Alain Savary, the leader of the UCRG, was elected to a newly-created post of First Secretary, the position of General Secretary being abolished to signify a movement towards a greater collectivity (though not proportionality) in the leadership. The strategy of the now formally constituted *Parti Socialiste* was to be more clearly Leftist, with Centrist alliances being explicitly excluded.[6]

Although many believed Savary was not the ideal leader, being somewhat reserved in manner, he had amongst his assets a sound record of having for many years supported moves to rejuvenate French socialism. (After resigning from Mollet's government in 1956 on its Algerian policy, he spent some time in the PSU before leading the UCRG). Writing about the new party and his vision of politics in 1970 he encapsulated what might almost be called the essence of the French socialist philosophy: 'The Left approaches politics as a collection of values to be put into practice: the Right considers politics to be a heritage which must be cultivated'.[7] With his own values not dogmatically held and with a belief that diversification of thought within the Party was not an unhealthy phenomenon, Savary seemed in many ways an admirable choice.

But he never dominated the Party, with the result that his position was never wholly secure. One reason for this was that Mollet, who had supported him for the leadership, continued to exercise considerable influence in the Party organisation. In addition, certain elements within the Party which were excluded from leadership positions inevitably wanted to see further changes. CERES, which had allied itself with the UGCS, was excluded on the Left, having proposed 'the unity of all socialist forces'. On the Right, some of those who had maintained their long-standing belief in a Centrist formula, were in a similarly isolated position. A third factor undermining Savary's position was that Issy had not brought all democratic socialists into the Party. In particular the CIR had voluntarily remained outside. By the end of 1970, however, Mitterrand was prepared to allow a merger to go ahead. After discussions with CERES on the need for a more vigorous Left-wing strategy he felt there was a chance of bringing the parent party under his control.

As a consequence of this change in the CIR's attitude, the third attempt at socialist reunification in two years took place at Epinay-sur-Seine in June 1971. Although the two previous congresses had established, to a certain extent, a new leadership and a rejuvenated membership,[8] they had obviously not been successful in uniting all members of the socialist family. Large sections of potential supporters had been unwilling to participate in the creation of a mere substitute for the SFIO. Epinay necessarily had to be more than that.[9]

Six motions were presented to the Congress, none of which had an overall majority on the indicative vote which emanated from the federation (departmental) congresses. They were:

(1)	Savary and Mollet	34 per cent
(2)	Mauroy and Defferre (The Leaders of the two largest federations: Nord and Bouches-du-Rhône)	30 per cent
(3)	Mermaz and Pontillon (CIR)	15 per cent
(4)	Poperen (UGCS)	12 per cent
(5)	CERES	8.5 per cent
(6)	The Clubs *Objectif 72* and *Vie Nouvelle*	0.5 per cent

Differences in content between the motions principally concerned organisation, and the extent to which the new party should pursue a dialogue with the Communists. These questions took second place, however, to what was really at stake: the leadership of the new party. Principles counted for little amidst the jostling of the factions to be part of a winning coalition. This was apparent when Mitterrand was able to rally, for a composite motion drafted by himself, support from the leaders of motions (2), (3) and (5) above. CERES delegates then had to be convinced that it was only by voting with the 'Right' (i.e. Mauroy and Defferre) that they would be able to change the Party to the 'Left'. Mauroy and Defferre had to convince their respective delegations that an alliance with CERES and the CIR was the only way to obtain influence within the new leadership. Mitterrand, who had of course only just joined the Party with the CIR, had to convince both CERES and the Mauroy-Defferre delegations that his socialist credentials were valid and that he was the right man to be leader. In his speech to the Congress he emphasised that his prospective leadership coalition did not 'have the same conception of the methods and organisation of leadership within the Party as the existing majority group and it was this that was at stake'.[10] In truth, the chord that bound the politically heterogeneous coalition which gave him a narrow victory on the final vote (by 43,926 mandates to 41,757 for the motion presented by Savary) went even further for many delegates: their vote was born of a desire to rid the Party once and for all of everything that Mollet had symbolised for the past quarter of a century.

It was recognised from the outset that there was likely to be a constant internal struggle in the newly enlarged Party. For quite apart from the open factionalism and bitterness of Epinay, new organisational rules had been adopted which resurrected the old Socialist practice of proportionality in Party elections. Hence, it was all the more important to have as quickly as possible a programme and a strategy which all sections could support. The programme, *Changer la vie,* was adopted early in 1972 following a Convention at Suresnes.[11] This paved the way for the strategy, on which there was a broad measure of agreement within the leadership (if only because there appeared to be no viable alternative), of seeking to establish a programmatic as well as electoral agreement with the PCF.[12] The signature of a Common Programme with the Communists in June 1972 confirmed this Leftist strategy and provided a launching pad for the further development of the Party.

Mitterrand always made it clear that he saw his main task as leader to be to 'rebalance the Left' and make the PS its main component. From Epinay until well into 1977 he made consistent progress in that direction, both in terms of membership and electorate.

Membership more than doubled between 1971 and 1977-8: from around 80,000 to over 180,000. (See Table 3.5). Though these figures are modest by PCF standards they clearly represent real progress. Moreover the expansion in membership is partly accounted for by the addition of new political elements. In particular, in the autumn of 1974 at a specially convened *'Assises du Socialisme'* the Party welcomed an influx of members from the small Left-wing party led by Michel Rocard, the Parti Socialiste Unifié (PSU), and also from the socialist-inclined trade union, the CFDT.[13] This *courant des Assises* as it was often called, grafted a strong *autogestion* (workers' participation) wing onto the PS and a current of thought which was noticeably less doctrinaire and less orthodox in its socialist principles than most existing tendencies in the Party. At the *Assises* there was also a small injection of support from the 'other side' of the democratic-socialist spectrum. Most notably, a few former supporters of the governing Majority, including Jacques Delors (who had been an adviser to the Gaullist premier Chaban-Delmas) and Edgard Pisani (an ex-Gaullist minister) joined the Party. Although both these men were, in Chevènement's phrase, 'politically unemployed' at the time, they were soon to become important political advisers to Mitterrand.

Electoral expansion from 1971 was no less impressive. The party which in 1969 had seen its presidential candidate gain only five per cent of the vote virtually achieved 'electoral balance' within the Left as early as 1973 as a result of its new, dynamic, and generally innovative image. With almost 21 per cent of the vote in the legislative elections it was less than one per cent behind the PCF.[14] In the 1974 presidential election Mitterrand was designated as the *candidat commun* of the Left and lost to Giscard by only the narrowest of margins on the second ballot. Parliamentary by-elections in late 1974 showed that the PS was emerging as the most popular party in the country and this was confirmed in the 1976 cantonal elections and the 1977 municipals. By mid-1977 opinion polls were showing that the Socialists might hope for as much as 30 per cent of the vote in the legislative elections which were due in 1978.

This expansion in membership and electorate coupled with what was increasingly seen by outside observers as the *dynamique de la gauche* naturally engendered great optimism in the PS in the mid-1970s. However this mood could not disguise the fact that the Party was always an uneasy coalition, held together by the prospect of power and Mitterrand's astute management. In fact, it was not even completely held together. At the very first Congress after Epinay, at Grenoble in 1973, there occurred what has since been a central feature of the internal struggle for control: the various tendencies within the Party organised their own meetings prior to the Congress in order to discuss the motions which had been submitted to Congress and to make plans to attain their different tactical objectives. In the event, the Congress was a personal success for Mitterrand since his motion, to which both Savary and Poperen rallied, was supported by 65 per cent of the delegates. But the Congress also heralded what was to become the most important breach in the Party in the mid-1970s: that between Mitterrand and his many varied supporters on the one hand, and CERES – whose motion attracted 21 per cent of the vote – on the other. At the next Congress, at Pau in January 1975, this division was consolidated rather than appeased when Mitterrand, his hand strengthened by the support of the new 'Rocard group', further imposed his authority on the Party by removing the increasingly critical CERES, which now commanded the support of 25 per cent of the delegates, from its leadership positions in the Secretariat. This formalised the existence of a 'majority' and 'minority' within the Party and greatly contributed to relations deteriorating even further.[15] CERES reproached the leadership for the *'phénomène de cour'* which existed around Mitterrand and was also strongly critical of the lack of regard for the views of the membership in the internal policy-making process of the Party. The leadership counter-attacked by accusing CERES of contravening Article Four of the Party statutes which disallows tendencies from having their own independent premises and resources. There was even talk of a schism if a code of good conduct was not established and the suspicion of a 'party within a party' was not quelled. The 1977 Congress at Nantes did little to resolve the situation. CERES indicated their willingness to compromise and insisted that 'the task of the Congress is to define the convergences of the Party and not to deepen the divergences'.[16] Mitterrand however, despite pressure to give a unifying speech to the delegates in advance of the legislative elections, adamantly refused to change the minority status of CERES. Doubtless an important consideration for him was an anxiety not to scare or deter that moderate section of the electorate that had been attracted to the Party since 1971.

It is worth saying at this point that Mitterrand's strategy to rebalance the Left, by expanding and consolidating its Socialist element, linked up in the early 1970s with developments in the Radical Party. During the Fifth Republic Radicalism had become a progressively weaker political force but it had still continued to be a significant component of the Left through its participation in the FGDS. But with the reduction of the Party in 1968 to only thirteen deputies, the collapse of the FGDS in the same year, and then the election to the position of Secretary General of the Party in 1969 of the Centrist inclined Jean-Jacques Servan-Schreiber (see Chapter 5 for details), a momentum developed for an alternative strategy. This resulted in an open schism at the 1971 Congress between the 'Leftists' – which included most of the deputies – and the 'Centrists'. The latter were victorious with the result that the former – led by Maurice Faure, René Billères and Robert Fabre – left the Party. In July 1972, as the *Groupe d'Etudes et d'Action Radicale Socialiste* (through which they had previously liaised *within* the Radical Party), they added their signature to the Common Programme and at much the same time set about the task of establishing a new Party, the *Mouvement des Radicaux de Gauche* (MRG).[17]

Political weakness and expediency were important factors in the calculations behind the creation of the MRG and its adherence to the *Union de la Gauche,* since most of the deputies who participated owed their election to Socialist support. The Party has since continued to be by far the smallest element within the 'established' Left. In classic Radical style it is essentially a party of *notables*, based principally in the South West, with only a loose organisation and a low membership.[18] That notwithstanding, however, the MRG has been a useful addition to the Left and to the PS in particular. Its representation at national level is small but not insignificant; 10 deputies elected in 1978 and 14 in 1981. At local level – where Radicalism has traditionally been strong – it retains some strength; in 1981 it had just over 160 departmental councillors, presided over 8 departmental councils and had around 10,000 municipal councillors. It has contested elections as part of the Left and the 1973, 1978, 1979 and 1981 contests saw it in harness with the PS. On each occasion it has contributed probably around three per cent of the jointly counted PS/MRG vote.[19] Perhaps, above all, its image of moderation, its mixture of economic conservatism and social progressivism, its firm insistence that individual liberties and freedoms must never be sacrificed to collectivism, have constituted in the eyes of many doubtful electors a useful 'liberal corrective' to the principal parties of the Left.

4. 1977-80: Rupture, Defeat and its Consequences

1977-8 marked a turning point for the PS. Since Epinay it had placed its faith in the strategy of electoral and programmatic agreements with the PCF and the MRG – the *Union de la Gauche* – and from this it had reaped considerable benefits. So much so that by 1977 it was commonly assumed by politicians and the electorate alike that the Left would win the parliamentary elections of 1978 and that the Socialists would be the largest component therein.

It came as a great shock to the PS leadership when the *Union de la Gauche* was brought virtually to a halt in September 1977 following a breakdown in negotiations to update the Common Programme. The reasons for this breakdown are discussed in detail in Chapter 5. At this point it is sufficient to note that in PS and MRG eyes the Communists had stiffened their demands to an unacceptable degree. CERES favoured some concessions but the leadership, anxious not to be seen as being dominated by the PCF, was prepared to make only marginal adjustments in its position. The Party thus spent the election campaign trying to convince potential supporters that a unitary strategy of the Left was still feasible, whilst an increasing barrage of criticism from the PCF seemed to demonstrate that it manifestly was not.

The rupture in the negotiations inevitably damaged the electoral standing of the Left. The PS, which had been the principal beneficiary of the advances made by the Left since the early 1970s, was the hardest hit. Its ability to lead a stable and united governing coalition was no longer so credible with the result that, for the first time since 1971, it lost popular support. In the March elections it still succeeded in becoming the largest party of the Left, and indeed the largest party in metropolitan France, but its 22.5 per cent of the vote fell way below its expectations of six months previously and was sufficiently low to give victory to the Right. (Given the static vote of the PCF, at around 21 per cent, the PS vote was always going to be the most crucial factor in determining the outcome of the election).

The election defeat brought to the surface divisions in the Socialist leadership which had been glossed over while victory had seemed possible. The whole strategy of the Party was brought into question and the different groups all had their scapegoats. So, Rocard, in a carefully prepared statement on television shortly after the results were announced, alleged that since the autumn rupture the significance of the Common Programme had been devalued to the extent that it had become nothing more than a platform for short-term gain.[20] CERES criticised the organisation of the election campaign – from which they had been partly excluded because of their minority status – and attacked Rocard for questioning the validity of the Common Programme. Other factions and personalities joined in with variations on these themes.

Dissension arising from defeat was no less apparent in the MRG. Its leader Robert Fabre resigned, disillusioned with the events since September, and the Party proceeded to divide over whether it should remain anchored to the Left, and if so, how strong its association should be with the PS. Michel Crépeau, a deputy and the mayor of La Rochelle, quickly replaced Fabre at an Extraordinary Congress held in May 1978. However this did not prevent a further weakening of the

Party since his election was a victory for the 'Leftists' and this resulted in departures by several prominent supporters who, like Fabre himself, preferred independence. The new leadership has since maintained its close ties with the Socialists, but it has also begun to seek ways of re-creating its own identity in the eyes of the public.

The divisions in the leadership of the PS became increasingly evident throughout 1978 as factions and new coalitions manoeuvred for advantage. These were exacerbated by the prospect of the 1981 presidential elections – to which attention now turned – as potential candidates, notably Mitterrand and Rocard, began to jostle for position. It was hoped in many Socialist quarters that the Metz Congress, held in April 1979, would resolve this damaging situation. As we show in the next section it failed to do so. No fewer than five major motions circulated in the federation meetings prior to the Congress and at Metz itself, in a political about turn that was audacious even by Socialist Party standards, Mitterrand created a new majority on the basis of a tactical alliance with his former adversaries in CERES. In so doing he put Rocard, who was now allied with Mauroy, into the minority. This was in spite of the fact that on many policy issues, such as Europe and defence, Mitterrand's position was closer to that of the new minority, than it was to CERES.

The factionalism so manifestly open at Metz undoubtedly harmed the political credibility of the PS.[21] However, even after the 1981 elections, it is difficult to envisage circumstances in which such factionalism will not continue to be a central feature of Party life. For the bases of the disputes, disagreements and struggles for control are located not simply in personality squabbles and naked power clashes – though they are certainly present – but also in the existence within the Party of individuals and groups who have come from different traditions, have had different loyalties, and in many cases have different visions of the nature of socialism. Moreover, as we shall now see, the organisational structure of the Party institutionalises these differences.

ORGANISATION

1. Guiding Principles

As has been shown the PS has been formed and shaped by the

merging, at different times, of many groups. Though having varied backgrounds and often subscribing to differing views they cling together because they are united by a desire to be part of a governing party which promises to radically transform the basis of the state and of society. To facilitate the ability of these strands to accommodate themselves within the PS, and to try and ensure that there are not periodic break-aways from the Party in the way that there frequently were from the SFIO, a set of organisational arrangements and practices have been adopted which put great emphasis on participation and democracy. There are three main aspects to this: representation on decision-making bodies, policy development, and candidate selection.

Representation on most of the key decision-making bodies of the Party is on the basis of open and genuinely competitive elections. The spoils of these elections are allocated by proportional representation, except above the level of the *Bureau Exécutif*. From there the *Sécretariat* is elected by the majority of the *Bureau Exécutif* and the First Secretary is elected by a majority vote of the *Sécretariat* (See Figure 3.1 There is a discussion below of the problems created by proportionality).

The development of policy is a rather complicated process, closely related to the factional struggles within the Party. The ideas which become integrated into official policy can come from a number of sources, all intermingling and interacting in an ever evolving fashion. Amongst the most important of these are committees of deputies, standing Party committees (which bring together specialists in specific areas), study groups (of which there are well over 100), and the factions (which vary in the extent to which they self-conciously exist and therefore also the extent to which they are organised). Ultimately all policy has to be approved by the national organs of the Party on which, as a result of proportionality, all shades of opinion are represented.

The participatory ethos was no more clearly seen than in the development, between 1978 and 1980, of the new Party programme for the 1980s, the *Projet Socialiste*. The process started in the summer of 1978 when questionnaires were sent out to each member so as to assess the views of the grass roots. The intention was that a working party would then be set up to evaluate the responses and to draft the outline of the programme which would then be presented to the Party at its Congress at Metz in 1979. However the divergences amongst the leadership which became increasingly apparent during the summer and autumn of 1978 effectively precluded a common approach and it was decided therefore to postpone the drafting until after the Congress by which time a new leadership would have emerged. After Metz events moved rapidly. Jean-Pierre Chevènement, now returned to the leadership with CERES, was placed in general charge of the elaboration of the *Projet*. As in 1972, when the first PS programme had also been elaborated under his direction, working groups were set up to plan each section. This time, however, they had the additional task of sifting through a sample of the responses to the questionnaires. (The task of trying to systematically analyse all the replies proved to be impossible). An *ad hoc* committee, on which all tendencies were represented, co-ordinated the task of drafting and in the late autumn the fruits of their discussions were presented to the *Comité Directeur* and the *Bureau Exécutif*. In November the document was printed and distributed to the membership via a special supplement of the Party's monthly magazine *Le Poing et la Rose*.[22] This heralded a period of two months of debate at local level during which many critical opinions were voiced.[23] These were transmitted back to the national level via the many informal channels which exist in the Party, and also through the election of delegates and the submission of amendments to a special Convention. The final text of the *Projet* was ratified by 96 per cent of the delegates at the Convention. It was then printed in book form with an initial run of 150,000, most of which were bought by the membership in the following months. Each *section* of the Party (the lowest unit) then organised meetings to discuss the finalised document and regional conferences were prepared in order to ensure greater publicity and a wider audience for the Party's programme for the 1980s.

Turning finally to candidate selection the democratic and participatory principles are again apparent. The selection of Socialist candidates for elections, at legislative and local levels, takes place at mass meetings of members of the Party. This means that for legislative contests (though not for the European Parliament because France votes on a list system) a number of *sections* meet to question and finally choose a candidate, who is subject to re-selection procedure before the next election. The choice is later ratified by a specially convened Party Convention. On occasions, a locally chosen candidate may be considered to be unsuitable by the national *Sécretariat* and in exceptional cases they may substitute a candidate of their own choice. Such a procedure is obviously divisive, however, and as a result is infrequently used.

For presidential elections there was, until 1980, no established procedure, the 1965, 1969 and 1974 contests each having taken place in different and – in their own way – special sets of circumstances. The 1981 election, however, established an agreed way of making the choice. (Because of the poor relations between the PS and PCF there was never any question, unlike in 1965 and 1974, of a joint Left candidate). Under the new procedure, which was set out in May 1980[24] a three-month election period began in the autumn in which all members of the Party could participate and cast a vote. This was followed by Federation congresses and culminated in a special national selection congress which was held at Créteil in January 1981. Though all candidates other than Mitterrand withdrew well before the final selection the formalities of the procedure were still respected.

This emphasis on participation and democracy is not to suggest that the PS is immune from the oligarchic temptations and tendencies observable in parties elsewhere. In any large organisation some voices are more influential than others, if only because they are better informed, are more motivated, or because there are a whole series of circumstances which demand that a lead be given. The negotiations in 1977 to update the Common Programme provide an obvious example of a situation in which decisions had to be made quickly and where only limited consultation was possible. Moreover, there is no doubt that factionalism, and more recently the struggle for 'the succession' in the Party, has resulted in the exclusion of certain individuals and *courants* from decision-making areas at particular times. This is no more apparent than in the way in which Mitterrand increasingly sacrificed a truly collegiate leadership structure to the authority of the First Secretary and at the same time sought to create a situation whereby any attack on him was perceived as being synonymous with a 'disloyal' attack on the Party. Doubtless, now the Party is in office, circumstances will dictate a clear shift in certain decision-making processes towards the upper echelons – above all where policy is concerned.

2. The Elected Organs

The *section* is the basic meeting place for Party members and is equivalent to a ward in the British sense. It is usually situated in a geographical locality but it may be in a workplace in which case it is called a *groupe* or a *section d'entreprise*. In 1980 there were over 6,000 sections of which 1,300 were in workplaces.

Sections meet regularly, usually twice a month, to discuss matters of general policy as well as to decide on local activities. They elect an

Executive Committee which, in turn, elects a Bureau if it is a large section. From their numbers a Secretariat is elected and it is this which is often the effective decision-taking body at local level, though on all matters their deliberations are preceded and conditioned by a full debate and vote in the section.

On the departmental level sections are organised into *fédérations,* with the area of competence of the federations extending over all matters directly concerning the *département.* The leadership of the federation is elected, in accordance with article five of the Party Statutes, by proportional representation at the Federal Congress which meets before the National Congress. At the Federal Congress indicative votes take place on the motions which are to be presented to the National Congress, with a list of candidates being placed as an annexe to each motion. It is on this basis that the Federal Executive is elected and the delegates to the National Congress are appointed. After the National Congress the Federal Executive Committee elects a Secretariat which in turn elects a First Secretary of the Federation.

Without affecting their autonomy within the *département,* federations may meet on a regional or inter-federation basis in order to co-ordinate activity over a wider domain. In some areas such meetings are quite common, for example in Brittany where there is a strong regional identity.

An important development in the Party since the demise of the SFIO has been a decline in the influence of the large federations as membership has increased elsewhere. The three federations which dominated the SFIO – the Nord, Pas-de-Calais, and Bouches du Rhône – commanded only 25 per cent of the votes between them at the 1979 Congress (see Table 3.6).

At the same time, federations have become less homogeneous and more prone to internal factional competition. For the Metz Congress, as Table 3.1 shows, only 42 federations – less than half – gave over 50 per cent of their votes to one motion.

Table 3.1 Percentages obtained by four main *tendances* in Federal Congress prior to the National Congress at Metz, April 1979

% Mandate	Mitterrand	Rocard	Mauroy	CERES
50+	37	3	0	2
45-49.9	15	2	1	0
40-44.9	8	6	1	3
33-33.9	12	6	2	1

Source: Maintenant, 9 Apr. 1979

Figure 3.1 Structure of the PS

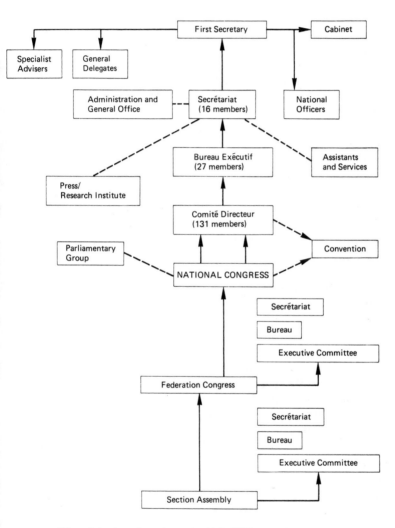

(Figures in brackets refer to the membership in 1980)

Although federations are thus divided, tendancies within the Party do nonetheless tend to have regional biases. For example, at the Metz Congress, although each of the principal motions received some support from all parts, Mitterrand drew his votes disproportionately from the South West (Aquitaine, Midi-Pyrenées, and Languedoc-Roussillon). Rocard was strongest in the West (Brittany is an old PSU area of influence) and in Yvelines where he is a deputy and a mayor. CERES did best in its stronghold of Paris and also in Eastern France.

Meeting every two years under normal circumstances, the *National Party Congress* is the sovereign organ of the PS. It is at the heart of the democratic process within the Party, but at the same time it is also the occasion for behind-the-scenes negotiations and bargaining between the different tendancies. What happens in the wings is at least as important as what happens outside in the public arena where the speeches are made and where the delegates sit.

To a great extent the general political debate is a purely formal exercise as the Federation Congresses will already have voted on the motions and delegates are bound to vote as mandated for the National Congress. Only those motions not counted in the Committee of Resolutions, because they did not break the five per cent barrier which is necessary in order to be represented, may have their votes redistributed. Composed of, in 1979, 62 members and elected on a proportional basis by the Congress, the Committee of Resolutions is responsible for determining the outcome of the hard-fought verbal battles waged on the floor of the Congress. All the leaders of the various factions will meet there, often late into the night, to thrash out their divergences and ultimately to form alliances on the basis of which the new Party leadership emerges.

Socialist Party Congresses are all milestones in the evolution of the Party. One talks of 'Epinay' where the Party in its present form was founded, of 'Pau' where the CERES group was excluded from the Secretariat, of 'Nantes' where Rocard emerged as the 'dauphin' of François Mitterrand, and of Metz where Rocard was excluded from the leadership and where CERES gained what has been described as their 'revenge' on the ex-leader of the PSU.

Delegates representing the various motions will meet a week prior to the National Congress in order to finalise their lists of candidates to the *Comité Directeur* which is elected at the Congress in proportion to the votes cast for the motions. These lists are then attached to the motions for consideration by the delegates.

The process may be illustrated by considering the 1979 Congress.

Seven motions were presented to the Congress, and the support gained by each one was as shown in Table 3.2.

Table 3.2   Support for motions to Congress of Metz

	Indicative vote %	Final vote %
Motion A. Mitterrand	40.11	46.97
Motion B. Mauroy	13.61	16.80
Motion C. Rocard	20.41	21.25
Motion D. Defferre	7.90	–
Motion E. CERES	14.32	14.98
Motion F. Pierret	3.24	–
Motion G. Femmes (Women's Movement)	0.30	–

The difference between the indicative vote (i.e. votes determined by the Federal Congresses) and the final vote (which determines the representation on the *Comité Directeur* arose from two factors: (1) The five per cent threshold prevented motions F and G being represented; (2) A synthesis was achieved at the Congress between motions A and D.

The results showed that Mitterrand would have to form an alliance with at least one of the other motions and their signatories in order to retain his position as First Secretary of the Party. Defferre, not wishing to be excluded from the leadership, pledged his support even before the Congress began, as soon as the indicative votes were known, but even then Mitterrand was still over three percentage points away from obtaining an absolute majority.

This created difficulties because the principle behind this type of election is that a coalition should be formed by groups who are able to reach agreement around a sort of composite motion or *synthèse* which states their general acceptance of a common policy option. So, at the Congress of Nantes in 1977 only two motions had been presented – one by Mitterrand to which most of the party rallied, and the other by CERES – and failure to reach a *synthèse* had left CERES in the minority and therefore excluded from the Secretariat. At Metz the situation was more complicated. Tactical considerations predominated, even more than usual, over clearly understood policies. Overshadowing the Congress were the forthcoming presidential elections and for Mitterrand, the prospect of a Socialist candidate declaring himself too soon constituted a significant handicap. By maintaining the post of First Secretary he would be able to keep all his options open. As Rocard was the alternative choice, though not avowedly so, it was in Mitterrand's interests to push Rocard and his ally Mauroy into the minority. (The Rocard-Mauroy alliance was essentially a marriage of convenience: Mauroy had become increasingly unhappy with Mitterrand's personalised leadership style, he opposed Mitterrand's determination to push Rocard into a minority position rather than seek an accord in the interests of Party unity, and he was against negotiating and compromising with the left-wing CERES group.) CERES were sympathetic to overtures from Mitterrand because they considered Rocard to be too close to the 'technocratic right' of the Party and also because they wanted to return to the Secretariat as their support in the Party had waned considerably since Nantes. They were therefore prepared to sink their differences with Mitterrand in order to enter the Party leadership again. So, far from being elected on the basis of common policy options, the new Secretariat emerged as a result of a tactical arrangement which posed a potential threat to the long term unity of the Party. As we shall see, the *Project Socialiste* was to provide a programmatic link to cement the new majority.

There are four bodies which have responsibilities for looking after Party business between Congresses. *National Conventions* bring together a delegate from each federation with members of the *Comité Directeur* and the parliamentary group. Conventions meet at least twice a year to provide a forum in which contacts between different sections of the Party may be maintained and to ensure that decisions made at Congresses are being respected. Special Conventions may be called from time to time, for example to try and resolve disputes in particular policy areas. The role of the *Comité Directeur* is to co-ordinate and implement Party decisions between Congresses and Conventions. Since, however, it, too, is rather unwieldy, having 131 members, most of the routine work is actually performed by the *Bureau Exécutif*. This has 27 members and is elected by the *Comité Directeur* on the usual proportional basis. The *Bureau Exécutif* is the highest level at which proportionality operates and as a result of this it has, since Metz, taken on more significance than hitherto because of the importance of the present 'minority'. Finally, drawn from the 'majority' within the *Bureau Exécutif* are the 16 members of the *Sécretariat*. Each of its members has a particular area of responsibility and within that area often enjoys a considerable degree of autonomy.

In a Party so divided as the PS the role of the leader – the First Secretary – is particularly difficult to fulfil. To assist him in his task he has a personal *cabinet* of close collaborators who attend to his briefings and manage many of his tasks. In addition he has the, often

Table 3.3   The Bureau Exécutif of the Socialist Party elected at the Metz
Congress 1979

Supporters of Mitterrand	Francois Mitterrand (S) (D) (M) – First Secretary
	Gaston Defferre (D) (M) – President of Parliamentary Group
	Lionel Jospin (S) – International Affairs
	Jean Poperan (S) (D) – Elections
	Pierre Beregovoy (S) – Relations with other parties
	Gérard Delfau (S) – Political Education
	Véronique Neiertz* (S) — Women's Affairs
	Laurent Fabius* (S) (D) – Press Spokesman
	Paul Quilès* (S) (D) – Organisations
	Christiane Mora* (S) – Communication and Propaganda
	Marcel Debarge* (S) – Local Affairs
	Michel Pezet* (S) – Environment
	Claude Germon* (S) (M) – Industry
Supporters of Mauroy	Françoise Gaspard (E) (M)
	Pierre Mauroy (D) (E)
	Daniel Percheron (E)
	Alain Savary* (D)
Supporters of Rocard	Michel Rocard (D) (M)
	Pierre Brana (M)
	Irène Charamande*
	Louis le Pensec* (D)
	Dominique Taddei (D)
	Michel de la Fournière*
Supporters of CERES	Jean-Pierre Chevènement (S) (D) – Study and Research Secretary
	Pierre Guidoni (D)
	Annette Chépy* (S) – Associations
	Michel Charzat (S) (E) – Nationalised Industries and Civil Service
Treasurer:	Pierre Joxe (S) (D)

KEY
S   – Member of Party Secretariat
D   – Deputy
E   – Member of European Parliament
M   – Mayor
*   – First elected at Metz

voluntary, services of a group of specialist advisers who may report either directly to him or through his *cabinet*. A number of 'General Delegates' are also nominated by the First Secretary personally and some, for example Georges Dayan until his death in June 1979, are extremely influential as general policy advisers.[25]

Perhaps the greatest difficulty facing the First Secretary is the need to impose some direction from above the mêlée whilst at the same time preserving a measure of Party unity. Until the 1978 elections Mitterrand balanced these two requirements with considerable success. On most occasions he was able to use his considerable tactical skills to see his views prevail whilst still being able to hold the Party together. But from the 1978 election defeat until he became the Party's presidential candidate in January 1981 his authority was by no means as complete as it had previously been. Frustrations following the defeat, the developing factionalism we examined earlier, and doubts about his capacity to present himself as a credible presidential candidate all combined to sap his authority, though not his prestige. The emergence of a new, younger generation of leaders also posed problems for him as the media increasingly began to concentrate on his possible successor.

The predominant institutional position of a nationally elected President of the Republic imposed a strong obligation on the PS until 1981 to choose a First Secretary whose appeal could reach beyond sectarian limits: he was after all, in effect, the Party leader. With the PS now in government there are clearly many ways in which ambitious Socialist politicians can project themselves other than through the inner Party structure. Where Lionel Jospin, who has replaced Mitterrand as First Secretary, will appear in the Socialist hierarchy remains to be seen. What is certain is that whatever status now comes to be attached to the position of First Secretary, the post will assume a key liaison role between the government and the Party in the country.

3. Mechanisms for Spreading Socialist Influence

The PS seeks to build up its support and extend its influence in a number of ways. The most obvious of these is through the direct efforts of its members. As with most parties, grass roots activism is most intense at election times but even between elections there is considerable 'visibility' in areas of Socialist strength. Posters, leafletting campaigns, public meetings and local *fêtes* are all commonly used devices to build up membership and 'spread the word'.

There are various organisations and groups through which the Party works or with which it has strong links. These fall into three broad categories. Firstly, there are those which are structurally part of the Party and which are principally designed to attract specific sections of the population to Socialism. The most important examples are the *Jeunesse Socialiste* and the *Etudiants Socialistes*. Secondly, there is the trade union movement. Although there are no formal links between the Party and the unions, as for example there are in Britain, there is an important Socialist presence in each of the three major industrial trade unions, plus the teacher's union. With the CFDT, the second largest industrial union, there is a particularly close relationship arising from a considerable overlap of membership and a shared ideological perspective at all levels. (The details of these party-union relations are discussed in Chapter 9). Thirdly, the PS is influential in a few ostensibly non-political clubs, societies and associations. The most significant of these are the *Foyers Léo-Legrange* which are, in effect, youth clubs and leisure centres. They have something like 50,000 members and are situated mainly in the Nord and Pas-de-Calais.

The PS presence in local government is also used to try to build up a favourable image of the Party. In areas where Socialists have long been entrenched in town halls, such as Lille and Marseilles, a well-established network exists, much of it informal, whereby it is generally known that it is through the Party that things get done. In areas where Socialist control of local affairs is more recent – and there have been major gains throughout France since 1971 – considerable efforts are being made to project an image of innovative reform coupled with administrative and technocratic efficiency. The considerable renewal which has taken place in local PS élites since 1969 has undoubtedly helped in this direction.[26] (There is an examination of the importance of the PS in local government in Chapter 8).

In creating images and disseminating political information the media, of course, has an important role to play. Since the Fifth Republic was established, the Left, with some justice, has accused the government of manipulation and interference in this respect. The 1978 and 1981 elections showed that little had changed. In spite of reforms in 1974 which were supposed to make radio and television less subject to government manipulation they continued to openly favour the Right. After the 1981 legislative elections it was hardly surprising when certain prominent figures in radio and television were pressurised into resigning and the new government initiated steps to make the services more genuinely impartial. The other branch of the media, the press, which is owned or controlled by highly conservative interests will doubtless continue to display its traditional hostility to the Left.

The PS is not, however, entirely without support in the national daily press. In recent years *Le Monde* has shown sympathy for many Socialist ideas, policies, and personalities. The paper's respectable and objective approach has done much, it may reasonably be supposed, to legitimise the Party's credentials amongst the better educated and moderate sections of the electorate. Since the latter part of 1976 a new paper, *Le Matin de Paris* (more commonly called simply *Le Matin*) has been avowedly Socialist, though it is independent from the Party. With a daily circulation of over 100,000 – compared to 450,000 for *Le Monde* – it has captured (by French standards) a respectable following in a short time. *Le Matin* is linked to the successful *Le Nouvel Observateur* which is an intelligent and well presented weekly news magazine with a circulation of nearly 500,000. Since its foundation in 1954 as *France Observateur,* it has supported progressive policies and since 1971 has backed the PS.

Since the disappearance of *Le Populaire* in 1969 the Socialists have had no daily newspaper of their own. In January 1981, at the start of Mitterrand's presidential campaign, a new attempt was made, with *Combat Socialiste*, but after the elections its closure was announced. In the regions, however, two daily newspapers are of considerable importance. In Marseilles, Gaston Defferre manages and runs *Le Provençal,* which is to be handed over to a co-operative ownership after his death. In the Nord, the daily *Nord-Matin* has supported the Socialists for many years. Both of these papers have been instrumental in helping to consolidate the Party in these most traditional bastions.

L'Unité is the weekly PS paper. It has a circulation of around 30,000 and it is very much the official organ of the Party, with its editorial content being supervised by the Party Secretariat. Another regular and general publication is *Le Poing et la Rose* which appears on a monthly basis. Special supplements of this are produced for Congresses and Conventions and most substantial Party projects and policy documents are circulated and discussed through its columns.

The Party also produces various reviews of a more specialised nature. *Communes de France* is intended for Socialist local councillors, *Combat* directs its attention primarily at the industrial sector, and *L'Unitè Agricole* is directed at rural supporters and sympathisers. There are several theoretically based reviews which are published either by the Party itself or by one of its factions. *La*

Nouvelle Revue Socialiste records symposium discussions organised by the Party's Research Institute, the *Institut Socialiste d'Etudes et de Recherche* (ISER), and also contributes to theoretical discussion within the Party as a whole. *Faire* is published by supporters of Rocard and is distinctly *autogestionnaire* in its sympathies. *Repères* was the well regarded journal of CERES, until, in an attempt to expand readership, it was replaced in mid-1980 by a new review entitled *Non*.

In order to publish books written by Socialists for an essentially Socialist readership the Party has established the *Club Socialiste du Livre*. Would-be authors can also look to the publishing company *Flammarion* which has published and distributed books by a number of prominent PS figures, most notably many of those written by Mitterrand and Chevènement.

The Party seeks therefore to transmit its message and project its image in various ways. We turn now to what is one of the major limiting factors on its activities.

4. Finance

For various reasons political parties tend to be reluctant to publish the details of their sources of income. The Socialists are franker than most. Since 1971 its financial position has been as shown in Table 3.4 (figures in francs)

Table 3.4 Socialist Party central organisation budget

Date	Expenditure	Receipts	Balance
25 June 1971			203,596
31 Dec. 1971	900,139	1,316,107	6,107
31 Dec. 1972	3,037,040	2,956,240	
31 Dec. 1973	5,030,440	5,125,482	
31 Dec. 1974	6,417,417	6,497,786	
31 Dec. 1975	8,772,656	8,738,078	
31 Dec. 1976	9,703,007	10,173,208	
31 Dec. 1977	12,216,667	12,164,214	
31 Dec. 1978	14,932,730	15,257,364	1,331,977

These figures represent the expenditure and income of the Party Headquarters. To these must be added the annual budgets of the

Federations. In 1977 these amounted to between 50-60 million francs and in 1978-9 they rose to over 70 million francs.[27]

Most of these funds are apparently obtained from subscriptions. According to Charles-Emile Loo, who was Party treasurer until 1979, membership fees account for approximately sixty per cent of the total.[28] The actual contribution of the individual is calculated as a proportion of his income. On average the figure is in the region of 100 francs.

Donations and fund raising activities also realise funds, with individual members being expected to periodically dig into their pockets, particularly at election times. Certain companies, firms and private individuals give lump sums but the total from this source is nothing like the amount received by the parties of the Right or the PCF. Amongst those who are known to give some assistance to the PS is the proprietor of FNAC in Paris, the owner of the Montparnasse Tower (where Mitterrand housed his campaign headquarters in 1974[29]), the managing director of Fournier Laboratories, and the Marquis Guy de Saint-Perier.

Another important source of income comes from the Party's various elected representatives. A Socialist deputy, for example, will normally pay over ten per cent or more of his stipend to the Party. This represents a contribution of about 1500-2000 francs per month. A Senator will give a similar sum and a municipal councillor of a large town will give approximately 750 francs per month. The increase in the 1970s in the Party's representation at both local and national levels has naturally significantly raised the income that is derived from this source, as has the success in the 1981 parliamentary elections.

Like other parties the PS also receives support from public funds. This comes in two main forms, 'open' and 'hidden'. The 'open' comes in the form of the printing and distribution free of charge by the State of national and local election literature. (This assistance is, of course, of even greater relative value to small parties, such as the MRG, which have only meagre resources). The 'hidden' support comes from the public funds which are available to pay the salaries of assistants of certain elected representatives. It is 'hidden' because though these funds are nominally intended for the exercise of public duties, a proportion of them, in practice, are indirectly channeled into party political activities. Being out of office until 1981 the PS has naturally not benefited from the large *cabinets* with which ministers surround themselves, but they have enjoyed the right of an assistant for each of their deputies and they have made liberal use of the ability of mayors in the large municipalities to be able to appoint 'advisers'.

Apart from direct income the financial position of the PS is also assisted by certain banking arrangements. It has managed to obtain favourable credit terms with the banks owned by the West German trade union organisation, the DGB, and the Swedish union, the LO. In France co-operative banks such as the *Banque Français de Crédit Coopératif* and the *Banque Centrale des Coopératives* have helped to finance a number of projects including the purchase of the political and administrative headquarters in Paris.

Turning now briefly to the expenses side, the Party has considerably expanded its activities and organisation since the demise of the SFIO. After nearly a decade in offices near the Palais Bourbon, which in 1981 were taken over by *Combat Socialiste*, the Party has moved into larger rented accommodation in the *rue Solferino*. Around 100 people are employed there on a full-time basis.[30] The Party bureaucracy is thus by no means as extensive, or indeed as rigid, as that of the PCF. Costs are kept down in a number of ways. The inability to establish a daily newspaper on a sound and regular basis is one aspect of the limited budgeting. Extensive use is made of unpaid voluntary assistance. So, at the centre, quite unlike in the PCF, many of the key Party figures and advisers who are not deputies are people with full-time – and often well paid – jobs outside: usually in academic life or in the liberal professions. Such limitations, however, should be seen in the overall context of the enormous financial and organisational improvement since 1971.

DOCTRINE AND POLICIES

The pressure for doctrinal change which built up in the West German Social Democratic Party (SPD) in the late 1950s, and which saw it adopt an explicitly reformist programme at Bad Godesberg in 1959, heralded the emergence of a period when ideological commitment fell into disrepute amongst most European social democratic parties. The SFIO was one of the exceptions. In practice, it was as reformist as many of the others, but formally, for a mixture of nostalgic, internal political, and electoral reasons it continued to cling to its traditional adherence to revolution and the class struggle. Some aspects of its doctrine were watered down in the 'Fundamental Programme' which the Party adopted in 1962 but the tenor of official vocabulary was still that of a party wanting to bring about 'fundamental' change, probably by a mixture of reformist *and* revolutionary means. Gaston Defferre's failure in 1965 to rally the Party behind his avowed reformism testified (amongst other things) to the continuing importance of the doctrinal inheritance.

It was only with the 1969-71 re-formation that the Socialists began seriously to re-evaluate their ideology and programme. Inevitably a problem from the very outset was the lack of internal homogeneity. The PS was, and is, the meeting place for different groups and factions, all of which have a contribution to make to the Party's ideological and doctrinal identity.[31] Currents range from those who draw much of their inspiration from the new lease of life given to radicalism in the late 1960s, to those who believe that cautious reformism is necessary in an uncertain economic world. As long as the Party retained its dynamism within the *Union de la Gauche*, and national office appeared to be imminent, these different strands could co-exist without too many difficulties. But after the 1978 defeat, ideological and programmatic commitments were called into question and could be so again now that in government it is not possible to fudge priorities.

This is not to suggest that the Party is wholly bereft of any common doctrinal base. On a general level there is what may be called a 'dominant attitude' which provides some measure of consensus on values. This may be summarised as a commitment to the abolition of injustice and inequality (the two are seen as inseparable) and the establishment of universal freedom and liberty. It is a humanitarian philosophy which is constantly supported by references to Jaurès and Blum and which is often supplemented by a recognition of the contribution made to socialist thought and analysis by Marxism.

On a more specific level there are two main elements which clearly differentiate the doctrinal perspective of the PS within the Left.

1. Analysis of Society: The Class Front

The concept of the class front goes beyond the original Marxist commitment to the working class by extending it to include a 'broad alliance incorporating all levels of society who are victims of capitalist exploitation'.[32] It was introduced to the Party by Jean Poperen and Serge Mallet who intended to take account of the new economic and social structures of modern society without denying the importance of the class struggle. In this way they hoped to steer a course between the 'traditionalism' of the PCF and the 'revisionism' of the advocates of a Third Force alliance.[33]

The PCF also accepts the need for class alliances but in its case they must be led and directed by the working class. This implies that those sectors of the population who do not belong to the working class must take a subordinate position within the alliance. Since the PCF presents itself as *the* party of the working class a subordinate position for other political parties is also assumed. For the PS such an analysis of the role of the class struggle is erroneous and quite unacceptable. It totally refutes the idea that there should exist a subordinate class within the 'class front'. The working class is accepted as having a 'motor function' in relation to socialism but this, it is argued, is not the same as exercising a hegemonic position *vis à vis* other social classes. The Party considers that the class structure of society is in a continual process of transformation which is leading towards an eventual 'fusion', within a single class, of different categories of working people. Hence, the 'class front' has at its heart the assertion that different social classes are undergoing a process of unification.

But the 'class front' is not simply a doctrinal assertion or a sociological analysis. It also contains a political strategy in which the anti-monopolist and anti-capitalist forces must go onto the offensive. This demands the need to participate in, but also 'to lead the struggle for unity'. Thus 'to cement the class front, a great Socialist Party is indispensable'.[34] *Union de la Gauche* is thus implicit, but only on the basis of a dominant PS. Since the PCF thinks in a similar way – except that in its case *it* must be the strongest element within the Left – there is a clear recipe for *disunity* in the class perspectives of the two parties.

2. Economic and Social Policies

Autogestion is one of the policy areas which most clearly differentiates the more dynamic character of the PS from its ideologically sterile predecessor. It acts as a powerful internal unifying influence, it underlines the Socialists' determination to express a distinct identity within the Left, and it is used to demarcate the Party as far as possible from the Soviet model of socialism.

The Party's interest in, and interpretation of, the concept has developed in stages. It was initially introduced by the CERES group in the late 1960s and quickly attracted attention as one way in which the Party might rejuvenate itself and also become identified with some of the ideas which had been generated during the 1968 crisis. (Although in fact the roots of *autogestion* can be traced back to early utopian socialism). In 1972 various proposals based on *autogestion* principles were included in *Changer la Vie,* the first programme of the post-

Epinay Party. In June 1975 a Party Convention was devoted to *autogestion* and a discussion document *15 Thèses sur l'Autogestion,* was debated and approved. In 1980 the Second Party Programme, the *Projet Socialiste,* re-affirmed and made more precise most of the earlier commitments.[35]

The term *'autogestion'* implies a major decentralisation of decision-making and social organisation within the context of a democratically produced national plan. The plan should be organised at local, regional and national levels so that popular participation can be encouraged as far as possible. The role of this planning machinery is to guide industry in such a way that the nation can decide on its priorities and social objectives. Within each industry the social ownership of the means of production would, according to this perspective, no longer be synonymous with the large state-bureaucratised organisations that are today's nationalised industries. Elected administrative councils where producers, consumers and the state are represented would control each company concerned.[36]

A cornerstone of autogestion, and indeed the Party's whole economic policy, is an extended programme of nationalisations. It is considered to be imperative that banking and certain major industrial concerns should be brought into public ownership in order that 'the mass of the population can be associated with the economic life of the nation'.[37] Amongst basic industries specifically identified are steel, chemicals and large engineering concerns. The *Projet Socialiste* also identifies as candidates for nationalisation and incorporation into a planning environment, areas of economic activity which are likely to assume greater importance in the future, e.g. companies providing materials for telecommunications, computers, aerospace and energy supply.[38]

Not surprisingly these policies have given rise to many criticisms from outside the Party. They have been described as watered-down communism (because of the collectivisation proposals), as hopelessly utopian (because of the participatory schemes) and as bourgeois (because they allegedly divert attention from the 'real task' of winning specific economic reforms for the workers). Naturally such suggestions are denied. Traditional Socialist commitments to narrowing wage inequalities, lowering working hours, improving social and educational provisions etc., are claimed – with justice – to have been in no way downgraded. On the contrary *autogestion* proposals are seen as supplementing and enriching the more long-standing concerns by bringing forward additional policies designed to cope with a world of increasing centralisation and automation.

But although there is a broad agreement within the Party on the basic premises of policy there are disagreements over priorities, over how far certain measures should aim to go, and at what speed they should be pursued. Two principal 'pole' positions may be identified. Rocard and his supporters – many of whom are the *autogestionnaires* who entered the Party in 1974 – tend to play down the statist aspects. They favour a rapid implementation of participatory schemes following a victory of the Left at the polls but believe this should be coupled with a careful and gradual approach to the implementation of the various collectivist proposals. (Many of Rocard's critics suspect such caution is but the tip of an iceberg. They believe that now the PS has come to office he will be amongst the first to suggest 'delays' in those policy commitments which involve major increases in public expenditure). CERES, on the other hand, with its explicitly Marxist influence, sees the prospects for *autogestion* in a longer term perspective. It, and its sympathisers, argue the need for an initial transitional and more centrally controlled period when priority must be given to consolidating an extensive programme of nationalisations and honouring promises to improve the economic conditions of workers. Mitterrand's position seems to be (as so often) somewhere in the pragmatic – some would say ambivalent – middle. With CERES, he believes the first responsibility of the Left after an election victory is to gain control of the State apparatus, for without clear central direction, moves towards a socialist society are likely to be disorganised and unsuccessful. But like Rocard, though less so, he does not think that centralisation on the scale envisaged by CERES is necessary. He is thus not too closely tied to either 'pole' and is seemingly well prepared to adapt to whatever circumstances the Socialists in office might find themselves.

In addition to these major aspects of PS doctrine there are three other important policy areas in which the Party holds distinct views.

(a) *Civil Liberties and Human Rights.* A special effort has been made to emphasise the importance of, and work for the protection of, civil liberties and human rights. This concern reflects a number of factors. For some, especially in the Centre and on the Right of the Party who are not convinced of the need for a major redistribution of wealth, it is an acid test for being of the Left. (It is interesting that the MRG, who in 1979–80 spent considerable time working on their own *projet* around the theme *'Un Socialisme du possible'*, are reducing their collectivist commitments but are putting a greater emphasis on liberties and the rights of man). For others, it displays a determination to throw off the still lingering shadow of one of the most sombre periods of Socialist history, when SFIO ministers became deeply involved in the Algerian conflict and many members resigned when evidence of torture and repression came to light. For all, it provides an opportunity to deflect criticisms that socialism is to be equated with the *gulag*. Of course it is the PCF which is most exposed to such accusations but the alliance strategy of the Left has also necessitated that the PS pay some attention to the question.

As a result the Party has frequently and consistently condemned political repression, from Chile to Argentina, from the Soviet Union to Kampuchea. It also proposes a range of measures, most of which the PCF also supports, for increasing liberties in France. These centre on a reduction in the power of the public authorities and include the introduction of Habeas Corpus, establishing a Supreme Court to ensure the constitution is properly applied, reducing police detention powers and abolishing Article 16 of the Constitution (the 'emergency powers' article).

(b) *Defence and Disarmament.* Traditionally French Socialists have been divided between those who have espoused pacifist principles and those who have considered themselves to be 'realists' on questions of defence policy. Since the division of Europe in the 1940s a second conflict has been superimposed on the first, with those who have accepted the need for (though not always the specific provisions of) the Atlantic Alliance being opposed by those who have favoured a neutralist position. Since the Party's 1950 Congress, when a majority voted to accept France's membership of the Atlantic Alliance and NATO, the 'realistic Atlanticist' position has not seriously been called into question.

But that has not prevented disagreements on specific issues. The policy of the post-Epinay party was typically fudged because of conflicting views and also because of disagreements with the PCF. On the most central issue of all, the 1972 signatories of the Common Programme committed themselves to 'general, universal and controlled disarmament', but they did not explain precisely how this was to be achieved. Because of such vagueness the Socialist's Defence Committee began deliberations from the end of 1974 with a view to establishing a more coherent policy.

In January 1978 a National Convention met to determine the

Party's defence and disarmament options. As is usual in such cases the Convention debated texts which had previously been circulated for comment and discussion. The first, and most important of these, was effectively the product of the Defence Committee's deliberations and was submitted by the *Bureau Exécutif.* Whilst not calling into question France's obligations in the Atlantic Alliance it confirmed the Party's intention to renounce nuclear weapons and it sought to create the conditions whereby general disarmament could be brought about. Until such time as general disarmament did occur the document proposed that the nuclear capacity be retained in its existing state, but without further technological development. It was also recommended that the 'final decision be left to the French people', i.e. a referendum be held. The second text, put forward by Patrick Viveret (a Rocard adviser), was circulated as an amendment to the first and it proposed specific disarmament measures such as the abandonment of the Mirage IV strike force and the unilateral de-nuclearisation of national territory by the dismantling of France's strategic and tactical nuclear missiles. The third text, distributed by CERES, favoured the retention of the nuclear deterrent. The Left-wing group argued that in prevailing conditions it was a guarantor of national independence and it could be necessary to protect 'the future Socialist Government' from external opposition.[39] (In taking this line CERES was adopting a similar position to the PCF which in 1977 had changed its position so as to favour the nuclear deterrent as long as it pointed 'in all directions').

After much manoeuvring and discussion at the Convention, aspects of the Viveret amendment were incorporated into the main motion and the CERES motion was not pressed to a vote. As a result the final agreed motion broadly reflected the submission from the *Bureau Exécutif.* The Party's policy on defence, confirmed in the *Projet Socialiste,* is thus that while France's 'half-in half-out' role in the Atlantic Alliance is generally acceptable, Socialists look forward to the nation's ultimate renouncement of nuclear weapons, but not on a unilateral basis. On taking office the Socialist government broadly reaffirmed, but in some respects also toughened, this position. France, it was announced, would play her full part in international negotiations on defence and disarmament but such negotiations should ideally wait until the West had achieved nuclear parity with the Soviet Union in Europe.

(c) *Europe.* It was the government led by Guy Mollet which did most of the groundwork in the negotiations which led to France becoming a constituent member of the European Economic Community in 1957. At that time, and during the 1960s, the SFIO, in common with most other French parties, broadly favoured the idea of European integration because it seemed to offer both political and economic advantages. Politically it provided some reassurance against the ever present French fear of a vigorously independent Germany, whilst at the same time it gave France herself an opportunity to re-assume a genuine international role. Economically, it offered the possibility for French industry to expand while her large agricultural sector remained protected.

Initially the PS, as on so many issues, was divided and uncertain in its attitude to Europe. Because of this a Convention was held at Bagnolet in 1973 to try and iron out internal differences and set a clear policy. It failed to do so. While a majority of those present made it clear they retained a commitment to the idea of Europe, there were differing degrees of criticism of the working of the institutions and of the extent to which multi-national interests were taking advantage of the Community at the expense of working people. In addition a significant minority, based on CERES and smaller groups, displayed an open hostility to the whole notion of the EEC as it existed.

Since the Bagnolet Convention there has been a further evolution of opinion with a much broader consensus now existing in the Party over the need for change and the direction in which changes should be made. This rallying round to a more united critical viewpoint is a consequence of two main developments. Firstly, CERES, particularly since they re-entered the leadership in 1979, have smoothed the edges of some of their criticisms for tactical reasons. Secondly, and more importantly, much of the enthusiasm of the pro-Europeans has waned as the EEC has clearly failed to live up to many expectations. On the whole it has not coped well with the economic problems that have been presented to it as a result of recession and in particular, from a Socialist perspective, it has often seemed to be insensitive to the individual, local and regional difficulties that have arisen from industrial reorganisation, regeneration and rationalisation.

This evolution is confirmed in the Party's manifesto for the 1979 European elections and in the *Projet Socialiste*. Although there is no suggestion that France should withdraw from the EEC the Party does seek a fundamental reform of the Common Agricultural Policy so that its dominance of the budget can be reduced and more funds can be available for other purposes, notably regional and social support.[40] Among the specific measures proposed in this respect are reductions in the subsidies on surplus products (which principally benefit the large and the rich farmers) coupled with a minimum wage for small farmers. An increase in planning at the European level is also advocated so that the less prosperous regions might develop their economic infrastructure. Planning would, it is felt, also help to limit the existing freedom of multi-national companies to move capital almost at will and without heed to the social consequences. The PS also calls for a strengthening of the European trade union movement, which it sees as representing a powerful ally against big capital interests, and seeks closer co-operation with other 'progressive forces' within Europe (which seems to include 'genuine' Eurocommunists) to help bring about a transformation and democratisation of the Community institutions.

Despite the factionalism and differences of opinion that exist in the PS it has been shown that there is a doctrine and there are policies to which the Party as a whole is committed and which clearly distinguish it within the French party political system. Within the general guidelines, however, differences of emphasis and interpretation are ever present. Though the 1980 *Projet Socialiste* was overwhelmingly ratified by the Convention specially called to discuss it, questions on doctrine and policy still remain. Many delegates who had reservations on particular points sank their doubts in the interests of Party unity or, in the case of those who perhaps aspired to the Party leadership, tactical necessity. In both cases they were assisted by a lack of precision in the *Projet* on certain controversial points. Later some of these points were given greater precision in Mitterrand's election manifesto which was drawn from the *Projet Socialiste*. It is the manifesto, as Prime Minister Mauroy has made clear, that forms the platform of the PS-led government.

MEMBERSHIP

1. Size

A characteristic of the SFIO throughout the post-war period was its declining membership. After quickly falling from a 1946 peak of over 350,000 (a similar fall was also experienced by the other parties which had initially benefitted from a good Resistance record) the Socialists hovered at just over 110,000 for most of the 1950s and were down to around 80,000 by the time of the 1969 re-formation.

Table 3.5 Membership of the SFIO-PS 1946-79

Year	Membership size
1946	355,000
1948	238,000
1949	156,000
1953	113,000
1956	120,000
1965	85,000
1968	81,000
1971	80,300
1972	92,232
1973	107,000
1975*	144,000
1976	160,000
1977	180,000
1978	188,216
1979	192,000

*The 1973-5 increase is partly explained by the expansion of the PS at the 1974 Assises du Socialisme. Reliable figures for 1974 itself are not available.

Since 1969 there has been a considerable renewal and increase in membership. This has affected the Party in three main ways. Firstly, it has undoubtedly contributed to a greater vigour and activism at the grass roots level. Secondly, it has resulted in a number of changes in the balance of political currents within the Party. For example, in the period of most rapid expansion, between 1971-5, CERES trebled its support from 8.5 per cent to 25 per cent of total membership, whilst other factions, such as Jean Poperen's ERIS, declined in strength. Thirdly, the influence of the large federations which so dominated the SFIO has declined as other federations have expanded. It is thus no longer so easy for a few key figures to dominate the affairs of the Party on the strength of their dominance of powerful federations.

But despite its expansion, PS membership at just under 200,000 remains weak by the standard of most West European social democratic parties. A major part of the explanation for this undoubtedly lies in the general French cultural trait whereby membership of virtually *all* political and economic groups (apart from the PCF and CGT) is comparatively low. Another reason is that the PS does not enjoy the membership benefits which accrue to many of its counterparts elsewhere from close links with trade unions. A third factor is that Socialist leaders, especially at local level, have often shown little interest in attempting to build a mass party. Thus in the recent period it has been clear that following a considerable renewal in local leadership between 1969 and 1973 the main concern in some places has been to consolidate positions rather than risk disruption by encouraging a rapid expansion in the number of activists.[41]

Table 3.6   Decline in strength of largest federations in the PS

	Percentage mandate to Congress		
	1971	*1975*	*1979*
Aude	3.7	2.7	1.9
Bouches-du-Rhône	14.3	10.3	8.7
Haute-Garonne	4.0	3.4	3.1
Nord	12.8	8.7	8.6
Pas-de-Calais	12.4	7.7	8.4
Puy-de-Dome	2.3	0.8	2.0
Paris	2.9	3.8	2.8
Haute-Vienne	2.1	1.6	1.3
Hauts-de-Seine	2.8	1.8	1.5

Since winning the presidential and legislative elections in 1981, the Socialist Party has begun to see its membership expand considerably, reflecting the desire of many people to be associated with the *élan* of the new government. This contrasts with the 1977–80 period which, particularly after the Metz Congress, was marked by a period of relative stagnation and even slight decline.

2.   Composition

Over the post-war period considerable changes have taken place in the nature of the Socialist Party's membership.

In sociological terms the most notable change has been the 'embourgeoisement' of the Party (see Table 3.7). Although around one third of PS members have working-class origins only about one fifth are in working-class occupations. This embourgeoisement reflects, of course, in part the demographic changes which have occurred in post-war France. In part too, however, it reflects the broadened geographical appeal of the post-Epinay Party and its particular attraction for the more educated sections of the middle class.

The 'bourgeois' nature of the Party becomes even more apparent if attention is directed to the background of the leadership (see Table 3.8) for, as with social democratic parties elsewhere, the middle classes are even more over-represented. Although many PS leaders have more modest family origins than their occupations might suggest (their social mobility often being a consequence of their having passed through one of the more prestigious institutions of higher education) the upper echelons of the Party are heavily dominated by university teachers, middle-level and higher-level managers and administrators (usually from the public sector) and liberal professionals. Of the 1978 PS-MRG parliamentary intake not one of the 114 deputies was a worker.

Table 3.7   Evolution of the class structure of the SFIO-PS[42]

	1951 %	1970 %	1973 %
Middle class	3	16	20
Lower middle class	53	61	61
Working class	44	23	19

Table 3.8   Composition of the PS by occupation 1973[43]

	Total PS %	Active PS %	Total population
Agricultural sector	8.7	11.3	9.2
Artisan – shopkeepers	7.7	10.1	8.6
Senior executives	8.1	10.6	6.4
White-collar clerical staff	7.6	9.9	9.9
Other non-manual staff	13.3	17.4	15.8
Manual workers	14.4	18.8	37.4
Educational sector	12.8	16.7	3.0
Retired	16.8	–	–

Of other characteristics of the PS membership, the most interesting is the renewal which has occurred since 1969.[44] The Party has always been a place where differing currents and ideas have jostled uneasily together. In recent years the changing image of the Party and the entry of new currents – from the 'generation of May '68' to dissident Gaullists – has made this even more the case. The transformation since 1969 is clearly brought out in a study made of the delegates to the

Party's 1977 Congress at Nantes.[45] A total of 74 per cent of the delegates had joined since 1969. Of these, 67 per cent had never been a member of any other political formation, 14 per cent had previously belonged to the PSU, 11 per cent to the CIR, only 4 per cent to the SFIO and 5 per cent to other formations. Moreover, as delegates to the Congress it is likely that they had more political experience than the ordinary member. (An assumption supported by the fact that 71 per cent of them had been a candidate of some sort at a public election). Such brevity of affiliation and lack of deep Socialist roots is an important factor in explaining the fluidity of movement between strains in the Party and the ease with which members are assimilated with one or other of the tendencies. In some cases members even appear to identify more with a *courant* than with the Party itself.

ELECTORATE

1. Size

From 1945 an electoral decline accompanied the SFIO's fall in membership. When Gaston Defferre could only muster five per cent of the vote in the 1969 Presidential election it was clear that only wholesale reform could revive the fortunes of the Party. (See Appendices for all election results).

That it should have fallen so low makes the 'reincarnation' all the more remarkable. In the 1978 legislative elections the PS polled the highest vote in mainland France. In the 1981 presidential elections Mitterrand obtained the highest ever Socialist vote, with 25.8 per cent on the first ballot. In the subsequent legislative elections the Party became by far the largest in France. With 37.5 per cent of the vote it polled 17 per cent more than its nearest rival. It thus assumed the status of a *parti dominant*.

A crucial factor in this post-1969 resurgence is an expansion in PS regional support. Traditionally the non-Communist Left has been strongest in the anti-clerical south and the industrial north and this continues to be the case, despite a stagnation in these areas in the 1970s. Considerable support however, now also exists elsewhere, as the accompanying map shows.[46]

The 'nationalisation' of the Socialist electorate is most clearly seen in the inroads that have been made in areas where the SFIO had virtually no support at all. These include Catholic and former Centre-

Right strongholds in the west and the east and Communist bastions in the Paris region. To give a specific example, in the conservative Vosges and Lozère the SFIO did not even present a list of candidates in 1956. (The electoral system was then a form of proportional representation). Yet in 1978 in the Saint-Die constituency in the Vosges the PS candidate managed to capture the seat in spite of powerful opposition from a government minister.

Map 3.1   Support for PS, March 1978

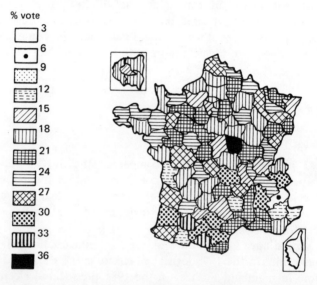

Source: N. Denis, 'Les élections législatives de mars 1978 en metropole', *RFSP* (Dec. 1978) p.989.

These gains provided a base for the expansion of the PS vote in the 1981 presidential elections and the landslide of the legislative elections. The increasing diversification and 'nationalisation' of the PS electorate, which many Socialists in the 1970s had seen as a hopeful sign, thus came to fruition. This was particularly seen in major gains in Catholic and Communist areas. In the West, the East and the Paris region the Right and the PCF were overtaken in some of their most traditional bastions. In the legislative elections there was not an area of France where the PS did not gain over 40 per cent of the vote in at least one *département*. In six *départments* it gained over 50 per cent: five in the south-west plus Mitterrand's base of *Nièvre*.

2. Composition

At the same time as increasing its geographical 'nationalisation', the PS has diversified the social nature of its electoral support. It now mirrors better than any other party the sociological make-up of the French population. (See Table 3.9 and Appendix 5 for details).

Table 3.9   The Socialist electorate

	Dec. 1972[1]* %	Mar. 1977[2] %	Total electorate Mar. 1977 %
Sex			
Male	49	53	48
Female	51	47	52
Age			
18-34 years**	29	38	35
35-49 years	32	39	25
50 and over	39	33	40
Occupation			
Agriculture	11	8	9
Artisan-shopkeeper	6	7	7
Liberal profession-senior executive	9	8	9
Clerical and junior executive	20	24	20
Manual worker	35	34	28
Pensioner, unemployed etc.	19	19	27

Source: [1]   IFOP, 16-21 Dec. 1972, cited in *Le Monde, 'Les forces politiques et les elections de mars 1973'*.
[2]   R. Cayrol and J. Jaffré, *Le Monde,* 22 Mar. 1977.
*   Strictly speaking, the survey concerns the PS and MRG (UGSD).
**   In the 1972 survey, the age cohort was 21-34 years.

The major areas of expansion in recent years have been amongst the young (only the PCF can boast a younger electorate), middle management and clerical workers (where it does better than any other party), and Catholics (who in earlier times scorned the Socialists because of their fierce anti-clericalism). These changes are partly a reflection of developments in the composition and attitudes of society. But they are also a consequence of the new image projected by the Party as innovative, technocratic and generally progressive. This has led some observers (mainly critics from the Left) to suggest that the PS is taking on the characteristics of a 'catch-all' party, wherein electoral gain is increasingly taking precedence over policy and ideological commitments. This is a misleading view. Certainly, like most parties, the PS trims its sails to win votes. But in so doing it can hardly be described as totally pragmatic in outlook or opportunistic in choice. While in the 1970s it certainly became the best placed party to attract the support of 'centrists' and 'moderates' who felt that after years of conservative government it was time for a change, it was not the central strategy of the PS to win that vote. Even when, after 1977–8, it was forced to seek more autonomy in relation to the PCF, Party leaders remained firm in their commitment to a government of the Left which would probably include Communist ministers.

For most of the 1970s the PS electorate necessarily appeared a somewhat fragile commodity when compared to the stable support traditionally given to the PCF. With the SFIO having declined for many years, and with the PS having so rapidly grown, it was legitimate to question the firmness of the Socialists' electoral base. By the late 1970s the support seemed to have settled at around 22 per cent but the fluidity of French party politics was, and is, such that major changes could never be excluded. The mushrooming of PS support in 1981 testified to this fluidity. In the legislative elections the Party gained a higher proportion of the vote in *all* social categories over *all* other parties. This included an unprecedented 44 per cent of the working-class vote (20 per cent more than the PCF) and 38 per cent of the 'top' social category vote (higher management, industrialists and liberal professions).[47] Naturally the startling 1981 election results raise further questions about the depth and solidity of the new support for the Party. Accurate assessments clearly cannot be made at this stage but it is worth emphasising that the decision of so many voters to support the PS was a 'rational' one, dictated by a desire for change. (The reasons for wanting change varied enormously). The nature of party politics in the Fifth Republic and the continuing bi-polarisation of political activity produced a situation in which the increasing number of people who were dissatisfied with the *status quo* felt they had nowhere else to go but to the PS. Their continuing loyalty will have to be earned.

CONCLUDING REMARKS

Since Epinay the Socialist Party has been rejuvenated and radicalised almost beyond recognition. After two decades of drift and decline it anchored itself in the early 1970s to a clear strategy and this helped it to become, by the mid-1970s, the largest party of the Left. More dramatically and importantly it also enabled it, in 1981, though – as we show in the Postscript – in not quite the way which had been anticipated, to win the presidency and a large majority in Parliament.

The return to government is likely to have a considerable effect on the future evolution of the Party. All the early indications are that it intends to press ahead without undue delay with its election promises. In presenting his legislative programme to the new National Assembly on 8 July 1981 the Prime Minister, Pierre Mauroy, announced a considerable list of measures ranging from nationalisations and income tax reform to the repeal of the previous government's oppressive security laws. As policies such as these begin to have an effect, if other election promises are not taken up, and if the general air of expectation is not fulfilled, the Party might find some of its new electorate turning away to 'opposition' parties either to the Left or the Right. With the 1981 elections having made the political and psychological breakthrough of putting the Left in power, the Left will doubtless now lose some of the mystique which it has in the past attracted as an almost virginal opposition force. It will have to demonstrate that its approach and its policies work.

Other questions are also raised by the Socialists' 1981 successes. The whole chain of responsibilities within the Party has been broken as many key figures have moved into the ministries or into the National Assembly. Many of the members of the Party's *Secrétariat* and *Bureau Exécutif* are now in government; many of the Party's assistants are now in ministerial *cabinets*; many others have found themselves rapidly promoted within the organisation and new staff have been brought in to replace them. Those who remain in an active capacity within the organisation now find themselves faced not only with normal duties but with the additional responsibility of ensuring that proper and coherent liaison channels exist between Party and Government. Too much independence by the latter could create a lack of responsibility and responsiveness which could, in time, lead to considerable friction.

The essence of the Party which was born at Epinay will doubtless remain much as it has been described in this chapter. The various tendencies will continue to compete with each other. This indeed was seen in a certain amount of jostling over ministerial posts following the presidential and then the legislative elections. (An interim government under Mauroy was appointed after the presidential elections.) But for a while at least such competition is likely to be held well in check. The initial task is to create the conditions for the consolidation of power in an atmosphere of liberty, responsibility and continued adherence to socialist principles.

4 The Communist Party

ENDURING FEATURES

From the early 1920s, when it was Bolshevised, until the present day the PCF has continually displayed three central features. Each has closely interacted with the other and each has seen its nature, emphasis and relative importance vary in accordance with changing circumstances. Taken together the three have combined to make up what may be described as the enduring core of the Party.

1. The Soviet Influence

To put the relationship at its mildest, the PCF has been heavily influenced by the Soviet Union. Historians and commentators dispute exactly what the linkages and channels between the Party and Moscow were and are but none question its central importance. From the mid-1920s until the mid-1960s the PCF was almost totally loyal. It never openly questioned directions taken by the Soviet Union, no matter how difficult or embarrassing they were for the Party's own interests, and it never criticised any aspects of the Soviet system itself. Furthermore, there can be no doubt that during this period, and arguably beyond, the PCF *objectively* served the foreign policy interests of the Soviet State. When circumstances required the PCF to integrate itself into the body politic it did so on each occasion: at the time of the Popular Front when the Soviet Union needed allies and wished to encourage anti-fascist fronts, in the immediate post-war period when the Soviet Union was attempting to consolidate its position in Eastern Europe and wished to reassure the West on the 'reasonableness' of communism, and from the late 1950s when Moscow began to seek an end to the Cold War and an accommodation with the Western powers. On the other hand, when a belligerent and uncompromising PCF was in Soviet interests the Party acted accordingly: at the time of the 'class against class' policy, during the Nazi-Soviet pact, and after 1947 and the onset of the Cold War.

This is not all to say that the PCF ought necessarily to be seen as having betrayed the cause of communism in France in the interests of a foreign power. Most of its leaders appear to have genuinely believed in an inextricable link between the defence of the Soviet Union and the communist cause in France. For the Thorez generation of leaders, (Thorez was General Secretary from 1930 to 1964), selected and trained by Moscow, this was especially so. The Soviet Union was at the centre of the communist world and they saw no conflict between obeying Soviet directives and serving the interests of the French working class.

Since the mid-1960s the relationship between the PCF and Moscow has not been so straightforward. This is partly because Soviet intentions in Western Europe, and France in particular, are not as obvious as they formerly were. The PCF in government has obvious attractions for the Soviet Union in terms of the de-stabilisation of the Western alliance, but it also has a number of potentially serious drawbacks. For one thing, it could threaten the detente which (the invasion of Afghanistan notwithstanding) has been a central plank of Soviet foreign policy for twenty years or so. For another, if the Soviet Union reacted favourably to a government of the Left – and it would find it difficult to avoid doing so – and that government then fell, the cordial relations which have been nurtured with France since the early 1960s, and which de Gaulle, Pompidou and Giscard d'Estaing all encouraged, might be endangered. A final danger, from the Soviet viewpoint, is that the example of a 'liberal' communist party in power – particularly as part of a coalition led by the 'Atlanticist' Mitterrand – could well make political stability more difficult to maintain in Eastern Europe itself. Because a government of the Left could thus threaten the *status quo* in various ways the Soviet Union has not been overly anxious to see it come about.

At the same time the PCF has revised its attitude to, and relations with, Moscow. From a tentative beginning in February 1966 – when the intellectual Louis Aragon protested in the Communist daily *L'Humanité* against the sentences passed on the dissidents Daniel and Siniavsky – criticisms of Soviet communism have frequently been heard. In the 1970s references to the 'defects' and 'deficiencies' of the Soviet regime unfolded with a positive rush as the Party sought to show its most liberal face to its Socialist allies and the French electorate. Most criticisms focussed on the lack of human rights though a few seemed to rest little short of a more complete disavowal. For example, in September 1977 Jean Elleinstein, assistant director of the PCF's Marxist Research Centre, a Party candidate in the November 1976 by-elections and a leading exponent of liberalisation stated 'I know very few Communists in France who would be able to live in the conditions of the Soviet Union or in other countries where there is no freedom of the Press or freedom of speech, etc... .'[1] Shortly afterwards in *France Nouvelle,* an official PCF publication, the Party spokesman on foreign affairs, Jean Kanapa forcibly expressed himself on the lack of individual and democratic liberties in *les pays socialistes:* '...we say that there is therefore between us and the communist party of these countries a divergence, and a very serious divergence, on the question of democracy and on the conception of socialism'.[2] A few days later in a meeting at the *Mutualité* Pierre Juquin, a PCF Deputy and a member of the Central Committee spoke at a 'Freedom' rally where no distinction was made between the political victims of right-wing regimes in South America and those of Eastern European Communism. The occasion clearly hit a raw nerve in Moscow which, through its news agency TASS, strongly attacked the French Communists for sending a representative to such a gathering.

As well as criticising aspects of the Soviet system the PCF displayed its growing independence from Moscow by asserting that there are many possible *pathways* to socialism and also many valid *conceptions* of socialism arising out of distinct political traditions and national heritages. To emphasise this the Party in the mid-1970s increasingly associated itself with 'Eurocommunism'. In fact it is questionable whether even at its height – between 1975 and 1978 – Eurocommunism ever really amounted to very much. It is true that the leaders of the French, Italian and Spanish communist parties did for a while appear to be converging around 'autonomist' and 'liberal' positions. A number of meetings were held and declarations were issued around these themes. The parties also actively co-operated, with others, in successfully resisting Soviet attempts at the 1976 East Berlin conference of European Communist parties to impose an acknowledgement of the leading role of the Soviet Union through a reference in the communiqué to proletarian 'internationalism'. But deep ideological and strategical differences, arising out of distinct experiences and situations, always existed between the constituent units of Eurocommunism. The PCF in particular always seemed to be less than wholehearted participants. Even after adopting the slogan *socialisme aux couleurs de la France* in the mid-1970s it never pursued so independent a position as the PCI or PCE. Nevertheless the fact remains, and its importance should not be underestimated, that the Party was willing to be identified with a movement which was widely seen as a regional communist grouping united in its desire for autonomy from the Soviet Union and in its commitment to individual and collective liberties, the latter being something the Soviet Union manifestly does not value.[3]

After 1977-8 the PCF drew in on itself, stiffened its positions and re-emphasised its more traditional characteristics. (We discuss the reasons for this below and in Chapter 5). As it did so, criticisms of the Soviet Union were less frequently heard and more emphasis was put on the Soviet achievement. In a phrase much used by PCF leaders from late 1978 the balance sheet of the Eastern European countries was *'globalement positif'*. At the same time Eurocommunism did, to all intents and purposes, cease to exist for the PCF. The party disagreed with the PCE, and even more so the PCI, on a number of points and quite consciously re-emphasised its links with Moscow. The most notable instance of this was with regard to the Soviet invasion of Afghanistan which the PCE and PCI both opposed but the PCF supported. Indeed in what could only be interpreted as a symbolic re-affirmation of the Party's 'special relationship' with the USSR, the General Secretary, Georges Marchais, for the first time in six years (an unprecedented gap) headed a PCF delegation to Moscow in January 1980, only two weeks after the invasion. During his stay he appeared on French television, direct from Moscow, to justify his Party's position.

This clear change in direction by the PCF can only be understood in the long-term context. Though the importance of the Eurocommunist 'episode' should not be underestimated – relations between the PCF and the USSR can never again be as they were – it was never quite as fundamental a break as it was sometimes presented. It certainly stopped short of denying that the Soviet Union is socialist and it did not involve a fundamental analysis of the Soviet system. That there was a point beyond which the Party would not go was made apparent in a much publicised and officially sanctioned book published by five PCF members in 1978, *L'URSS et nous*. Though it was designed to finally 'set the record straight' no real attempt was made to come to terms with the whole repressive apparatus which still produces thousands of political prisoners, repression of individual liberties and a total lack of any participatory democracy.[4]

The fact is that the Soviet Union has always been seen by the PCF, and is still seen on the whole, as a force for good. Its achievement is

lauded and its strategy, as manifested in its foreign policy, is
supported. (The 1968 invasion of Czechoslovakia – when the PCF's
Politbureau expressed its 'surprise and reprobation' and the Central
Committee its 'disapproval' – is the only occasion when criticism has
been voiced. Even then the 'normalisation' of relations between the
Soviet Union and Czechoslovakia was soon welcomed). In the last
analysis the Soviet system is deemed to be superior by virtue of the
(claimed) fact that since production is for the general good, and not
for profit, it does not contain the economic contradictions of
capitalism. It might also be added that even if any PCF leaders were to
be deflected from this general faith they could not openly admit to it
without running the risk of opening a Pandora's box in which the
whole history, nature, distinctiveness, coherence and unity of their
Party would be threatened. The Soviet influence has thus remained
and is likely to continue to do so.

2. The Revolutionary Party

The PCF has always described itself as revolutionary, although it has
become increasingly clear that a large number of Communist electors
(though not members) do not share the Party's revolutionary aspira-
tions. According to one survey, in 1977, only 46 per cent of PCF
sympathisers are in favour, to some degree, of revolution; 46 per cent
take a 'middling' position on the question of social change, and 9 per
cent want society changed as little as possible.[5] Attempts to satisfy
both 'revolutionary' and 'non-revolutionary' elements have been an
important source of the tension, caution, and uncertainty that has
been apparent in PCF strategy in recent years.

The revolutionary claim jars somewhat with the behaviour of the
Party at certain key points in its history. On the three occasions since
its foundation when there *perhaps* was a potential for revolution in
France – 1936, 1944-5 and 1968 – leaders spent most of their time
attempting to defuse the situation. The official explanation is that on
none of these occasions was there any real chance of a revolution and
that precipitate action would have led only to the repression of both
the Party and the working class. In the post-Liberation period, for
example, it is claimed (probably correctly) that the 'Anglo-Americans'
were ready to intervene in the event of a Communist uprising. In
words which it echoed in May-June 1968 the Party said of 1944
'Communists are revolutionaries, not adventurers'.

Many outside observers have not been totally convinced by the official explanations and have put forward other interpretations for the Party's 'conservatism' in the three situations. Two alternative views are most frequently heard. The first detects, in 1936 and 1944-5 particularly, 'the hand of Moscow'. It is argued that on none of the three occasions was revolutionary action in Soviet interests and appropriate instructions were therefore given to French Communist leaders. (As was noted in Chapter 2, there is direct evidence to confirm this view for 1936. For 1944-5, and even more so 1968, evidence is largely circumstantial). The second view, which is not inconsistent with the first, is that the Party at some stage – and there are different ideas as to when – lost its revolutionary ambitions. The more charitable would say this was occasioned by a realistic appraisal of the limited opportunities for a successful direct seizure of power in an industrialised state. If not all the leaders realised this in the 1930s they had no option but to do so by the early 1960s when the significance of the post-war division of Europe into spheres of influence could no longer be ignored: the Soviet Union would not directly intervene to assist an attempted Communist takeover. The more cynical (or realistic?) prefer to emphasise organisational reasons for the avoidance of revolution. They point to the bureaucratic conservatism of the Party machine and suggest that as the number of full-time officials has grown, the organisation has taken on a life of its own, wherein functionaries regard the structure as having an end and an importance in itself. Upheaval and turbulence are not to be risked for they could threaten the organisation – and with it the careers of the officials themselves.

In addition to its 'non-revolutionary' practice the Party has, since the early 1960s, considerably modified its revolutionary rhetoric. Increasingly it has emphasised its commitment to 'a peaceful road to socialism'. Neither the practice nor the rhetoric are seen, however, as undermining the fundamentally revolutionary nature of the Party. This, it is vigorously asserted, is still manifestly apparent in Party aims, strategy and organisation. The *aim* is 'to assure the democratic and socialist future of France' and to achieve this a total break with capitalism is said to be necessary. The *strategy* is to raise the political consciousness of the masses around a united Left in which 'the revolutionary party of the revolutionary class' has a directing role to play. Party *organisation* provides an essential mechanism via which the revolution is to be achieved. It is based on the principles of democratic centralism in which, in theory, democracy is allied with the revolutionary necessities of discipline and unity.

After the rupture of relations with the Socialist Party in 1977-8 this revolutionary claim of the Party began, like the Soviet link, to receive renewed emphasis. Indeed in February 1980 the National Congress of the *Mouvement de la jeunesse communiste de France* (MJCF) adopted as its manifesto *'Vive la révolution'* and Marchais stated in his address to the Congress that the Communist intention was to *'faire la révolution'*.[6] It must be emphasised however that the post-1977 developments do mark only a change in *emphasis* and do not signify, as some observers have suggested, a fundamental ideological change in *direction;* even in its most 'liberal' phase in the mid-1970s, the Party always made clear its determination not to be confined to mere electoralism or to be confused with an advanced form of reformist democratic socialism.[7]

3. The Party of the Working Class

The PCF has also consistently emphasised its *ouvrièrisme*. Even though it has never attracted much more than one third of the working-class vote or had more than one half of its own electorate from the working-class, special links with and responsibilities for the workers have always been claimed. In classic Leninist terms it sees itself as the 'vanguard', the 'avant-garde', the 'revolutionary party' of the working class. The working class, in its turn, is the revolutionary class. In the words of the Party's 1968 *Champigny Manifesto:*

> The working class, in effect, is the fundamental revolutionary force of society in our time. It is the one which is most directly subject to capitalist exploitation. But it is also the one which does not exploit and which does not aspire to exploit any other social class. As 'The Communist Manifesto declares', the working class is the revolutionary class par excellence because it has only its chains to lose and it has a world to win with the socialist revolution.[8]

The quote could be taken from almost any important policy document at any time.

Even when the PCF has been at its most expansive, *ouvrièrisme* has remained a key concept. So, the appeal which was launched after the 1976 Twenty-Second Congress for a grand alliance based on 'all those who are exploited by the great monopolies' – a 'union of the French people' – carefully referred to potential supporters as 'the natural allies of the working class'. Salaried employers, technicians,

ntellectuals etc., were *couches sociales* who could not hope to aspire
o such a clear consciousness of their position in society as the working
class. They must, therefore, expect to be led by that class or, more
accurately, its political expression, the PCF.

At the same time as displaying these permanent features the PCF has
also been characterised, as we saw in Chapter 2, by twists and turns in
its strategical orientations. This has arisen from its attempt, since the
mid-1930s, to maintain a balance between influences, interests and
strategies which have not always been reconcilable. Until well into the
Fifth Republic the main tension arose from the Party being, at one
and the same time, firmly within the Soviet Union's orbit of influence
but also being part of the French political system. When the demands
of the former clashed with those of the latter it was the former which
always prevailed. Thus were produced *les grands tournants* of the
Popular Front, of the Nazi-Soviet pact, of the Resistance and
Liberation, and of the Cold War: periods of internal political
integration alternating with isolationist, pro-Soviet periods.

In the Fifth Republic, as the Soviet influence on the PCF has
become less direct, a second and closely related source of tension has
emerged to supplement the first. On the one hand the Party has, more
determinedly than ever before, sought to integrate itself into the
domestic political system and thereby open the way to a return to
office by democratic means. Whilst pursuing this end, however, it has
been unwilling, as we have just seen, to wholly renounce those
enduring features which link it with its past and which help determine
its distinctive and special role within the system. As a result it has
found itself attempting to become a party *comme les autres* while still
clinging to its claim to be a party *d'avant garde*. Conflicting
alternatives have thus jostled uneasily against one another as
temptations to break with the past have competed with pressures to
preserve continuity.

A consequence of this is that the recent history of the Party is less
easy to divide into distinct periods. Certainly there has been an
apparent continuation of the established pattern; the isolationist Cold
War period, which was installed in 1947, was followed by an
integrationist period from the early 1960s to 1977-8 and that in its turn
– until 1981 – was succeeded by a return to isolationism. But the
'breaks' between these periods are much less definite and clear cut
than they were when the determining factor was simply Soviet
interests. So, the integrationism from the early 1960s developed only

gradually and was by no means continuous; at one point indeed, from the autumn of 1974 until well into 1975 it was temporarily suspended following a marked 'stiffening' in the PCF's attitude towards the PS. More importantly, the isolationism which developed from the late 1970s was less than complete on two counts. Firstly, though fairly rigorously applied at the national level it was, despite difficulties in some places, by no means fully extended to local relations between the PCF and PS or indeed to relations between the Communist dominated CGT and the non-Communist trade unions. Secondly, the integrationism from the early 1960s involved, unlike earlier periods, not only a switch in strategy but also major ideological and policy developments; for the most part these survived the post-1977-8 break with the PS and helped to provide a base for the PCF's return to government in 1981.

LA VOIE DÉMOCRATIQUE

During the 1950s the PCF pursued no clear strategy for gaining power in France. Whilst its loyalty to Moscow brought about internal political isolation it was increasingly obvious that the Soviet Union would not be prepared to go to its aid, if it were to engage in serious revolutionary activity. The Party was thus confined to an unproductive political ghetto.

From the early 1960s serious moves got under way to leave that ghetto. The motives behind the development were many. Some were external. The Soviet Union itself, to the initial dismay of PCF leaders, opened the way with the 1956 provision for 'the peaceful road to socialism'. This was immediately seized on by the PCI whose leader Togliatti developed the notion of 'polycentrism' in which the international communist movement no longer had a 'single guide'. This assertion of independence, which the Italian Communist Party began to fully develop from 1961, resulted, as many in the PCF noted, in *growth*. The PCI's position reflected the way in which the whole communist world was becoming more complex and heterogeneous. Yugoslavia and China had rejected the Soviet model. A Bolshevik style revolution no longer appeared likely in the West and alternative avenues to power were increasingly discussed. On top of all this the Soviet commitment to peaceful co-existence, coupled with the now obvious strength of the Soviet State, reduced the need for a rigid PCF defence of the 'motherland of socialism'.

Internal pressures also provided an impetus to a reappraisal of the

Party's position. Because of its political isolation the PCF had performed disastrously under the new two-ballot electoral system in the 1958 parliamentary elections, winning only ten seats. It was clear that a major improvement in its fortunes would necessitate finding electoral allies. At the same time, with the newly resurgent Right rapidly establishing itself in positions of power and with its own electoral fortunes declining, the non-Communist Left began to look towards the PCF for some sort of 'arrangement'. Just as the interests of the two 'sides' coalesced in this way the PCF's principal tie, both real and symbolic, with Cold War Stalinism, Maurice Thorez, died in 1964. He was replaced as General Secretary by the more flexible and, as it turned out, more 'liberal' Waldeck Rochet.

From the early 1960s the PCF thus slowly sought to integrate itself more into the political system. To this end it adapted aspects of both its strategy and ideology. One of these adaptations, the partial rupture with Moscow, we have already considered. There are three others.

1. The Analysis of Capitalism and the Pathway to Socialism

In classic Marxist style the capitalist system is seen by the PCF to contain contradictions which will eventually and inevitably lead to the victory of socialism. Driven by the mechanisms of competition, accumulation and exploitation, societies based on the capitalist mode of production can, it is alleged, do no other than lurch from crisis to crisis. These crises moreover are not just economic in nature but are also political, social, cultural and moral. They are, however, no longer seen as foreshadowing the imminent collapse of capitalism. This is because of the perceived ability of the capitalist system, at both international and national levels, to adapt itself to changing circumstances. It is claimed that the linking chord between the two levels lies in the development of State Monopoly Capitalism (SMC).[9]

At the international level SMC is seen in the increasing integration and concentration of the forces of capital. Less likely now to be characterised by ruthless competition and imperialist wars, capitalism has sought to stabilise itself on the basis of an American dominated economic and political imperialism. Three principal features characterise the present period of international capitalist development, each of which is principally designed to provide mechanisms for the maximisation of profits at a time when the outlets for profitable reinvestment of capital are falling. Firstly, there is a growth of multinational corporations, which have as their major advantage an ability to speedily transfer investment capital to areas yielding the quickest and highest profits. Secondly, financial markets are increasingly co-ordinated. Thirdly, mutually beneficial and politically protected trading zones are of growing importance.

At the domestic level – and the PCF describes the crisis as *'avant tout nationale'* – SMC is seen in the emergence of increasingly authoritarian states, working in the interests of monopolies. In France *'le pouvoir et le patronat'* are alleged to pursue a whole series of policies carefully designed to boost profits: deliberately stimulating inflation, resisting wage demands, pillaging public funds, merging enterprises to extend monopolisation, favouring unemployment etc.

In response to this two-fold 'defence' by capitalism the PCF advances a complementary dual strategy for building socialism in France.

At the international level it expresses its support for the forces of 'progressive democratic socialism' and also gives its backing to the attempts of *'les pays socialistes'* to resist 'imperialistic capitalist expansionism'. In specific terms these mean two main things. Firstly, it supports Soviet foreign policy. Secondly, it fiercely argues the need for the preservation of national sovereignty. Infringements on the political and economic independence of France have long been presented as signifying further capitalist penetration and increasing American influence. In recent years, especially after Giscard assumed the presidency, this has led to particularly bitter attacks on the EEC. Thus, with regard to the proposals to enlarge the Community to include Greece, Spain and Portugal, the PCF has attacked them at two levels. An immediate threat is seen to be posed to certain French industries, especially in the south and west, from the low wage, low social welfare economies of the applicant states. Taking a longer term view the Party has presented enlargement as part of a remorseless movement towards German and American economic hegemony. The fear has been constantly articulated along the following lines: 'This enlargement is linked to the wish to integrate France into a West European and Atlantic conglomerate dominated by the Federal Republic of Germany and operating under the general supervision of the United States'.[10]

With national independence thus (it hopes) preserved, and with the crisis of capitalism being 'primarily national' in origins, the second arm of the PCF's strategy for building socialism naturally emphasises the domestic possibilities. Wholesale transformation of society is now seen to be possible without a full scale frontal assault on the 'facade of bourgeois democracy' and without even the overthrow of the state. From the doctrinal re-analysis of the role of the state which is part of the theory of SMC the PCF has concluded that it is only necessary that it be 'transformed' by 'democratic forces'. The increasing economic powers that it has assumed in its role as an agent of the large monopolistic interests opens the way for the use of the machinery of the state by others. The 'democratic forces' could change the existing apparatus in such a way that it would serve their purposes. In other words SMC provides the opportunity for the Left to take over the state machinery and introduce socialism through it. Clearly therefore, as Jean Elleinstein, is fond of saying, 'the revolution is no longer what it was'.

The whole process would take place, it is claimed, via legal and constitutional channels. Although this is not seen as restricting the Party exclusively to parliamentarianism – 'social struggle' still has an important role to play – it does put the ballot box at the centre of the pathway to socialism. This in turn, because the Communists cannot themselves hope in any foreseeable circumstances for an overall election victory, has led to faith being placed in an alliance with the non-Communist Left. From 1972 to 1977-8 this was centred around the Common Programme of Government in which both the PCF and the PS pledged themselves to create over a five-year period in office an 'advanced democracy'. For the PCF this was to be an interim stage on the way to socialism. Constantly giving the Programme a maximalist interpretation the Party emphasised the social progress implicit in measures such as nationalisations, re-distribution of income, 'democratic planning' (the meaning of which has never been clear), and curbs on authoritarian political practices. The Party could proceed from this base to the building of socialism itself.

In opting for this strategy of *Union de la Gauche* in the early 1970s the PCF was acting in a quite different way from its neighbour, the PCI, which at much the same time was proposing to the Italian people an 'historic compromise' in which it would work in government with the largest Italian party, the Christian Democrats.[11] The difference between the two communist parties arose mainly from the contrasting strategic situations in which they found themselves. In France party politics were becoming increasingly bi-polarised and as they did so a united Left came to have an excellent chance of winning elections. In Italy there was no strong socialist party and the PCI saw little to be gained from long term alliances with the smaller parties. Still much influenced by the 'hegemonic' theories of its former intellectual Gramsci, and more deeply affected than the PCF by the fate of Allende's government in Chile, the PCI came to believe that it could win *and hold* power only by appealing to the widest possible area of support. (Many PCI leaders doubted whether a narrow election victory by the Left in France would really give it power. Only a major victory, as was to be achieved in 1981, could overcome the opposition that would be met in the administration and financial circles and elsewhere.

Even in the early 1970s, when most enthusiastic about *Union de la Gauche,* the PCF always made it clear that the arrangement with the Socialists must meet certain requirements. The most important of these was that the working class, and therefore also the PCF, must have a central role in the *Union.* Since the PCF sees itself as the only true revolutionary party it follows that it also sees itself as providing the only guarantee that a Left-wing alliance will not be deflected into reformism. It is in this context that the 'Union of the French People' – the appeal launched to all 'anti-monopolistic' elements in the mid-1970s – should be seen. It was a device to build Party support and it rested on the claim that under monopoly capitalism only a few of the population are not exploited, and as a result many *couches sociales* are now ready for socialism. The fact that this appeal had only limited success and the PCF found itself becoming the junior partner in the *Union de la Gauche,* played a major part (as we show in Chapter 5) in persuading the Party to change its tactics and bring about the virtual collapse of the *Union* in September 1977.

After that collapse the PCF continued to pay lip service to the *Union* but in practice it was clearly not interested in restoring it except on conditions much more favourable to itself. As that was obviously unacceptable to the PS, the Communists were apparently in a position where they had no serious strategy for winning national office. Conscious of this the Party, from mid-1979, tended to put less emphasis on the benefits to be accrued from political office and more on the possibility of making progress through social struggle. The idea of advanced democracy was largely replaced by the suggestion that reforms of an incremental nature could be wrestled from the State through the direct efforts of the working class. This in turn was closely linked to what has long been a major aim of the PCF: to establish a strong presence in the State apparatus. Whether this presaged a further 'permanent' switch in Communist strategy was unclear, though looking at the situation from an historical perspective, it was always tempting to conclude that rhetoric, as so often in communist parties, was being used as a rationalisation for political reality. The dramatically changed circumstances of 1981, and the eagerness shown by the PCF to accept ministerial posts, seemed to confirm this view. (See Postscript for details of the PCF's return to government.)

2. The Nature of Socialism: Economic Features

Paralleling the changing views on the means of achieving socialism there have been modifications in the vision of the future socialist society itself. More than ever its distinctiveness and essential Frenchness is emphasised. It is not possible, the Party claims, to look at any other country to see what a socialist society in France would be like because there is not, and cannot be, a model. Socialism will be made *'aux couleurs de la France'*.

Close inspection, it must be said, suggests that in socio-economic terms the projected society does not differ so radically from that which the PCF has always envisaged. Despite Party denials it still seems to be broadly based on the Eastern European systems. The intention remains to build a society in which production 'will be organised on the basis of individual and collective needs rather than profit', and a society in which the productive effort 'will be to the benefit of all' rather than merely a small exploiting minority. In more specific terms this means a society in which measures will be taken to narrow social inequalities, to extend social service and educational provisions, to improve working conditions, to eliminate unemployment etc.

Key pre-requisites for the effecting of such a society are the taking into public ownership of *'les grands moyens de production'* and movement towards 'a more rationally planned' social and economic system. Inevitably this has brought forth accusations that the PCF's vision of socialism is essentially centralist, interventionist and uniformist. In an attempt to deflect such charges the Party has in recent years cautiously tempered some aspects of its policies. Amongst its 'concessions' it has supported the continuance of a small private sector under socialism, of some differences in income (based on the 'quantity and quality of work') and of some forms of inheritance. It has also laid stress on the decentralised and participatory features of the future society (The 1979 Party resolution went so far as to say that the intention is to build a *'socialisme démocratique, autogestionnaire'*).

It would be fruitless to speculate in any very specific way on what the PCF's economic proposals will add up to now the Party has entered government. Much will obviously depend on the conditions prevailing at the time, both within the coalition – of which the Party in 1981 is only a small part – and in the wider political and economic environments. All that can be said with reasonable certainty is that the movement will be collectivist and centralist and that the Party will seek to ensure, as it did when it was last in office after the Liberation, a central role for itself in all key social and economic structures.

3. Parliamentary Democracy and Individual Liberty

As the Party sought to leave the political ghetto it began to 'liberalise' its position on what for many non-Communists is the touchstone of its commitment to re-integration: its attitude to the norms of parliamentary democracy and the liberties and freedoms normally associated with it. Would these be respected by the Party on its way to socialism and, ultimately, if socialism was ever achieved?

Communists themselves often try to trace the beginnings of their 'democratic' evolution back to a famous interview Thorez gave to *The Times* in 1946. In the interview he stated, 'The progress of democracy throughout the world, in spite of rare exceptions which serve only to confirm the rule, permits the choice of other paths to socialism than the one taken by the Russian Communists'.[12] We can safely dismiss this as having any real significance. It was said in the context of trying to reassure the West at a time when the PCF was in government and the Soviet Union was seeking to extend its influence in Eastern Europe. It in no way modified the deep Stalinisation of the Party and in any case Thorez was referring only to the *means* of achieving socialism and not the ends themselves.

It was from the Fifteenth Party Congress in 1959 that the first steps away from orthodoxy began. Less emphasis was given to the inevitability of the class and the proletarian revolution and the central one-party doctrine gradually and cautiously came to be questioned. Speaking to the Central Committee in May 1963 Thorez said the theory of a single party doctrine in a socialist regime was an error of Stalin's. By 1963 he is also reported to have been privately questioning the Party's position on such issues as individual liberties and the role of 'the dictatorship of the proletariat'.[13] Nothing much was made public, however, until the Seventeenth Congress in May 1964 when new Party Statutes were adopted which strongly expressed a desire for a peaceful transition along a French road to socialism.

The 'liberal' awakening was to be a slow and, for many outsiders, an unconvincing process. Declarations of new found 'flexibility' had long to be seen in the context of the dead weight of a still dominating rigidity. The effect of 'concessions' was frequently spoiled (as it still is to some extent today) by a tendency of Party spokesmen to hedge or to hold back on key commitments, such as whether or not parliamentary elections were the *only* valid path to power for Communists, whether a socialist regime would permit non-communist parties to exist, whether the Communists would withdraw from government if rejected by the electorate, and whether there would be full respect in a socialist regime for all existing individual liberties. The frequency with which Communists referred to Eastern Europe as socialist, democratic, and multi-party was enough to raise serious doubts in many minds on the genuineness of the conversion.

It was only through a long and gradual process that the PCF, under no little pressure from the non-Communist Left, 'conceded' on the essential questions. This process can be followed through in a series of policy documents which came out with some frequency after 1968 as the movement towards unity on the Left gathered momentum. In 1968 itself in a joint declaration with the FGDS in February and then later in the *Champigny Manifesto* the possibility of achieving socialism through gradualism was first openly recognised. In 1971 in the policy statement *Changer de cap,* and then in 1972 in the Common Programme, more *specific* commitments were given to multi-partyism and *alternance*.[14] The sincerity of the changes were however, by the PCF's own actions, continually brought into question. So, in 1973 Georges Marchais, in his book *Le Défi démocratique,* after having laboured at length that socialism did not imply *'le parti unique'* wrote 'In Poland, in East Germany, in Bulgaria organised and influential non-communist parties participate today at the side of communists in the management of the affairs of the country'.[15] It seemed a curious view of multi-partyism and raised serious doubts about the long-term commitment of the PCF, particularly as its spokesmen still continued to refer to the 'irreversibility' of socialism.

The Party was not deterred by the doubters and in 1975 turned its attention to the question of civil liberties. In May a Declaration of Liberties, *Vivre libres!,* was presented to the public for discussion. This affirmed the PCF's commitment to what in earlier periods it had described as 'bourgeois' democratic freedoms and it proposed that they be introduced into the Constitution of the Republic in a similar fashion to that of the Bill of Rights in the United States

Constitution.[16] Confirming the Party's position on these issues, Marchais, in November 1975, met with the General Secretary of the PCI, Enrico Berlinguer, and they issued a joint statement in which they extolled the virtues of 'All those liberties which are the fruit of the great democratic bourgeois revolutions or of the great popular struggles of this century which had the working class at their head...' They also emphasised that 'The French and Italian Communist Parties favour the plurality of political parties, the right of opposition parties to exist and to act, the free formation of majorities and minorities and the possibility of them alternating democratically'.[17]

In February 1976 the Twenty-Second Party Congress took as its theme *la voie démocratique*. With democracy, freedom and independence as its themes the Congress in many ways marked the culmination of the process which had been under way since 1959. The 'French road to socialism' via the 'union of the French people' were widely proclaimed. Individual liberties were constantly stressed and, in a move which had been made known the previous month, (and which in truth, was merely a formalisation of actual Party doctrine, though it had great symbolic significance) the dictatorship of the proletariat was dropped from the new programme. It was claimed to no longer correspond with Communist policy. As Marchais said in announcing it 'We are now in 1976, the French Communist Party is not stagnant. Neither is it dogmatic. It knows how to adapt to contemporary conditions. At present the word "dictatorship" does not correspond with what we seek in any way. It contains a significance which is completely contrary to our hopes, and to our plans'.[18]

Since the 1976 Congress these commitments to 'bourgeois' liberty and democracy have remained firm despite the turn of events since the breakup of the *Union*. The Resolution adopted by the 1979 Congress, in a section entitled '*Libertés, Démocratie, Autogestion*' specifically refers to and affirms the commitments of *Vivre libres!* Nonetheless, as with other aspects of the PCF's 'liberalisation', the return to 'fundamentals' after 1977 resurrected (or confirmed) non-Communist's doubts over these commitments. The announcement by the Party in February 1980 that it was creating a *Comité de defense des libertés et des droits de l'homme en France et dans le monde* hardly allayed the critics. For, amidst great publicity, the announcement was accompanied by the issuing of a list of 130 infringements of human rights over the previous 20 years; on the extensive list the only reference directly involving the Soviet Union – and then it was not mentioned by name – was the 1968 invasion of Czechoslovakia![19]

As the possibility of communist accession to office in certain major countries of Western Europe became a real possibility in the early 1970s, a debate was sparked off on the whole notion of Eurocommunism. Many observers – academics, politicians and journalists amongst them – questioned whether parties such as the PCF, PCI and Partido Communista de España (PCE) had *really* changed. It was suggested that the new image conveyed by these parties, with its stress on acceptance of democratic methods and procedures, was little more than a facade, likely to be discarded at the first opportune moment. In the French case it was pointed out that 'Socialism in French Colours', 'The French Road to Socialism', and 'Union of the Left' could not possibly be reconciled with the continued emphasis by the PCF on its revolutionary spirit, its exclusive relationship with the working class, and its directing role in the building of socialism.

There is much in these arguments. As we have seen, *la voie démocratique* has been built on persisting characteristics which link the Party firmly with its past. The democratic development has jarred with these permanent features and has imposed very real restrictions on how far the Party can go without bringing into question its very nature and *raison d'être*. This is why changes have often been less than wholehearted. The Stalinisation of the PCF was thorough and it cannot be easily thrown off. The Party, or at least its leaders, feel obliged to keep in touch with their ideological origins and not to forget the 'historical mission' laid down for all communist parties. It was such feelings that led them in 1975, though not without some embarrassment, to support, in the interests of communist solidarity, the Bolshevik strategy of the Portuguese communists.

There is therefore a tension within the Party arising from change within continuity. A desire to be part of the mainstream of political life clashes with a determination not to be simply reformist and electoralist. The Party will not pay any price for power and, as we show in Chapter 5, it was a belief that it was in danger of paying too high a price that led it in the autumn of 1977 to stiffen its doctrinal and policy positions and apparently quite deliberately turn its back on the prospect of governmental office. (See Postscript for the 1981 price.)

But at the same time as recognising the limitations of the PCF's 'conversion' the real changes which have taken place within the Party should not be underestimated. Whilst too much should never be read into the documents and pronouncements of political parties, especially when they have long been out of office, they should not be dismissed as inconsequential verbiage, particularly when they have been developed, as in the PCF, over a long period.

But in any case even if ideological change is dismissed as mere political candyfloss the 'threat' of real Communist intentions in power must be seen in the context of two other restricting factors. The first is that, as we show below, the liberalisation of doctrine has been accompanied by a massive turnover in membership. Over two thirds of members have now joined since 1968, many of them attracted by *la voie démocratique*. Their loyalty since 1977 has been shown to be far from unquestioning to any 'hardening' in the Party line. The second restriction is that there are no foreseeable circumstances in which the PCF will come to power and not be greeted by widespread hostility and suspicion in the army, the security services, the police and the administration. In addition they will probably be, as in 1981, the junior partners in government to an ever watchful Socialist Party.

It is, of course, possible to argue that no matter what the *real* intentions of PCF leaders may be, and no matter what the safeguards erected by non-communists are, the *logic* inherent in a communist party will always drive it in the direction of the destruction of liberal democracy as it is known. In this connection the internal practices of the PCF are often seen as evidence that this is the case.

ORGANISATION

1. Structure

Formally the PCF is organised on the basis of democratic centralism. In theory, this allows for a balance between democracy and centralisation. On the one hand members may participate in policy formulation via free and open discussion and may also play a full part in the election of the Party leadership at all levels. On the other hand, once policy has been decided, the requirements of discipline, unity and, if necessary, acquiescence are demanded.

In practice, the system is grossly distorted with the centralist aspects far outweighing the democratic. Both the electoral and decision-making processes are so arranged that power is firmly located in the highest echelons of the Party. The opportunities for members *really* to make their influence directly felt are minimal.

Below the national organisation there are three main levels in the Party: *cells,* which are organised either in neighbourhoods or in workplaces; *sections* which are normally based on part of one of France's

96 *départements* or on a town, though some bring together cells in a large industrial enterprise; and *fédérations* which provide the departmental structure. At each level two sorts of elections take place. (See Figure 4.1). Firstly, representatives are elected who will act on behalf of that level in between full meetings of cells, section Congresses, federation Congresses and the National Congress. Apart from in the cells, this is a two-stage process, whereby the Congress elects a committee, which then elects a bureau and a secretariat. Secondly, delegates are elected to the congresses of the next highest level.

These elections are not genuine contests. Their outcome is decided before the formal vote takes place. This is because at each electoral level and in every type of election (for representatives, office holders, and delegates) the number of candidates always equals the number of places to be filled. Furthermore, apart from in the cells, where control is less tight, the whole process of the selection of candidates is carefully channelled through *commissions des candidatures.* The *commissions,* which are also formally elected by the congresses are made up of trusted 'loyalists'. At the section and federation levels such faithfuls are mainly drawn from their respective bureaux and secretariats, supplemented by at least one representative from the next highest level. For large federations this means that *permanents* (full-time officials) usually dominate. At the national level the *commission* is controlled by senior figures at headquarters.

As Figure 4.1 indicates, elections are layered so there is no opportunity for members at the lower levels to put forward names or vote for candidates at the highest levels. A new candidate for the Politbureau will, therefore, probably have gone through five stages; from a cell, to a section, to a federation, to the National Congress, to the Central Committee and, finally, to the Politbureau itself. In most cases, the whole process will have taken at least twenty years. (See Table 4.1). At each stage the candidate will have been more closely vetted than at the last, with his biography (which he has to complete periodically and which contains an account of aspects of his personal and political life), his record and his activities all being thoroughly checked. This exhaustive process ensures that those who last the course and reach the upper echelons have, at the very least, a powerful emotional attachment to the Party. With full-time officials – which includes all the Politbureau and Secretariat and a high proportion of the National Congress and Central Committee – this attachment is supplemented by a financial dependency, since dissent means instant dismissal.

Figure 4.1   Formal structure of the PCF

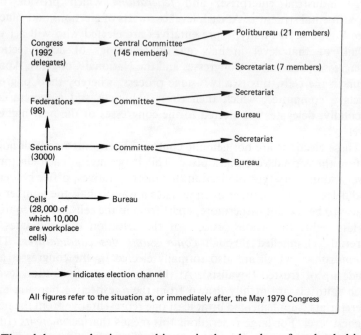

All figures refer to the situation at, or immediately after, the May 1979 Congress

The elaborate election machinery is thus largely a facade, behind which the real process of co-option takes place. Any *responsable* who questions official policy is likely to be removed from his post at an early stage. Inevitably this makes for a highly cautious, even conservative, Party machine. Members rise to the top by displaying conformity and compliance rather than initiative and innovation. It is doubtless partly because of this that the Party has traditionally had difficulty in adapting itself to new situations and new ways of thinking. In recent years alone it has been far slower than the PS to react to emerging issues such as workers' participation, regionali-sation, women's rights, and environmental protection. There are very powerful vested interests in the machine, with a highly developed sense of self-preservation, who see their entrenched positions challenged by new currents of thought, whether they are demands for internal democratisation or calls for new analyses of Party strategy. As a number of commentators have suggested, bureaucratic centralism is perhaps a more accurate description of the functioning of the PCF than democratic centralism.

Apart from electoral manipulation there are also other ways in which the Party hierarchy maintains its dominance.

Firstly, and most importantly, there is a constant monitoring of the activities of lower levels by higher levels. This takes place in a number of ways; through reports, records, meetings between officials, but above all through what are known as *rapporteurs*. These are representatives of higher bodies who attend meetings of lower bodies – especially congresses – to ensure the latter are running smoothly and in an approved manner. If there are problems, the *rapporteur* is likely to play an interventionist role. He may perhaps be called upon to explain changes in national policy or to advise lower organs on how national strategy is to be translated into local practice. On questions which are a source of controversy this may give rise to some acrimony. So, for example, after the rift with the PS in 1977 and the subsequent election defeat, *rapporteurs* from members of the Central Committee downwards, had to deal with hostile receptions at many meetings. Usually, however, explanation and persuasion are sufficient, if not to convince everyone of the merits of the official line, at least to keep criticisms within bounds. Disciplinary action is usually avoided where possible.[20] Where words are not enough and a firmer response is deemed necessary this will normally take place not in open Party forums but in meetings between *rapporteurs* and appropriate committees and office holders. Most typically, pressure will be brought to bear to replace 'suspect' *cadres* with more acceptable figures.

The whole monitoring and controlling process is orchestrated through an extensive bureaucracy of *responsables* from the National Secretariat at the top to cell secretaries at the bottom. In all there are probably well over 100,000 members with an official position of some kind in the Party. Of these, many are full-time officials, though exactly how many is unclear. The Party itself puts the figure at less than 1000,[21] but this does not take into consideration all sorts of categories: employees of the Party press and commercial enterprises, employees of PCF run municipal authorities who spend most of their time on Party work, officials of the CGT and other PCF-linked organisations. A total of 10,000-15,000 people are probably, *in practice,* engaged in more or less full-time work on the Party's behalf.

To ensure that the *responsables* and *permanents* carry out their duties in an acceptable way the careful selection procedures we have noted are supplemented by training programmes in which Party schools have an important role to play. These are held at section, federation and national levels and centre around a core curriculum of subjects such as Marxist doctrine, Party policy and strategy, the history of Communism, and socialist economics. The courses run at national level are the most intense and cater for 'influentials', e.g. *permanents,* federation and section officials, councillors, and representatives from specialised groups. The extent of the courses may be partly gauged from the fact that of the 1992 delegates to the May 1979 National Congress only 15.7 per cent had attended no Party school at all; 12.8 per cent had attended an elementary school, 32.5 per cent a federal school, 23.6 per cent a central school of one month duration, and 15.2 per cent a central school of four months duration.[22]

Secondly, there are virtually no opportunities, other than to some extent in cells, for genuine debates to take place between ordinary members. The Party structure is rigidly vertical with horizontal contacts – across cells, sections or federations – strictly forbidden. It is not, therefore, possible for like-minded individuals and groups, who may wish to challenge the leadership on certain questions, to come together to exchange views, let alone plan strategy. The official justification for this is that a revolutionary party fighting for the transformation of society cannot afford to have its defences lowered, its resolve weakened and its energies dissipated by factions who snipe at 'democratically agreed' decisions. Accordingly when some members did succeed in establishing horizontal contacts in 1978 (see below) the leadership quickly attempted to isolate them and branded their activities as *fractionnelles.*

On the only occasions when open debate is legitimate – in the Party press before Congresses – contributions can be made only via properly constituted Party bodies. So, perhaps to set an example, it was publicly announced by the *commission* in charge of the pre-1979 Congress debate that one of the critical texts it had received (which was from activists grouped around the review *Luttes et débats*) could not possibly be published since its signatories included members from five different sections and two federations. This constituted 'a total break with the principles and rules of procedure of the Communist Party' and was in a very clear way *'un travail fractionnel'* of Trotskyite inspiration.[23]

Thirdly, and more subtly, the hierarchy feeds on and encourages the tendency of members to think of themselves and their party in a special way: the PCF is *'le' Parti.* Such feelings partly arise from the whole history of the Party and its self-presentation as *'un parti pas comme les autres'.* It is further stimulated by attempts to immerse

members in Party life via political and social activities; to draw them
in to what a number of observers, notably Annie Kriegel, have called
the counter society' of the PCF. Propaganda also aims in this
direction of exclusiveness, with a defensive posture continually being
struck in official pronouncements, in addresses to Party gatherings
and in the Party press. Enemies are said to be everywhere and
Communists are exhorted to be ever on their guard. A 'we-they'
mentality is thus fostered in which the values of loyalty, unity and
discipline are constantly emphasised and a Communist 'sub-culture' is
maintained.

As a result of these many mechanisms and devices, dissent above
the level of the cell, and even more so the section, is rare. Internal
critics are usually kept firmly at the base and are accorded little legitimacy. As Georges Labica, a member of the Federal Committee of
Hauts-de-Seine has said, disagreements with the official line are
viewed not as a normal function of political activity but as problems
that need to be resolved. Drawing a medical analogy he has compared
dissenters with patients and Party functionaries with doctors. Either
the patient is restored to full health or is declared incurable and
rejected.[24]

At best internal critics can expect to be presented as unwitting and
misguided tools of the Party's enemies. At worst they are the enemy
within. The few who do attain positions of prominence are usually
quickly relieved of their responsibilities. There is much in the
suggestion of Louis Althusser, one of the *enfants terribles* of the
Party, that the PCF organisation is similar at one and the same time to
the military model of a closed, vertical and absolute structure, and to
the model of the parliamentary bourgeois state where decisions are
taken (in Althusser's view) by a corps of co-opted specialists.[25]

This is not to say that conformist 'identikit' members are always
elected to congresses, committees and official posts. Mavericks,
adopting distinctive positions, have periodically appeared at even the
highest levels. Usually, however, they have been quickly drummed
out, though often their views have been subsequently adopted. As has
been widely observed the mistake of Doriot, Servin, Casanova,
Garaudy and others who have been purged from the Party, was to
have been right too soon.

But if occasional individualists cannot by themselves seriously
threaten the structure of the Party a more broadly based dissatisfaction with the leadership could do so and in this context important
developments have taken place in recent years with the task of central

control having been made increasingly difficult by the more demo
cratic image that French Communism has projected since th
mid-1960s. The emphases on liberty, democracy and pluralism hav
inevitably resulted in accusing fingers being pointed at the Party's ow
internal procedures. At the same time the rapid expansion in member
ship during the 1970s, from around 300,000 at the beginning of th
decade to, it is claimed, 700,000 at the end, has produced not just a
larger Party but a more heterogeneous and critical one. Over two
thirds of the members in 1980 had joined since 1968, during th
period of *la voie démocratique,* and there is therefore less willingnes
than hitherto for leadership decisions to be accepted unhesitatingly
This was clearly shown in 1978 when, following the election defea
and the Party's apparent return to a 'hard-line' policy, attacks on ar
unprecedented scale were launched by members on the leadership.

The leadership, despite the impression given by sections of the
media, never really lost control of the situation, however, though i
was certainly seriously embarrassed. Less than 100 cells (out o
28,000) officially expressed their disagreement with the Party leadership. The critical letters and articles, though an unprecedented phenomenon, came principally from 'marginal' intellectuals. Of the
petitions which circulated among members the most successfu
attracted no more than 1500 signatures. According to one independen
estimate, a maximum of 3000 members, out of the 700,000, signed ar
article, letter or collective text of some kind.[26] These figures are, o
course, only partial indicators of the dissatisfaction that was felt. But
the comparatively low level of open dissension is in itself an indicator
of the success of the leadership for, according to many reports,
rapporteurs met disillusionment and resentment at almost every
turn.[27] It is significant that most of the dissatisfied did not choose to
fight but either fell into line or quietly withdrew from participation in
Party affairs. A similar process was apparent in 1980, when the open
return to a pro-Soviet position (as witnessed particularly by the
endorsement of the Afghanistan invasion) was greeted by the re-
emergence of protests of various kinds, but mainly by a fall off in
attendance at cell meetings and by difficulties in mounting Party
activities.

Power therefore lies firmly at the top. Decisions are taken with
virtually no reference to the membership at large. In recent years alone
there have been many examples of sudden and quite unexpected
changes of policy and strategy. For example, in January 1976, shortly

before the Twenty-Second Congress – but after the documents which form the basis of discussion within the Party had gone out – Marchais casually announced in a television interview that it was proposed to omit the reference to 'the dictatorship of the proletariat' from the Party programme. In 1977, after the PCF had for a long time bitterly opposed France's nuclear deterrent, it suddenly became, on certain conditions, acceptable.[28] The break up of the alliance with the PS in September 1977 and the subsequent campaign against its former partner was also generally unforeseen. Everyone then had to wait to see if a second ballot electoral pact would be authorised. The re-establishment, early in 1980, of open links with the Soviet Union, and Marchais' visit to Moscow, at the very time that his fellow Euro-communists in Italy and Spain were condemning the invasion of Afghanistan, also came as a surprise.

Given then, that power lies at the very top, exactly *where* is it located? This is a question which is difficult to answer, in any precise way, about most political organisations. In the case of the PCF it is doubly so, because of the well-guarded secrecy which surrounds most of the activities at headquarters. Only general indications can therefore be given.

In the institutional sense there is no doubt that the influence of the General Secretary is not as great as it was when Thorez occupied the post. It is still the single most powerful and prestigious position in the Party but both Waldeck Rochet and Marchais have been circumscribed by a more collective style of leadership than their illustrious predecessor. Foremost amongst the bodies with whom the General Secretary shares power are the Secretariat (which in 1981 had seven members) and the Politbureau (twenty-one members). Within these bodies individuals have specialisms and areas of responsibility which, it may be assumed, results in their own personal authority and influence varying according to the question under consideration. (See Table 4.1). Those who are members of both the Politbureau and Secretariat, which usually means *all* the Secretariat, presumably enjoy extra political weight.

Below the apex of the Secretariat and Politbureau a vast and complicated apparatus exists of committees, advisory bodies and officials. The most important of these are the *Commissions Centrales* which are staffed by members of the Central Committee plus others, such as trade unionists or Party journalists, who have a particular contribution to make in a specialised area. The most important *Commissions* are those for Candidates, the Promotion of Officials,

Political Control (which includes 'ideological orthodoxy'), and Finance and Administration. Overlapping with the *Commissions* are the *Sections Centrales* which are made up of full-time Party experts and administrators. The more important of the *Sections* are usually presided over by a member of the Politbureau. Formally the *Commissions* are the more powerful of the two bodies but in practice, because the *Sections* are more directly involved in the execution of policy, relations are more complex and variable. The Finance and Organisation *Sections* appear to enjoy particular influence.

Table 4.1 Politbureau elected in May 1979

Name	Age	Year joined the Party	Year first entered Polit- bureau	Former em- ploy- ment*	Special res- ponsibilities
Gustave Ansart (D) (E)	55	1944	1961	Metal Worker	Chairman of the Central Committee of Political Control. The Work of the European MP's
Mirielle Bertrand	37	1959	1972	Assistant Chemist	Health, quality of life, and consumers' section
Jean Colpin (S)	50	1952	1972	Employee	Workplace Section. Immigrant workers
Charles Fiterman (S) (D)	45	1951	1976	Electrician	Propaganda and Communication Section. Youth relations with political parties
Maxime Gremetz (S) (D) (E)	38	1958	1976	Metal Worker	Foreign Policy Sect- ion. Relations with Christian organi- sations
Guy Hermier (D)	38	1958	1972	Academic	Intellectuals, culture and Education Section
Phillippe Herzog	39	1965	1979	Academic	Economic Section
Pierre Juquin (D)	49	1953	1979	Academic	Propaganda and information
Henri Krasucki	55	1940	1964	Metal Worker	Deputy General Secretary of the CGT
André Lajoinie (D)	49	1948	1976	Farmer	Agriculture Section. Relations with the Parliamentary groups.

Paul Laurent (S) (D)	53	1946	1961	Technician	Party Organisation Section. Co-ordination of the federations of the Paris region.
Francette Lazard	42	1952	1979	Academic	Theory and research.
René Le Guen	58	1944	1979	Engineer	Secretary of *l'Union générale des ingénieurs cadres et techniciens* CGT
Roland Leroy (D)	52	1943	1964	Railway-man	Director of *L'Humanité* and *L'Humanité Dimanche*
Georges Marchais (S) (D) (E)	58	1947	1959	Metal Worker	General Secretary
Gisèle Moreau (S) (D)	38	1958	1979	Bank Employee	Women's Section
René Piquet (E)	46	1951	1964	Mechanic	Regions Section
Gaston Plissonnier (S)	65	1935	1964	Farmer	Aid to the promotion of militants' section. Co-ordination of Politbureau and Secretariat.
Claude Poperen	48	1949	1970	Metal Worker	Liaison with the federations and co-ordination of the work of the regional committees
Georges Séguy	51	1943	1956	Railway-man	General Secretary of the CGT
Madeleine Vincent	58	1938	1970	Employee	Elections Section. Liaison with PCF local councillors

S   = Member of the Secretariat
D   = Deputy
E   = Member of the European Parliament
Information compiled from: *Le Point,* 27 Feb. 1978; *L'Humanité,* 14 May 1979; *L'Humanité,* 22 June 1979.
*It must be emphasised that this category is only of limited value. Firstly, because the information available is vague in some cases. Secondly, because most of the members of the Politbureau have been full-time employees of the Party for many years.

In individual terms analysis of the distribution of power between the principal figures of the Party is not a fruitful task. Since the late 1960s commentators have frequently sought to explain the twists and turns of Party strategy in terms of the changing fortunes of personalities and groups in the Politbureau, but events more often than not have forced them to subsequently re-evaluate their views.

A recurring theme in this context has been the supposedly more liberal composition of the decision-making bodies, as old Stalinists have died or retired and a new generation has risen to take their place. Such alleged liberalism did not however prevent the marked stiffening of both policy and strategy from September 1977. The fact is that labels such as 'liberal', 'conservative' and 'moderate', which need to be used with care in any political setting, are likely to be particularly misleading when applied to the power structure in the PCF. The whole training and selection procedure is not one which encourages individualism or lack of conformity. Different perspectives on the questions of the day, though they certainly exist, are always likely to be marginal. Judgements on what is best for the Party in any particular circumstances will not necessarily be related to a consistent liberal or conservative pattern. This is illustrated by Charles Fiterman who, when he was first elected to the Politbureau in 1976 was widely described by outsiders in the media as a 'liberal' and a supporter of Marchais' democratisation. Yet according to a reliable report he voted with the 'conservatives' when the Secretariat divided in April 1978 on whether to open the Party press to an internal debate on the election defeat.[29]

A further point which should be noted on this question of a liberal-conservative division is that the 'newness' of the Politbureau is often exaggerated. It is true that by 1979 over half had joined since 1970 (thirteen out of twenty-one). But, as can be seen from Table 4.1, only one had been in the Party for less than twenty years. In other words all, apart from Phillipe Herzog, had spent formative years in the Party while Thorez was still General Secretary and while Stalin and Stalinism were still revered.

A related theme taken up by commentators has concerned the personal authority of Marchais. Many have suggested that he has gradually increased his power and as evidence they point to key promotions in the Party, especially since the 1976 Congress. Certainly it was widely assumed that each of the three members elected to the Politbureau at the Twenty-Second Congress – Charles Fiterman, Maxime Gremetz and André Lajoinie – were sympathetic to the policy of *ouverture* Marchais apparently favoured. Again, at the Twenty-Third Congress his position seemed to be further strengthened by, on the one hand the election of his young associates Phillippe Herzog and Gisèle Moreau to the Politbureau (and in Moreau's case to the

Secretariat too), and, on the other, the removal of Roland Leroy, a so-called 'hard-liner' and supposed opponent of Marchais from the Secretariat. If this interpretation of events is valid and Marchais has strengthened his position it would not be altogether surprising. For in virtually all communist parties the post of General Secretary carries with it a highly strategic position when it comes to the replacing and appointment of personnel. But to know that Marchais's position has improved does not tell us a great deal about the overall direction of the Party, for all the evidence indicates that he cannot be meaningfully categorised as a 'liberal' or a 'conservative'. Essentially he seems to be a pragmatist who is prepared to lead the PCF in the direction of *la voie démocratique* when it is clearly in the Party's interests, but who is equally at home presiding over retrenchment when that seems to become the requirement. As many commentators have suggested his greatest merit is perhaps his ability to adapt rapidly to changing circumstances, to jump on the train which is already moving or, to use another analogy, to lead with the prevailing wind behind him.

2. Towards Greater Democracy?

Since the mid-1960s demands for more internal Party democracy have greatly increased in number and in intensity. This has partly occurred because society itself has become less conformist but it has also been stimulated by the ideological liberalisation of the Party and by changes in the composition of its membership. In response to these pressures a number of modifications in internal Party life have taken place. In the 1970s there were no exclusions of prominent dissidents after Roger Garaudy, a Politbureau member and for years the leading ideologist, was forced out of the Party in 1970 (though see Postscript for a partial reversal of this policy in late 1980). Many critical works have been published by members (mainly intellectuals) which have not resulted in direct disciplinary action. A greater flexibility in discussions at the lower levels of the Party is now permitted. Changes in the Party Statutes have also been seen. In 1964 the secret ballot was introduced for elections to section and federal committees and to the Central Committee. The publication of voting figures for certain leading Party organs, including the Central Committee, was introduced for the 1979 Congress. In the new Statutes adopted by the 1979 Congress provision was made for *tribunes de discussion* to be opened, apart from those which precede the National Congress, 'when the Central Committee authorises it, because of a political situation or an important event'.[30] In addition the Congress established a new consultative organ, a *conseil national,* which, again on the initiative of the Central Committee, will bring together members of the Central Committee, Deputies, Senators, federation secretaries, and secretaries of sections from the industrial sector.

Accompanying these various changes there have been more assertions than ever before by the hierarchy on the truly democratic nature of the Party organisation. Frequently their testimonies have taken a defensive form. Paul Laurent, for example, alleges that the critics of democratic centralism are people clearly not interested in seeing the Party act efficiently on behalf of the working class and the popular masses. Such critics are frustrated because the PCF is not characterised, like the other parties, by constant inner debate and factionalism. He also makes the point (with some justice) that external critics rarely comment on the lack of inner democracy in their own organisation. More positively he claims, 'Democratic centralism allows for the conscientious and active participation of all communists as much in the elaboration as the putting into effect of the policy of their party'.[31]

Despite such claims, the fact is however that very little has really changed. The modifications have been cosmetic and marginal rather than substantive. Those holding unacceptable views are as far removed from power and influence as they ever were. The machinery and devices we considered earlier see to that.

Because this is so voices of protest against the rigidity of the structure were increasingly heard during the 1970s. After the disappointment and disillusionment of the March 1978 election defeat they reached a level which the Party had not experienced since the days of the Nazi-Soviet pact. As usual intellectuals led the way. From the 'Eurocommunist Right' Jean Elleinstein, Jean Rony and others accused the leadership of having wanted to dominate the Union of the Left and of taking the Party back into sectarianism when it became apparent that this could not be achieved. From the 'Left' Louis Althusser plus a number of sympathisers took quite the contrary position. They argued the leadership had become far too opportunistic and should now return to a true revolutionary theory and strategy. The ideological gap between these currents was thus considerable. Notwithstanding that, many of the proponents on either side were agreed on one central point and formed what almost amounted to an unholly alliance around it: there must be more democracy and liberty in the Party. When the leadership made it clear that there would be few, if any, concessions in this direction, and refused to allow the columns of the Party press to be opened to the circulation of such ideas, many of the *contestataires* went elsewhere; they published in the 'bourgeois' press, in particular in *Le Monde, Le Matin* and *Le Nouvel Observateur.*[32] (The latter two are sympathetic to the PS). Some also became involved, along with members of the PS, in the establishment of a new non-aligned weekly newspaper *Maintenant.* In taking such action the *contestataires* were breaking fresh ground. Unlike their 'predecessors' in 1956, when internal unrest followed the Party's acceptance of the Soviet invasion of Hungary, and 1968, when there was opposition to the leadership's moderation during *les événements,* they were choosing to challenge official policy from within rather than resign.

The *contestataires* were always a minority and the official reaction was at first to dismiss them as of little significance. The liberal image was even reinforced by a statement from Marchais that there would be no exclusions. As the campaign developed however, to take an unprecedented open form, a firm response became necessary if the Party structure was not to be seriously disturbed. Accordingly, many of the old devices were brought out in an attempt to marginalise and isolate the critics. The response was not to engage in debate but to repress. The methods were traditional:

(a) *Rapporteurs,* from the highest level to the lowest, were dispatched to explain and smooth over the various sources of grievance: the changes in tactics which had seen a firm line in the negotiations on the Common Programme in September 1977; an apparent capitulation to the PS on 13 March after the first ballot and a return to antagonism towards it after the second ballot; the claim by the Politbureau that the Party carried 'no responsibility' for the election defeat; and the refusal to allow an internal debate on these questions.

(b) *Responsables* who had voiced criticisms or who had allowed discussion to go too far in their cells, sections or federations were replaced. In Paris, where the traditionally more independent intellectuals had been particularly vociferous, direct pressure from the Politbureau led to the replacement in early 1979 of the federation's First Secretary, Henri Fiszbin, and the resignation of five of its Secretariat.[33]

(c) It was strongly hinted that some members might be better off leaving the Party. Critics, it was said, sapped the Party of its revolutionary strength and diverted it from its true tasks.

(d) The Party press far from opening its columns to the views of the *contestataires* saved its comments for attacks and condemnations. Publicity was not given to those criticisms which went to the very heart of the role and nature of the Party: what is the purpose of democratic centralism? why had the Party apparently 'demanded everything in September, then conceded everything in March'? was it still a revolutionary Party? what was now its strategy for achieving power? (e)　Where the publishing side had stepped out of line measures were taken to bring it back under control. *Paris Hebdo,* the unofficial organ of the restless Paris federation, was quickly closed. A number of journalists who had displayed sympathy for criticisms were relieved of their functions, or not discouraged from resigning. Under the guise of financial reform a major reorganisation was begun in some quarters. Most notably, *La Nouvelle Critique* (a literary, intellectual monthly) which published many critical articles – some going as far as calling for 'a true break with the Stalinist heritage and the introduction of *real* democratic centralism'[34] – was eventually merged with the (then) organ of the Central Committee *France Nouvelle* (which itself had displayed some sympathy for the criticisms).

The whole process of 'normalisation' was more gentle than it had been in the past. The Party was, after all, attempting to strike a difficult balance between its traditional, revolutionary and *avant-garde* role on the one hand and its new democratic image on the other. No-one was excluded. Though pressures were exerted behind the scenes, the critics still enjoyed unheard of latitude. In December 1978, a special meeting, which was quite contrary to the 'vertical principle', was even arranged between the leading intellectuals and the Politbureau. All in all persuasion was more important than it ever had been. But the end result was much the same in terms of the balance of power within the Party. A price was paid, in that the limits on internal dissent have had to be extended, and many members seem to have drifted, in their disappointment, into inactivism, but the leadership was prepared to accept these as necessary, if regrettable conditions for the maintenance of the traditional structure.

That nothing fundamental has changed may be illustrated by briefly considering some of the events which occured prior to and at the Twenty-Third Party Congress in May 1979. The period prior to a Congress is supposedly the time when the democratic side of democratic centralism comes most fully into its own. Ordinary members are encouraged in Party publications to participate in the election of their delegates to the section congresses and to express their views on the documents which are published by the Central Committee about three months before the Congress and which serve as the focus of the debate.

The Party hierarchy certainly tried to give the impression that democracy had reached new heights. Writing in *La vie du parti* (an internal publication intended for officials and activists) Charles Fiterman, a member of the Secretariat, called for a truly far-ranging and free debate. Somewhat ominously, however, he also pointed out that opponents of the Party were hoping to see tendencies and personal ambitions in open conflict. Care must therefore be taken to ensure that these opponents did not impose the pattern of the debate, oppose comrades against one another, and at the end of the day make 'our Party incapable of assuming its responsibilities of the revolutionary party and the party of the working class'[35] When launching in February the documents for discussion, the amended Party Statutes and the *projet de résolution* Marchais also expressed his hope that the debate would be 'the most free, the most frank and the most profound'.[36] At the Congress he stated that his hopes of February had been confirmed. Etienne Fajon, then a Politbureau member, who opened the Congress, went so far as to say in his speech that the debate in the preceding months had been 'the most free, the most sincere and the most meaningful that our party has experienced since it was founded'.[37] Neither he, Marchais, nor any other spokesman saw fit, however, to discuss the manifestly non-democratic features surrounding the Congress and its preparations. For example:

(1) It was made clear at a meeting of federal secretaries held in February that no cell could send to a pre-Congress section conference a delegation including *both* supporters and opponents of the texts issued by the Central Committee. (There was, of course, no question of permitting the submission of *alternative* texts.) This rubric was clearly designed to reduce the influence of *contestataires*. It was further emphasised that those delegates who did hold critical positions should not get, except in rare cases, beyond the section conference.[38]

(2) Though dissenting views were expressed in the *tribune de discussion* held in *L'Humanité* and *France Nouvelle* they were carefully managed. As usual, the only information given to readers about the signatories of contributors was their cell, section and federation. This allowed a very high proportion of published contributions to be written by *permanents* and *cadres* without it being blatantly obvious. On the two main controversial themes of the debate, the Union of the Left and the degree of socialism in Eastern

Europe, the two polar points of criticism were often placed side by side or were published on succeeding days. So, on the Union of the Left, contributions appeared alleging the PCF was too conciliatory to the Socialists, whilst others argued it was too inflexible. This strategy allowed the leadership to appear to be taking a reasonable middle way. Another tactic saw opposing viewpoints paralleled with, or quickly countered by, contributions supporting the official position. A particularly graphic illustration of this was seen when critical articles in *L'Humanité* by the 'liberals' Antoine Spire and Jean Rony were directly replied to the very next day. This meant that the *commission* which had the responsibility for choosing the texts to be published (which was presided over by Marchais) had taken steps to prepare a reply at least two or three days before the publication of the original letters.[39]

(3)   Charles Fiterman, who presented the report of the *Commission de la résolution* to the Congress, attempted to demonstrate in his speech the breadth of discussion and near unanimity of views in the Party on the new *resolution*. He claimed that of the 28,000 cells only 82 had rejected the resolution, and this included 20 which had adopted it but with modifications of its overall orientation. He further stated that of 20,446 delegates who had participated in the 98 federal conferences only 63 had voted against the *projet de résolution* while 151 had abstained.[40] He made no mention of the careful filtering process we have described. Nor did he refer to the fact that in many cells and even a number of section conferences the numbers participating in debates had been unusually low.[41] The circle thereby closed. Such overwhelming approval was taken to justify the exclusion of critics from Party platforms: clearly they represented but a tiny and insignificant minority.

(4)   The lists of candidates for the various national bodies elected by the Congress and the Central Committee saw a few names omitted because they had become associated with dissent. Two were especially noteworthy. Jacques Chambaz, the member of the Politbureau responsible for relations with intellectuals and who had expressed some sympathy for them, was dropped, though he retained his place on the Central Committee. François Hincker, editor in chief of *Nouvelle Critique* which, as we noted above, had seen the expression of dissident views, was removed from the Central Committee. At the highest level, and in a way which highlights the almost complete secrecy of the inner workings of the top leadership, Roland Leroy, director of *L'Humanité* and long thought of as an opponent of the whole *Union*

de la Gauche strategy, was dropped from the Secretariat. This came as a complete surprise to everyone outside the privileged inner elite.

From what we have seen it is thus apparent that, despite all the publicity and propaganda concerning the democratic nature of the Party, little has *really* changed in its internal functioning. Whatever may be claimed there is no escaping the fact that arrangements are such that power rests firmly in the topmost levels of a well organised, secretive, and tightly controlled machine.

MECHANISMS FOR SPREADING COMMUNIST INFLUENCE

Annie Kriegel has described the PCF as being made up of a series of concentric rings. From the permanent apparatus at the centre, where commitment and involvement are greatest, the Party spreads out to its membership and from there to the distant circles of the Communist press and voters.[42] To keep in touch with and to encourage the development of these various levels the Party makes use of many devices in addition to the formal internal channels of communication with its members.

1. Press and Propaganda

The most obvious of these devices is the publication and distribution of an enormous range of literature. There is a constant outpouring from the Party presses of books, policy statements, pamphlets, newspapers, journals, newsletters, etc. Naturally the 'flow' of some types of publication varies according to circumstances. For example, 'official' books examining aspects of Party policy and Party life have increased in recent years in response to internal and external debate on the Party and also as a result of the increasing PCF mood of self-justification. The number of publicity leaflets and handouts also varies, with passers-by being subject to the greatest barrage at election times. But there are also many regularly produced publications and their total exceeds that of all the other major parties put together. Counting daily and weekly newspapers, and weekly and monthly journals and magazines, the total is over sixty. In addition there are many local editions of newspapers plus innumerable periodic newsletters and newsheets of federations, arrondissements, sections and even communes.

Many publications are directed primarily at members. These include theoretical and discussive journals such as the monthly *Cahiers du Communisme;* technical and professional reviews such as *Fédération des Postes* and *Tribune des Mineurs;* and regional and local reviews such as *La Semaine en Haute-Savoie* and *Nouvelles de l'Yonne.* Naturally the style, purpose and content of such publications vary enormously. This may be illustrated by brief reference to two important national journals. The monthly *L'Elu d'Aujourd'Hui* is directed principally at PCF councillors and therefore focusses much of its attention on particular problems and experiences in local government, especially in municipalities dominated by the PCF. It frequently also contains technical discussions of matters as various as urban development and sewage disposal. The weekly *Economie et Politique* on the other hand is more theoretically orientated and devotes considerable attention to questions of socialist economics.

Unlike the semi-internal publications we have just mentioned the Party's newspapers are intended to reach not only members and positive sympathisers but also a wider, mass audience. They can hardly be said to succeed in this aim. The number of daily newspapers published by the Party has declined from over thirty after the Liberation, to twelve in the mid-1950s, to four today. There has been a corresponding fall in the number of daily Communist newspapers sold from 2,770,000 in 1947, to 800,000 in 1955 to around 250,000 at present. Nonetheless, compared with the press of the other political parties, circulation figures are still highly respectable. *L'Humanité,* the Party's principal daily – and which, with its regular publication of Party communiqués, detailed accounts of Party activities and rigid ideological orthodoxy, can hardly be said to be light reading – sold in 1979 a daily average of 150,000 copies and had an estimated readership of 608,000. *L'Humanité Dimanche* (which is much less political) sold an average 400,000 copies and had a readership of 1,373,000.[43] The other three daily newspapers are all provincial: *L'Echo du Centre* (based on Limoges), *Liberté* (Lille) and *La Marseillaise* (Marseilles). One other important newspaper is the weekly *La Terre.* Aimed at farmers and peasantry it claims to 'go into' 212,000 families in the countryside and to be read by nearly 800,000 people per week. Doubtless these figures are inflated, but there can be no disputing that the paper is widely read and that it plays an important role in focussing the attention of rural sympathisers on one of the Party's favourite themes: the danger to French farmers posed by enlargement of the Common Market.

2. The Importance of Activism

All the different publications do, therefore, naturally have their own style, emphasis and clientele. There is one theme, however, which constantly recurs – apart from the obvious need to support the Party – and that is the need to *work* for the Party. Members are constantly exhorted to be *active*. This at first sight may seem rather curious to outsiders, given the general supposition that communists everywhere are always enthusiastically committed. In the case of the PCF this is by no means the case and for many members being a Communist means little more than holding a Party card. Publications direct much of their attention therefore at combatting passivity. *L'Humanité,* because of its relatively wide audience, naturally has a central role to play in this respect and it continually encourages activism and reinforces the many appeals and campaigns which are launched and transmitted through the federations, sections and cells. Other publications perform a similar service, though of course they tailor their encouragement to their audience. This may be seen, for example, in *La Vie du parti,* a publication intended principally for office holders at cell level. It is clear from reading its columns that many small cells, especially industrial cells, are unable even to find the five or six members necessary to make up a *bureau* or to take on the key posts of secretary, treasurer, *L'Humanité* officer and propaganda officer. *La Vie du parti* therefore frequently offers advice to its readers on how enthusiasm in the cells might be generated; though mainly office holders, they may not themselves be as active as is desired. It even tries to induce involvement by playing down responsibilities, claiming that jobs do not take up *that* much time. As a last resort, where a cell or bureau cannot be formed, it is stated that the section leadership should be called in an attempt to find a solution. If necessary they will make available an active colleague from a neighbouring cell.[44]

Apart from special appeals, such as at election times or during periods of industrial strife, there are many permanent tasks to which members are constantly exhorted to give their assistance. For example, the distribution of *L'Humanité* is constantly emphasised as being of crucial importance, not only because it is the principal mouthpiece of the Party, but also because it is highly dependent on street sales. At the turn of each year a major campaign is always launched encouraging members to promptly renew their Party cards, to chase up laggards, and to bring in, wherever possible, new recruits.

Members who subsequently do not attend cell meetings, which are supposed to be held monthly, may, in active cells, find themselves subsequently visited by concerned comrades. Throughout the year, but particularly during the summer months when many *fêtes* are organised, members are prompted to participate fully in and help make a success of the various events which are open to the public and which have recruitment as a major aim. To this end local targets for increases in membership are often set, published in *L'Humanité* and successes reported as an encouragement to others.

Another form of activism which is strongly encouraged is involvement in the *organisations des masses*. The most obvious and successful manifestation of this is the Communist dominance of the main trade union the *Confédération Générale du Travail*. The details of the relationship between the PCF and the CGT are examined in Chapter 9 so it need be only stated here that for most practical purposes the direction of the affairs of the CGT is firmly in the hands of PCF members, and prominent members at that. According to the CGT's General Secretary Georges Séguy, about 500,000 of the 2.3 million members the union claims to have belong to the PCF.[45] At the higher levels in the union's structure this proportion of PCF members is greatly increased. This has not made the CGT a completely pliable PCF agent but it is a fact that there has been no fundamental disagreement between the two since Communists gained control of the union just after the Liberation.

Apart from the CGT there are many other organisations which the Party strongly influences or controls, even though they are not part of the official PCF structure. The importance of many of these satellites has declined in recent years, but they still serve as useful propagandist outlets. Among the best known are the *Mouvement de la Paix* (a peace movement which focusses particularly on the de-stablising influence of Western imperialism), *Secours Populaire Francais* (which attempts to speak for and defend victims of repression – especially in the Third World), and the *Mouvement de défènse de l'exploitation familiale* (MODEF, which is basically a small farmers pressure group). Other associations represent women, the aged, students, youth, war veterans, immigrants etc.

Activism of all kinds is, therefore, constantly encouraged. It is seen as the way to extend the influence of the Party and to ensure that it is the dominating force of the Left. It also, though this is not its official intent, has an important role to play in reinforcing the identity of members with their Party. Constant involvement in Party affairs,

rom social events to selling *L'Humanité* outside a Metro station, can
help to stimulate feelings of belonging to something rather distinct
and rather special. In other words activism can have its own internal
function by fostering the idea of *le parti* and hence contributing to
Party unity and Party discipline.

FINANCE

At the Twenty-Third Congress in May 1979 Armand Guillemot,
chairman of the Central Commission of Financial Control, estimated
that the Party's total income for the year would amount to around 160
million francs.[46] (Around £17 million). This officially declared income
comes from three main sources:

(1) *Membership dues.* Making up about 40 per cent of total income
the collection of subscriptions in the PCF is unusual in two ways. In
the first place, payment is not an annual affair, as in many parties, but
is on a regular monthly basis. Cards are issued at the beginning of the
year and are stamped up as payments are made. The idea behind this
procedure is that ordinary members are kept in regular contact with
the activists and can be regularly encouraged to participate in, and
work for, the Party. (The scheme also creates problems and results in
many cards being far from complete). The second distinctive feature is
that, apart from the lowest levels of income, the subscription paid is
supposedly equivalent to one per cent of salary. (Again, in practice,
this has created administrative problems).

(2) *Returns from elected members.* This amounts to around 25 per
cent of income. Deputies, senators, members of the European Parliament and elected local representatives hand over their salary to the
Party. In return they are paid the same salary as all Party *permanents,*
which is the average of a skilled worker. In the case of Deputies this
has usually meant they have received about one quarter of their parliamentary salary.

(3) *Other income.* Making up the remaining 35 per cent, by far the
largest component of this comes from special subscriptions and donations. In addition to having a permanent national appeal special
collections are made on a number of occasions; to support
L'Humanité (whose accounts are kept separately from those of the

Party), to fight election campaigns, to buy property for the Party, to hold a *fête* etc.

Beyond these 'official' returns the Party is known to supplement its income in a number of ways, though to what extent is a matter of fierce debate. Two principal sources are known to exist and a third is alleged.

Firstly, in municipal councils dominated by the Party all sorts of devices exist for generating income or offsetting expenditure. (Some of the procedures, it should be said, are not unknown to other parties). Employees who in practice spend much, if not all, of their time engaged in Party activities are hired by councils. This may occur directly or through the agencies and organisations with which councils deal. Many council 'trading' activities, from buying materials to seeking technical advice on specialised matters, are channelled through firms which are controlled by, or are sympathetic to, the Party. Donations and assistance are given by councils to organisations which are allied with or are sympathetic to the PCF. Municipal publications and public facilities are used to transmit the Party's views.

Secondly, the Party is known to have interests in a number of commercial enterprises. The official position is that these are directly related and limited to essential work of the Party: bookshops, printing works, distribution of literature, research, improvement of publicity etc. Few outside observers take this claim at face value, however, for there are known to be interests in a whole range of other activities. Amongst the ventures in which the Party is believed to be involved are banking, finance, tourist agencies, import-export offices (often acting in a liaison capacity between Eastern and Western Europe), co-operatives, and property. According to two recent studies the Party's commercial sector is made up in all of around 300 business ventures.[47]

How much of the profit of this 'capitalist empire' finds its way into the Party's treasury is, of course, another, and quite unknown factor. The degree of interest in individual firms and enterprises varies, and whilst those which are directly controlled may be assumed to regularly 'contribute' in one way or another those with looser ties may give only indirect and intermittent assistance. Calculations simply cannot be made as long as the present secrecy persists. Outsiders bandy figures around – an average of ten per cent of profits being 'paid over' is a frequently heard estimate – but they are quite impossible to substantiate. All that can be said is that the Party must reap considerable benefits since some of the enterprises have a turnover well in excess of £10 million.

The third, alleged, 'unofficial' source of revenue is direct assistance from Eastern Europe. Allegations of 'Moscow's gold' have been made against the Party throughout its existence and there is no doubt that until comparatively recently financial assistance was received. Until the Popular Front it seems indeed that most of the PCF's revenue came from Comintern (and hence the Soviet Union). Furthermore, in the early post-war years many of the enterprises which the Party sought to build up were initially heavily funded from Moscow.

Today, however, the Party appears to be financially independent. Accusations that it is still in the pay of the Soviet Union are still to be heard, mainly from Right-wing political opponents. The best known of these is Jean Montaldo. He has documented in great detail the way in which the PCF and associated organisations do much of their business through, and hold most of their deposits in, the Soviet-owned *Banque Commerciale pour l'Europe du Nord'* (BCEN).[48] He claims that through the bank the funds of the PCF are 'scrutinised, managed and manipulated' and he strongly implies that a great deal of direct financing is involved. In the eyes of most detached observers Montaldo is wrong. The PCF certainly opens itself to criticism by banking with the BCEN. It may also receive indirect forms of assistance such as favourable terms to finance commercial activities, (which, of course, it can be argued, amounts to the same thing as receiving subsidies). But there is no evidence to suggest, or indeed even reason to believe given the sources of many of the Party's ventures, that direct funding still takes place. The Party itself certainly denies that it does. Shortly after the appearance of Montaldo's second book early in 1979 it issued a statement that it receives not *'un centime de l'étranger'*. The point was reinforced at the Twenty-Third Congress when Guillemot emphasised 'It [the Party] receives money neither from the State, the industrial bosses, or abroad'.[49]

Turning to the expenditure side of the PCF's finances, total figures are not given. There is even uncertainty over the relative proportions of spending. The Party tends to speak vaguely of about one half being spent on propaganda and the other half being evenly divided between salaries and administration. Jean Elleinstein has suggested rather different proportions by strongly implying that propaganda, administration and salaries account for about one third each.[50] In either case the categories are hardly illuminating.

The only exact figures published are those for the Central Committee. In 1979 these showed a total expenditure of 63 million French francs; this was 39 per cent of the Party's *total* declared *income* for the year.[51] (The expenditure total was not given.) The major expenditure items of the Central Committee were given as salaries at 45 per cent and publications at 28 per cent. These cannot, however, be necessarily taken as an accurate guide to the national expenditure pattern, since the Central Committee's responsibilities are naturally different to those of the federations, sections and cells, (which are each supposed to receive one quarter of membership dues).

Exact information on the Party's finances is, therefore, difficult to obtain and much has to be left to surmise. What is without doubt, however, is that the party which claims to represent the under-privileged and the exploited is itself by far the richest of all France's political parties.

MEMBERSHIP

1. Size

Apart from the periods of the Popular Front and the Liberation, the PCF until the mid-1960s did not seek to maximise its membership but preferred the Leninist conception of a smallish, well-disciplined van-guard. Since the development of *la voie démocratique* however and the *Union de la Gauche* it has openly sought a mass membership and to this end it has organised successive recruitment drives. Its efforts in this direction are most openly seen at rallies, local assemblies, and the annual *Fête de l'Humanité*. On every occasion great attention is paid to the number of new members recruited; sometimes there are even illuminated signs, which relay new registrations as they occur to the assembled gathering.

The recruitment strategy of the Party is therefore a crucial factor in determining its size. A large membership may not necessarily imply a period of increased Communist popularity but may be a consequence of a more 'open door' policy in which the emphasis is on quantity rather than quality and in which the entry requirements have been facilitated. Such has been the case in the recent period when a higher membership has been sought, because it raises internal morale and helps to establish the representative claims of the Party. The near doubling in Party size in the 1970s (see Table 4.2) should not therefore be necessarily taken as evidence of major inroads into hitherto barren areas. Much of it is explained by the strategical change which has allowed for easier entry, less taxing demands on members, and, as a consequence, a higher ratio between members and pre-existing sym-pathisers.

Table 4.2 Membership of the PCF

1921	110,000	1969	380,000
1925	60,000	1972	392,000
1932	30,000	1973	410,000
1936	150,000	1974	450,000
1937	327,000	1975	500,000
1946	800,000	1976	530,000
1956	430,000	1977	600,000
1961	300,000	1978	690,000
1964	330,000	1979	700,000
1966	350,000		

The above figures can only be approximations since actual membership varies according to the criterion taken. For the recent period the figures refer to cards sent out to the federations and not to those taken up by members. This probably leads to an official PCF over-estimate of around 10 per cent. In addition, of those taken up many will not be fully stamped, i.e. the full annual subscription will not have been paid.

A large membership is not of course simply a consequence of strategical calculation by the Party leadership. There are many reasons why people join the PCF. In some established Party bastions it is a natural consequence of family and social background, in others a result of a more conscious political choice. With regard to the latter it is clear that events of national significance have a mobilising effect on parts of the population: the Popular Front, the Resistance and Liberation, the expectation in the mid-1970s of a new Popular Front government have all coincided with membership peaks. The specific factors behind the mobilisations at these peak times vary considerably. Thus after the war new recruits associated the PCF with the fight for liberation, whilst in the aftermath of the 'events' of 1968 – which was another period of increased recruitment – many of those joining spoke of their sympathy with the way in which society had been called into question and their search for an alternative, which the PCF maintained it could provide.[52]

Since the mid-1970s the PCF has set itself the goal of ultimately attracting one million members. A major difficulty it faces in achieving this is that although much new blood has been attracted since the expansionist strategy was set in motion in the 1960s the Party has great difficulty in holding onto its recruits. In the past the annual turnover has been in the region of 10 per cent; since the mid-1970s it has increased to around 15 per cent. This fluctuation is occasioned by a number of factors. One of the most important is that the level of commitment required of an active member is not always sustainable over a long period. Amongst younger members in particular family and other social responsibilities may come to have prior claims with the consequence that their membership lapses. Other members may become disillusioned as a result of a change in official policy. This has clearly been the case since 1978, with many of those members who joined on the momentum of the *Union de la Gauche* failing to renew their cards because of the rigid line of the leadership on internal democracy and alliance strategy. Some members may leave simply because the reality of Party life does not live up to their expectations. This problem seems to have been exacerbated in recent years with the near doubling in membership in the 1970s for, inevitably, this expansion with its laxer standards of entry has meant that more 'marginal' and heterogeneous elements have entered, many of whom are lacking the dedication the Party has traditionally sought.

There is clearly something, therefore, of the *'parti passoire'* about the PCF. But the case should not be overstated. Underlying the turnover is a solid and continuing base. According to official figures in 1979 the Party still retains 38,000 members who joined before the last war, and nearly 100,000 who first obtained their card before 1948.[53] At the 1979 Congress it was reported that 57.4 per cent of delegates had joined before 1972.[54] Most importantly of all, as we have already seen, those with responsibilities in the topmost echelons of the Party are all long established and experienced figures.

2. Social Composition

The ideological and strategical emphasis which is placed on the predominant role of the working class is reflected in the social composition of the Party's membership. Although the proportion has declined in relative terms, in part because of changes in the infrastructure of French society, the industrial working class still comprises over half the total membership, according to official figures (see Table 4.3). This has three major consequences for the internal life of the Party. Firstly, it helps to confirm and legitimise the Party's perception of its historic mission as *the* party of the working class. Secondly, it assists internal discipline since the industrial working class are, on the whole, more willing than other social categories to accept decisions made at higher levels. Thirdly, because the working class are less well-educated

than other classes, there is felt to be a need to politically inform them
so as to mould them into effective members. Many of the Party
schools are therefore organised for this purpose.

Table 4.3   Socio-economic composition of PCF membership

	1966 %	1979 %
Farmers and agricultural workers	9.9	3.4
Artisans and shopkeepers	5.8	4.1
'Intellectuals' (teachers, engineers, architects, doctors, writers etc.)	8.8	13.5
Clerical staff	18.6	28.0
Industrial workers*	56.9	51.0

Source: Censuses conducted by the PCF Organisation
          Department.
*It should be said that many observers regard the PCF's use
 of this term as excessively liberal.

Corresponding to the decline in the working-class base there has
been an increase in the proportion of non-manual recruits. The
growth in the number of office workers has been particularly noticeable. This reflects changing occupational patterns and the willingness
of the Party to aim its appeals beyond the 'traditional' working class
to other 'underprivileged' sectors of the population: *'les couches
sociales les plus défavorisées'*.

The Party has also actively sought to recruit amongst the female
population. Normally under-represented in political parties, women
have been joining the PCF in ever-increasing numbers since the late
1960s. According to the Party's own 1979 study over 250,000
members are now women (35.7 per cent) as compared with 90,000
(25.5 per cent) in 1966. As customs have changed and women have
been given more equality and responsibility within society, efforts
have been made to involve them more directly in the life of the Party.
They are still grossly under-represented but it is clear that in both the
Party organisation and in its candidates for public office women have
been chosen as a result of deliberate policy decisions to give them an
increased proportion.

In terms of age structure the Party has 'grown younger' in recent
years. Whereas in 1966 9.4 per cent were less than 25 years and 33.1
per cent were aged between 26 and 40, these figures in 1979 had risen

to 11.8 per cent and 39 per cent respectively (see Table 4.4). Over half
the Party are thus under the age of 40.

Table 4.4   Age distribution of PCF in 1979

	Number	%
Under 25	83,000	11.8
25-30	106,000	15.0
30-35	97,000	13.8
35-45	132,000	18.8
45-60	170,000	24.1
Over 60	115,000	16.0

Source: Census conducted by PCF
Organisation Department.

3.   Geographical Distribution

Traditionally the PCF has reaped most of its active support in urban
areas and this continues to be the case. Membership remains strongest in
and around Paris with the seven federations in the region containing just
over one quarter of the total Party membership. Other areas of strength
are Rhône-Alpes, Provence-Côte d'Azur, the Nord and Picardy, which
between them make up over one third of the total.

Despite the strong urban bias there have always been Communist rural
pockets and these have remained as the Party has increasingly
championed the cause of French farmers. In recent years it has reaped
political dividends from its opposition to the enlargement of the EEC,
which in the South and South-West poses a serious threat to the
livelihoods of farmers.

ELECTORATE

1.   Size

Three things are striking about the PCF vote in the post-war period. The
first is its remarkable stability. Despite the vastly different situations in
which the Party has found itself, it consistently polled, until 1981,
between one fifth and one quarter of the vote. In the Fifth Republic,
in all national elections, the range of its vote varied in a narrow band
between 19.2 per cent in 1958 and 23.4 per cent in 1969 until it fell to
15.3 per cent in the 1981 presidential election. The second is that, the

stability notwithstanding, there has been an overall decline. This is most marked between the Fourth Republic – when it never achieved *less* than 25.9 per cent – and the Fifth – when it has never achieved *more* than the 1969 23.4 per cent. (In legislative elections its best result was in 1967 when it polled 22.5 per cent). The third characteristic is that, bearing in mind the *overall* decline, the Party has done best *relatively*, when it has emphasised its Frenchness and its desire to integrate itself into the national political system. Just as the Popular Front brought an increase in its vote before the war so did the Resistance and Liberation, and the *Union de la Gauche* after it: the four poorest results in the Fifth Republic – 1958, 1968, 1978 and 1981 – have all coincided with periods when the Party has, or has been perceived to be, pursuing a 'non-French' (1958), 'revolutionary' (1968), 'isolationist' (1978) or 'sectarian' (1981) path. (See Appendices for election figures).

2. Geographical Distribution

As is to be expected there is a strong correlation between the Party's membership and its electorate. The main areas of electoral support lie in the working-class areas of the Paris region (from where many of the Party's deputies are elected), in the industrial areas of the North, in the Mediterranean coastal region, and in parts of Central France.

During the Fifth Republic there has been an improvement in the Party's position in certain areas, notably in the poorer and de-populating South-West and West. But the overall trend has been of stagnation and in many places decline. To take just the changes between the 1973-8 elections there was slight progress in 8 of the 22 regions (principally in traditional Socialist or Radical strongholds) but a decline in the majority.[55] The most marked, and for the Party most worrying fall-off was in the Paris region where a trend which had set in in the late 1960s was confirmed with a drop from 27.1 per cent of the vote to 24.2 per cent. In 1981 this fell to below 20 per cent.

The rather odd regional spread of the PCF electorate is explained by the fact that the Party attracts different types of support, which vary in their relative importance between areas. So, in its urban bastions it draws heavily on the historically poor integration of the working class into the political mainstream and the existence in these areas of feelings of oppression and alienation. In less industrialised areas its success seems to be primarily a consequence of it having inherited traditions of voting against the establishment, against Paris, or for the most credible left wing candidate. (Many of its rural strongholds were

Radical-Socialist in the latter part of the nineteenth century, Socialist before 1914 and Communist after 1920.) These differing motivations have enabled the Party to build up local Communist traditions, which are securest in the most *ouvrièriste* areas. This is because, as Bon has observed, 'the higher the Communist vote, the more homogeneous the social milieu, the older the establishment [of the Party], the more the Communist voter finds himself in an environment which favours the perpetuation of his political attitudes.'[56]

Map 4.1   Support for PCF, March 1978

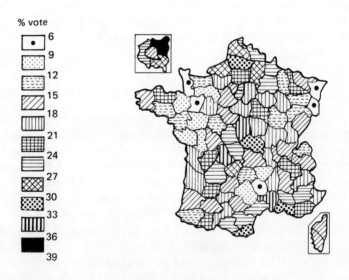

% vote

Source: N. Denis, 'Les élections législatives de mars 1978 en metropole', *RFSP* (Dec. 1978) p.987.

3.   Social Composition

As can be seen from Table 4.5 there have been changes in the social composition of the PCF's electorate in the post-war era. The most significant of these are the decline in the proportion of the agricultural vote and the increase in the proportion of manual workers. Until 1981 (see below) the latter constituted over half of the Party's electorate, while over one third of all manual workers voted Communist.

Table 4.5 Socio-economic structure of PCF electorate

	1952 %	1966 %	1976 %
Agriculture	13	9	4
Liberal professions, commerce, industrial managers	9	9	8
Clerical and white collar	13	21	15
Manual workers	38	46	52
Other categories	27	15	21

Source: Adapted from IFOP surveys.

The changes observable in Table 4.5 are mainly to be explained by the post-war transformation of the French social structure. The decline of PCF rural support has gone hand-in-hand with the decline of this sector of the population, while the increase in the proportion of manual workers reflects the increase in industrialisation and urbanisation. As workers have left the land they may not have changed their political allegiance but they will have changed their position in the statistician's tables.

Of other social and demographic variables three are particularly noticeable. Firstly, the Party's electorate is less male biased than it used to be; 51 per cent are men and 49 per cent women. Secondly, as is to be expected, there is a strong correlation between lack of religion and voting PCF. Thirdly, the average age of the Communist voter is younger than that of the whole population and the Party is the strongest of all the major parties in the younger voting categories (see Table 4.6).

Table 4.6 Age structure of PCF electorate 1977

	PCF %	Total population %
18-24	31	15
25-34	23	20
35-49	26	25
50-64	18	20
65 and over	12	20

Source: Louis Harris Poll, *Le Matin,* 30 Sep., 1977.

This young age structure, which was re-confirmed in 1981, could possibly provide a basis for future PCF growth. But it may be a faint hope since it needs to be seen in the context of the widely observed tendency of voters to become more conservative as they age.

CONCLUDING REMARKS: THE ROLE OF THE PCF IN THE FRENCH POLITICAL SYSTEM

From 1977 the PCF toned down and in some respects abandoned *la voie démocratique*. However in 1981, after Marchais' poor performance in the presidential elections, it returned to 'moderation'. A useful way of analysing these and the other about-turns in the PCF's history is through the different roles the Party performs within the political system and the different priorities these have been accorded at different times.

Ronald Tiersky in his much praised historical analysis of the PCF identifies four main roles: 'The classic role of *revolutionary vanguard,* and its hard line counterpart, the role of *countercommunity,* are opposed to the moderate and collaborative roles of *popular tribune* and *government party'*.[57] The first two, which draw on Annie Kriegel's writings, highlight the Party's revolutionary tradition and its attempts to instil in its members feelings of distinctiveness and of being 'apart' from the rest of French society.[58] When emphasising these roles priority is given to the Party's 'maximum' position: the revolutionary transformation of the political, social and economic systems. The second two roles owe something to the work of Georges Lavau who has built on general comparative functional literature to emphasise the integrative role which the PCF performs within the French political system. Focussing particularly on the 'tribune' role Lavau argues that the Party, amongst other things, articulates the grievances of discontented groups and channels then in non-revolutionary directions.[59] By claiming to speak for the 'plebeian' classes, whilst being fundamentally non-revolutionary, the Party, in Lavau's view, contributes to the stability of the political system whilst at the same time reaping advantages for itself. These self-advantages are electoral – the Party widens its appeal – and doctrinal – contradictions are masked by a mixture of traditional rhetoric and a good dose of opportunism. This tribune role, along with Tiersky's government role (which sees the Party competing for power at all levels) thus tends to push the PCF towards a 'minimum' position in which moderation and reform are emphasised.

Clearly the 1977-81 period saw an attempt to alter the balance between these roles, so that an emphasis on the more moderate roles did not pave the way for an unfettered electoralism which would deprive the Party of its other functions. In seeking to redress the balance in this way the leadership highlighted how they were seeking to walk a number of tightropes: attempting to make the PCF part of the system, whilst remaining 'special' within it; being the largest and strongest party in France, but remaining tightly organised and homogeneous at the same time; satisfying the demands of both the revolutionary and non-revolutionary elements of the Communist electorate; and wanting a solid union of the Left, but not being merely supportive therein.

The elections of 1981 suggested that the post-1977 strategy had failed. The balance of power within the Left shifted dramatically as the PS captured the presidency and a parliamentary majority and the PCF lost a quarter of its electorate: its vote fell from 20.7 per cent in 1978 to 15.3 per cent in the presidential elections and 16.2 per cent in the parliamentary elections. Moreover this decline included a dramatic loss amongst the working class with which the Party has always claimed such a special relationship: in the presidential elections Marchais attracted only 30 per cent of the working-class vote, as opposed to 33 per cent for Mitterrand; in the legislative elections the PCF working-class vote fell to 24 per cent, as against a staggering 44 per cent for the PS.[60]

The reaction of the Party leadership to these reversals was highly pragmatic. After unconditionally, though not with any great enthusiasm, supporting Mitterrand in the second presidential ballot, it rediscovered the virtues of *union* after his victory. This blatant opportunism was designed to recapture in the parliamentary elections those Communist voters who had not supported Marchais and also to reap a share of the new *dynamique de la gauche* which Mitterrand's victory had created. Though this failed to work, the Socialists – anxious to demonstrate their unitary spirit and not wanting an 'internal' opposition – still offered the PCF government posts; but only on what amounted to humiliating terms. The terms nonetheless were accepted and the PCF bowed to the Socialists' position on such important matters as the range and pace of economic change, Poland and Afghanistan (see Appendix 6 for extracts from the contract).

In signing this document the PCF was trying to rescue something from the wreckage of Marchais' presidential vote and the loss of half of the Party's deputies in the parliamentary elections. But in exchange for the considerable PCF policy concessions the PS gave relatively little away. Of 44 ministerial posts the Communists were given only four: Transport, Health, Civil Service and Administrative Reforms, and Vocational Training. This relative marginality could well encourage the PCF to reappraise its presence in government at a propitious time in the future.

5 The Left in the Fifth Republic: The Struggle for Unity

THE IMPETUS TO UNITY

Attempts to achieve some sort of Left-wing unity are not peculiar to the Fifth Republic. As we saw in Chapter 2 efforts were made throughout the Third and Fourth Republics to heal, or at least paper over, the divisions which have been so much a part of the history of the Left and such a source of its weakness. These efforts ranged from attempts to bring about organic unity between the SFIO and the PCF to temporary and tenuous electoral alliances between the SFIO and the Radicals.

In the Fifth Republic the search for unity has continued, but at a brisker pace. New factors have arisen to give an added impetus and a greater urgency to the whole process. Each has played its part in stimulating and encouraging the development of more systematic and integrated forms of co-operation. They may be classified under three broad headings.

1. The Electoral Systems

There are three main levels at which elections are conducted in France and each puts a high premium on co-operation and coalition building between the political parties.

For **parliamentary elections** France in 1958 reverted to the system which was used for most of the Third Republic: the single member constituency with two ballots. To be elected on the first ballot a candidate must obtain 50 per cent + 1 of the votes and not less than 25 per cent of all registered votes. On the second ballot a simple majority suffices. Between the two ballots candidates who attract less than a minimum percentage of the vote are eliminated. (The figure in

147

1958 was set at 5 per cent. By the 1978 elections it had climbed to 12½ per cent). In addition, and crucially, any candidate may voluntarily withdraw between the two ballots.

This system was adopted principally because when used in the Third Reublic it had assisted moderate parties and discriminated against extremists. It had done so for two reasons. Firstly, the use of the single member constituency allowed *notabiliste* parties, which were mainly of the centre, to reap the maximum benefit of local loyalties and allegiances. Secondly, the moderate parties were usually capable of negotiating beneficial electoral agreements between the two ballots, whereas the extremists normally remained isolated. Thus the *Cartels des Gauches* of 1924 and 1932 provided for mutual withdrawals between the Socialists and the Radicals after the first ballot; the sole candidate on the second ballot being the more successful of the two on the first. In this way the parties did not split the 'non-Communist left' vote on the second ballot but shared it by drawing on the support of the candidate who had dropped out. The Communists however, who were not part of the *Cartels,* could do little more than poll their first ballot vote.

The 1958 elections did not work out as had been anticipated. The PCF was certainly dramatically punished for its electoral isolation; it won a paltry 10 seats, despite having gained 19.2 per cent of the vote on the first ballot. But, unexpectedly, the non-Communist Left also lost seats heavily; the SFIO fell from 99 to 44, even though its vote, at 15.7 per cent, was much the same as in 1956 and the Radicals saw their parliamentary representation fall by almost two-thirds, from 94 to 32, though their electoral support had fallen by less than half, from 15.2 per cent to 8.3 per cent. The strong tide of Gaullism, which succeeded in attracting much of the moderate vote on the second ballot, was a major reason for the losses of the two parties. Another and equally important factor was that the PCF was now an electorally more important force than it had been when the electoral system had last been used before the war. The lack of an electoral agreement with the PCF was, therefore, now more 'expensive' for the SFIO and Radicals.

The very mechanics of the parliamentary electoral system thus forced a reappraisal of election strategies. Both Communist and non-Communist Left needed to eliminate second ballot competition between their overlapping electorates if they were to regain a significant representation in Parliament. It was, after all, now theoretically possible for the Left to win as much as 66 per cent of the second ballot vote in a constituency and yet still lose the seat if its share was so divided that none of its parties gained over 33 per cent whilst a single opponent gained 34 per cent.

The effects and implications of the electoral system were demonstrated again in 1962 when the SFIO and the PCF agreed to a limited number of mutual second ballot withdrawals. The PCF increased its vote by a moderate 2½ per cent, to 21.7 per cent, yet saw its seats quadruple to 41; the SFIO actually *lost* 3 per cent – falling from 15.7 per cent to 12.6 per cent – yet *gained* 22 seats. In 1967 when there was a *national* agreement of withdrawal between the PCF and the FGDS the benefits were again apparent: the PCF gained a further 32 seats (to take its total to 73) although its vote increased by less than one per cent; the *Fédération de la Gauche Démocrate et Socialiste* (FGDS) won 116 seats with 19 per cent of the vote – compared with a combined SFIO and Radical total of 105 seats on a slightly higher vote in 1962. Not surprisingly, in the light of this clear relationship between electoral unity and electoral prospects, the parties of the Left have negotiated a national second ballot agreement in each subsequent general election; 1968, 1973, 1978 and 1981. This is despite the fact that in 1968 and 1978 their relations were otherwise extremely strained.

Presidential elections impose the need for unity in an even starker way. Again there is a two ballot system, but with the difference that only the two leading candidates on the first ballot may proceed to the second. Some form of bipolarisation is thus institutionalised. At the same time, by their very nature, presidential elections are national in scope and demand the mobilisation of many disparate and divided interests. As in the USA, though in a less fluid way, the successful candidate for the Presidency is the one who can build the largest coalition. Pompidou and Giscard, in 1969 and 1974 respectively, owed their victory, in large part, to the fact that they took the opportunity of the presidential elections to extend the boundaries of the governing Right-Centre coalition. For the Left to succeed it too must capture part of the so called 'centre ground' in addition to its natural constituency. This implies the need to engage in some coalition building. Mitterrand's strength over Rocard, his main rival for the PS nomination in 1981, owed much to the fact that he could appeal to 'Centrist' voters, yet still implicitly incarnate Left-wing unity in spite of the candidature of George Marchais. Mitterrand's firm credentials as a man of the Left thus constituted an integral part of his appeal to the electorate in 1981. Had another, more 'right-wing' candidate represented the Socialists, there would have been much more explicit first ballot divisions on the Left than there were, and this would have damaged the potential for a second ballot victory of the Left.

The effects of division were no more clearly seen than in the 1969 presidential election. The Left, in a state of disarray following the up-heavals of 1968 put forward three main candidates: Defferre from the SFIO, Duclos from the PCF, and Rocard from the PSU. Their votes split in such a way that two non-Left candidates – Pompidou and Poher – led the poll. The Left therefore had no second ballot candidate.

Even **local elections** are so designed as to encourage maximum co-operation. In 1964 the electoral system was changed so that in towns with over 30,000 inhabitants arrangements were as follows: (1) The town is treated as one constituency (there are modifications in a few of the very largest towns). (2) Lists are presented to the electorate and the one which gains an absolute majority on the first ballot or, if none does, a relative majority on the second, takes *all* seats on the council. (3) A list with less than 12½ per cent of the vote on the first ballot (10 per cent until 1976) is eliminated. (4) The composition of lists presented on the first ballot cannot be changed in preparation for the second. The system thus puts very strong pressure on parties to draw up joint lists before the first ballot, and, as we show in Chapter 8, this has been precisely its effect; in the last municipal elections, in 1977, the PCF and PS competed against each other in only 17 of the 221 largest towns.

The electoral systems to the three main elective bodies thus each encourage close co-operation between like-minded parties, particularly if they are competing for the support of similar sections of the electorate. The Right has long realised this and, facilitated by its relative lack of ideological divisions, has until recently found it easier to present a united front. In parliamentary elections from 1967 to 1978 it presented a single candidate on the *first* ballot in the great majority of seats. In the presidential elections of 1969 and 1974 a Gaullist did compete against a Centre-Right candidate on the first ballot, but there was a very quick rallying around the 'victor' for the second. In 1981, however, the position was reversed. A powerful presidential campaign by the 'Gaullist' Jacques Chirac, which was followed by a less than whole-hearted recommendation to support Giscard on the second ballot, resulted in insufficient electoral discipline on the Right. On the Left, by contrast, the bitterness of the first ballot campaign was dissolved when the PCF supported Mitterrand without attaching any conditions. In the ensuing parliamentary elections the Left again presented a more united face.

2. Constitutional Developments

Under the Third and Fourth Republics Parliament was the centre of
political struggle. Multi-partyism and the lack of a political grouping
or coalition with a stable majority ensured that power was shared
amongst many parties and individuals. The constant making,
collapsing, and remaking of governments meant that only the
extremists and those who excluded themselves could not hope to
participate directly in the exercise of government at some time. Thus,
during the Fourth Republic, all the major parties except the PCF
enjoyed extended periods in office.

In the Fifth Republic the balance of institutional power has clearly
changed. Parliament, though by no means toothless, has declined,
and the Presidency, which during the Fourth Republic was little more
than a ceremonial office, has become, to use de Gaulle's words, 'the
cornerstone of the Constitution'. Virtually all major policy initiatives
since 1958 have originated in the Elysée. From Algeria to the
European Monetary System in foreign affairs, from administrative
and constitutional change to economic management in the domestic
sphere, the President's hand has usually been firmly at the helm. As in
the USA, the Presidency has thus become the major political prize to
be won.

This was only slowly realised by many politicians of the Left. De
Gaulle's magisterial occupancy of the Presidency was reluctantly
accepted in the early days because it was thought that only through
him could the Algerian problem be solved. But this was generally
assumed to be a temporary measure, a necessary evil, something to be
suffered in advance of a return to a modified parliamentarianism. As
it gradually dawned that this was an illusion, at least as long as the
Gaullists and their allies kept winning elections, a reappraisal was thus
forced on the parties of the Left as to how they might again regain
power.

Presidential*ism* as a form of government, over and above the
mechanics of the Presidential electoral system, has, therefore, also
forced the parties of the Left to think about unity. The widespread
public approval of the office as an institution, and its ever-extending
power under its first three occupants, has meant the Left has had no
choice but to give it attention. At the very least, the fact that the President does command so much power forces on the politicians and the
public the bi-polarising question: are you broadly, in the last analysis,
for him or against him?

3. Party Political Changes

During the early years of the Fifth Republic, important changes took place in the fortunes of political parties, which were not just a result of the vagaries of the electoral system.

Most obviously the Right, principally through Gaullism, established itself, for the first time in its modern history, as a united and coherent force. Furthermore, it enjoyed immediate electoral success. The Gaullist party, the *Union pour la Nouvelle République* (UNR), won 199 seats on a first ballot vote of 19.5 per cent in 1958. In 1962 it went further and became the first party this century to win over 30 per cent of the vote: 31.9. With their allies, the Gaullists, from 1962, held a permanent majority in parliament.

The emergence of this powerful, united, and successful Right has deprived the Left of its earlier luxury of deciding *whether* it should participate in government. From the early days of the Fifth Republic it was excluded from office and seemed likely to return only by winning an election. With much of the attraction of the Right stemming from its ability to provide (more or less) stable government, it was clear that the more the Left could present itself as a coherent force, and therefore a viable opposition, the more its prospects would be improved.

Paralleling this consolidation and expansion of the Right was a decline in the Centre and the Centre-Left, over and above the losses experienced as a result of the effects of the electoral system. The 'non-Left' elements of the Centre, of which the MRP and Independents were the main components, were the hardest hit and by the end of the 1960s had been largely swallowed up by the governing coalition. For the Centre-Left the process, though more gradual, was just as apparent. In 1958 the SFIO held on to its 1956 vote of just over 15 per cent; the Radicals, however, lost almost half of their electorate and fell from 15.2 per cent to 8.3 per cent. In 1962 both declined further: the SFIO to 12.6 per cent and the Radicals to 7.8 per cent. In 1967 and 1968, when the two were combined in the FGDS, the trend continued, the total FGDS vote being 19.0 per cent in 1967 and 16.5 per cent in 1968. The nadir was reached in the 1969 presidential elections when the Radicals failed to put up a candidate and the Socialist, Defferre, gained a miserable 5.1 per cent.

There are many reasons for this withering of the Centre and the Centre-Left (some of which are considered in Section 4 below). The gradual fading of the clerical issue, as a divisive political force, harmed the MRP and the Independents. The widespread appeal of Gaullism bit deeply into the support of most parties. Industrialisation and the consequent decline in population of small town and rural France deprived most Centrist parties, but particularly the Radicals, of their most 'natural' supporters. Finally, the parties brought much on themselves by clinging to old loyalties and attachments, being reluctant to engage in wholesale reform, and generally showing an inability to detach themselves from memories of the discredited Fourth Republic. All these developments assisted in a decline of the Centre, contributed to the bi-polarisation of political life, and had three major consequences for the strategy of the Centre-Left.

In the first place it meant the idea of a Third Force, bringing together the many disparate elements between Gaullism and Communism, was increasingly less attractive in electoral terms. Secondly, it made unification of the non-Communist Left increasingly urgent. Finally, it implied that even if the non-Communist Left could reorganise itself it would still have to negotiate, at the least, electoral arrangements with another political force if it were truly to challenge for power. Since the PCF retained a steady 20-22 per cent of the vote, it was the obvious potential ally.

But even an electorally united Left did not command a majority in the country. Whereas the total Left vote had always exceeded 50 per cent during the Fourth Republic, until 1981 it never did so in a parliamentary or presidential election in the Fifth and in the 1960s was nowhere near it. From having captured 56 per cent of the vote in 1956, the Left fell to 43 per cent in 1958 and hovered around that figure in the 1963, 1967 and 1968 parliamentary elections. In presidential elections it did even worse. Mitterrand's 1965 bid, which was heralded as a great success, had seen the Left gain only 32 per cent on the first ballot, though this rose to 45.5 per cent on the second with assistance from Centrist and even Right-wing anti-Gaullists. Again, in 1969, the combined first ballot vote was just over 32 per cent. The message was thus increasingly clear: electoral coalitions in themselves were not enough. To increase its electorate, the Left would have to improve its credibility. This, in turn, appeared to demand evidence of a *real* understanding between its various parts.

4. Socio-Economic Transformations

There is a long and continuing debate amongst political scientists over the exact determinants of party political systems. At one end of the spectrum there are those who put the main emphasis on institutional factors, notably the electoral system. At the other end, the social, economic and cultural context of politics is emphasised.

We have just seen the effects of the post-1958 parliamentary electoral system in stimulating unity. Yet a very similar system was used for much of the Third Republic without the same results. It stimulated electoral deals between political parties but its overall effect was short term. It certainly did not produce the evolution towards electoral bi-polarisation that has been apparent since the mid-1960s. This is because party political systems are the creatures of a number of factors, closely interacting with one another in a dynamic and ever-changing way. In the pre-war period there were many factors inhibiting bi-polarisation; institutional arrangements, the relative strengths of parties, ideological loyalties and, perhaps above all, the socio-cultural environment.

A principal reason for France's traditional multi-partyism has been the divisive nature of French society. Stemming from the Revolution and beyond, issues have arisen which have been deeply felt and which have divided Frenchmen politically. Religious, regional, class, and constitutional cleavages have been the most important. Moreover, since these cut across, rather than cumulated on one other, they provided a base on which highly sectionalised parties grew. To give an example, anti-clericalism at the turn of the century, when the role of the Church was *the* key political issue, was not embodied in one party because *fundamental* divisions between Radicals and Socialists over social and economic reform precluded it. Alternatively, a major reason why a successful social democratic party was not created in France after 1945 was that the SFIO saw itself as a defender of secular France, while the MRP was Christian Democratic.

Since 1945 there has been a loosening of many of these old divisions and hostilities as rapid economic change has transformed French society. The 'stalemate society' of the inter-war period has been completely undermined by rapid population expansion, changes in the composition of the workforce, urbanisation and rural de-population, and much greater social and geographical mobility. As these processes have unfolded there has been, in two senses, a greater potential for, and also a greater need for, co-operation between 'related' political parties.

In the most direct way, some parties, of which the Radicals are the prime example, have seen their electoral base decline. With the proportion of the workforce engaged in agriculture falling, from around 40 per cent in 1939 to just under 10 per cent by the late 1970s, and with urbanisation and 'modernisation' undermining the classic political appeal to the 'little man', the Radicals were simply forced, for reasons of self-preservation, into new electoral alliances.

Less directly, the climate of opinion has changed in a way which has allowed for more meaningful discussions between parties. The withering of the clerical issue, which was assisted by the *Loi Debré* in 1959 (under which Catholic schools receive state funds), has permitted Catholics to participate more fully in the Left. The 'nationalisation' of party political life, brought about in large part by the development of the media and communications, has reduced, politically at least, the importance of geographical sectionalism. Economic modernisation, with its raising of living standards and its expansion of the tertiary sector, does appear, though this is a rather more controversial point, to have reduced the perceived significance of the class struggle. Finally, the long and deep controversy over the constitutional framework has waned. It would be premature to say it is over, since it has yet to be put to its ultimate test. But now there is not, as there was in all previous regimes, a powerful party or faction in the country committed to its complete demolition. The Left (apart from the extremists) wish to amend it, but not destroy it.

This mutation, though not disappearance, of many former antagonisms has gone some way to providing a shared context in which discussions can take place within political 'families'. The comparison may be made with the USA which, though also a fractured society throughout its history, has seen political bi-polarisation made *possible* (not *created*) by a common acceptance of fundamentals: on the Constitution, the role of government, and the basic structure of the social and economic systems. This is not to suggest that France is becoming a consensual society. Divisions between and within the Left and the Right are still sharp. But there are more shared assumptions than there were a generation ago and this has facilitated discussions and accommodations.

In addition to domestic socio-economic change, developments in the international environment have also stimulated and permitted Left-wing unity. The thaw in the Cold War from the early 1960s encouraged the PCF to adopt a less disruptive and intractable line towards the political system as a whole and other Left-wing parties in particular. At the same time the development of détente and the increasingly cordial relations between France and the USSR made the PCF more acceptable in the eyes of its potential political allies.

The specific recognition by Khruschev in 1956 that there were 'peaceful roads to socialism' also helped to facilitate a dialogue within the Left. In reality this was little more than an open acknowledgement of a logic emanating from the Yalta conference at the end of the Second World War when Europe was divided into Eastern and Western spheres of influence. But its implications had remained hidden by the image of Stalinism and the tensions of the Cold War. From the mid-1950s it became more obvious. As Hungary in 1956, and later Czechoslovakia in 1968 and Portugal in 1974-5, all showed, neither the USA nor the USSR would directly intervene to promote 'revolutions' in the other's zone of influence. A classic Bolshevik-type, Soviet-supported revolutionary coup in Western Europe was no longer on the strategical agenda. The PCF, if it wished for institutional power, therefore had to adapt. Accordingly, from the early 1960s, it was in the forefront of calls for joint action of the Left.

As we have previously noted, Left-wing parties were involved in many different agreements and coalitions prior to 1958. In the Third Republic periodic challenges to the system and also electoral arrangements both gave a strong stimulus to co-operation of various kinds. During the Fourth Republic, as post-war modernisation gathered pace, as associated socio-cultural changes occurred, and as the extremes of Right and Left attempted to disrupt 'normal' political life, so then did the Centre-Left and the Centre *and* the Centre-Left frequently come to work together.

In the Fifth Republic many of these arrangements have been taken up again, but they have been more fully developed. Institutional, party political and other factors have all interacted in a highly complex way to produce a clear development towards a bi-polarisation of political groupings (though not, of course, of parties). On the Left this has involved three main processes. Firstly, agreements *involving* Left-wing parties have increasingly been *restricted* to these parties, i.e. the Left-Centre options of the Third, Fourth and early Fifth Republics have gradually been removed. Secondly, agreements have come to be more national in scope. What is negotiated between party leaders in Paris has increasingly been accepted at the grass roots and, as a result, there is no longer such a varied pattern of local arrangements. Finally, most of the moves towards unity have gone or have sought to go further and be of a more permanent nature than the essentially short-term agreements of the pre-1958 period.

We shall now proceed to examine the nature of this developing unity.

THE THREE APPROACHES TO UNITY

At first sight the varied manoeuvrings between the parties of the Left during the Fifth Republic are bewildering. There appears to be no ordered development in the many different forms of co-operation, coalition and integration that have been attempted. Some have sought to bring together most of the elements of the Left, whilst others have been restricted to specific sections. A few have taken root and have fundamentally changed the nature of the Left, whilst other have made no lasting impact or have even been aborted altogether. Others again have appeared to be making progress but then have experienced sudden and sharp reversals of direction.

There are a number of reasons for this inability of the Left, despite the pressures on it, to progress in an ordered way to unity. We shall consider these in detail presently but, briefly, they fall into two broad categories:

1) The non-Communist Left throughout the 1960s, and to some extent in the 1970s, was divided over the direction in which it wished to go. Some sections pulled towards the Centre, some to the Centre-Left and some towards a firm alliance with the PCF.

2) The long history of ideological division and electoral and organisational rivalry between parties of the Left has persisted. Whilst most of the sharper edges have been smoothed within the non-Communist Left, underlying suspicions and antagonisms between it and the PCF have continued. The two sides may have needed each other but mutual mistrust has continued.

The divisions and tensions arising from these two factors have produced a rather confusing history, but it is possible to identify, amidst the many manoeuvrings, three major strategies being pursued.

1. Attempts to Create a Third Force

From September 1963 the weekly magazine *L'Express* published a series of articles in which it was argued that a political campaign should be launched to support a candidate who would have a realistic chance of defeating de Gaulle in the 1965 presidential election. This candidate, called *Monsieur X,* should have an established political reputation, should not be too tarnished with the image of the Fourth Republic, and should have an appeal which could extend across the centre ground of politics. It soon became clear that the candidate it had in mind was the prominent SFIO Deputy and Mayor of Marseilles, Gaston Defferre. In December 1963 he formally asked his party for permission to declare his candidacy and at an extraordinary National Congress, held in the following February, he was unanimously nominated as SFIO candidate.

But Defferre aimed to be more than just the Socialist's candidate. His short-term goal was to mobilise behind his campaign as much as possible of the political spectrum which lay between Communism on the Left and Gaullism on the Right, i.e. those who had voted for the censure motion against Pompidou's government in 1962 and who had gone on to constitute the *Cartel des Non* in the subsequent referendum. He recognised that this might not constitute an overall electoral majority but he ruled out any negotiations with the PCF, hoping that his candidacy would prove to be so successful that the Communists would have no option but to support him, on the second ballot if not the first. In the longer term Defferre hoped to bring the Centre together on a permanent basis.

To try and bring about this aim he distanced himself from his own party in a number of ways. His programme *'Horizon 80'* was drawn up independently of the SFIO by himself in collaboration with a number of supporters. In the spring of 1964 he established a *Comité Horizon 80,* which in turn encouraged the development of local committees. Though individual members of political parties were welcome to join there were no formal party links. Most ambitiously of all he increasingly associated himself with, and in April 1965 formally launched, the creation of a new political force: a Democratic Socialist Federation, uniting the parties of the Centre and the Centre-Left and also the many *forces vives,* which sympathised with the project. The Federation was clearly intended to serve as a base for the ultimate creation of a new political party.

Initially the candidature attracted interest and support. Each of the three main potential partners in Defferre's plan – the MRP, SFIO, and Radicals – were still attempting to understand and come to terms with the institutional arrangements of the Fifth Republic and their own electoral decline. They were unsure over their future strategy and were susceptible to a scheme which appeared to offer the opportunity of a new dynamism. Furthermore the Radicals and the SFIO still had reservations over the institutions of the new regime. In the SFIO in particular there were many who believed the Party should devote its energies to restoring parliamentary government rather than giving presidentialism legitimacy by becoming actively involved in the election campaign. Because of such uncertainties none of the parties had devised a procedure for choosing a presidential candidate. Defferre was the first to act.

In June 1965, after National Congresses of both the SFIO and the MRP had agreed to go ahead with talks on the proposed Federation, negotiations began. They collapsed almost immediately. Within days Defferre had renounced his candidacy and the whole *Projet Defferre* was at an end. Why had it failed?

A major reason was that the scheme had originated from outside the political parties and as such had raised all sorts of suspicions and jealousies. The fact that his nucleus of advisers included many political 'newcomers' – from journalism and from the 'political' clubs which had sprung up in the early years of the Fifth Republic – hardly allayed such resentments. His scheme clearly challenged the party machines and was inevitably resisted by party officials. In his own SFIO the leaders of the three most powerful *fédérations* – Mollet (Pas-de-Calais), Augustin Laurent (Nord) and Claude Fuzier (Seine Saint Denis) – were hostile and each played a part in fuelling the criticisms which circulated in the Party: Defferre had jumped the gun; he was acting too independently of the Party; he was attempting to use his Socialist base to destroy the Party.

Even more serious than organisational protectionism were the ideological and strategic barriers to unity. In the SFIO Mollet's commitment to a cohesive, pure and independent party still received much support. Those subscribing to this view were generally suspicious of Defferre's moderate programme and argued that, if the SFIO did have to become part of a broader grouping, it should be via an arrangement with the PCF rather than the clerical MRP. The Radicals, too, were divided. When, after the 1962 elections, they had found themselves too small to constitute a parliamentary group their President, Maurice Faure, had attempted to promote a new centrist force grouped around the Radicals, MRP and moderate Independents. This failed but he did succeed in forming a smaller group, the *Rassemblement Démocratique*, made up of Radicals, *Union Démocratique et Socialiste de la Résistance* (UDSR) and various non-attached Deputies. There were, however, many in his party who were opposed to this enterprise and who looked towards the SFIO for an agreement. Finally, the MRP were also floundering. Some of their leaders (like much of their electorate) were attracted by Gaullism and the prospect of government, some to a reformation of the Centre Right, some to a Third Force without the SFIO, and some to genuine Third Force of the kind proposed by Defferre. With such divisions in all three prospective partners it was no wonder Defferre's grand coalition of *tous les républicains* was still-born.

In the late 1960s, as the Centre parties withered, several more modest attempts were made to reconstitute a Third Force. For example, Edgard Pisani (a former Gaullist Minister of Agriculture) and Michel Soulié (a Radical) sought to create a 'progressive alternative' option on the Centre-Left of the political spectrum. Pierre Abelin (who had been a leading figure in the MRP) tried a similar strategy. None of the projects came to anything, largely because they were made without any real party support.

It was Jean-Jacques Servan-Schreiber, the Director of *L'Express* and the inspiration behind the Defferre campaign, who was to achieve most in the Third Force direction. Not without opposition from those Radicals who favoured ties with the Socialists, 'JJSS', as he is popularly known, became General Secretary of the Radical Party in October 1969. His aim was to rejuvenate the Party but also to use it as a platform for a new Centre-Left coalition. In the first instance that required preventing the unitary Left strategy, which the new Socialist Party began to seek in 1969.

Servan-Schreiber's approach was not lacking in aggression. In somewhat grandiose language he talked of a need to put moral considerations above the laws of politics and of a necessity for reform through growth. In January 1970 a new manifesto was published based on a policy of 'revolution by reform'.[1] It advocated a range of measures which, it was claimed, would open the way to true social justice. Among the specific policies proposed were regional devolution, the phasing out of hereditary wealth, and various improvements in social services. The whole scheme was based, and this damned it in the eyes of many Socialists, on a liberal economic policy, which was strongly committed to Europe.

A by-election at Nancy in June 1970 saw him enter parliament and also gave him an opportunity to project his 'dynamic' image, but the momentum gained from this was short-lived and in retrospect it can probably be said that he was working against long term changes which precluded any real chance of his sought-after political re-alignment. As it turned out his scheme virtually collapsed by the year's end when his maladroit intervention and personalised style in a by-election at Bordeaux earned him the hostility of many of those whom he had hoped to attract. Excluded a short time later from the Socialist group in the National Assembly he went on to divide the Radicals. One section, under his leadership, joined up with the *Centre Démocrates* (who were mainly the remnants of the MRP) to form the *Mouvement des Réformateurs*. With the election of Giscard d'Estaing to the presidency in 1974 they entered the governing Majority alliance. The other section, who wanted continued association with the PS, formed the Left Wing Radical Party (MRG) as described in Chapter 3.

Despite the failures of Defferre and Servan-Schreiber, the idea of a Third Force still lives on in some quarters. Not least with Valery Giscard d'Estaing. In his much publicised and discussed book, *Démocratie Française,* written in 1976, he claimed:

> Contrary to glib assertions, France is not divided in two over major social problems.... . If one had to trace lines of cleavage on the majority of important issues, none would go down the middle. Our country's sociological centre already possesses real unity and the figures suggest that it comprises much more than half the population.[2]

There was something to be said for this view of French society. The combined vote of the PS, MRG and the 'centrists' within the governing coalition – the latter being loosely united in the *Union pour la Démocratie Française* (UDF) – was 46% in March 1978 and 51% in the European elections of June 1979 (27.5% for the UDF, 23.6% for the joint PS/MRG list). Public opinion polls suggested they could retain most of that support were they to come to an 'arrangement'. For example, a *Sofres* poll in March 1979 found that 27% of UDF voters favoured a UDF-PS government and a further 46% favoured a government made up of the then governing Majority (i.e. UDF plus the Gaullist *Rassemblement pour la République* (RPR)) enlarged to include the PS. At the same time 29% of Socialist voters favoured a UDF-PS government and 13% favoured the PS entering government with the existing Majority coalition. Furthermore such an alliance could even have hoped to attract support elsewhere, for the same poll showed 56% of RPR voters would have liked to have seen the PS enter government with the UDF and RPR.[3]

Attractive though this strategy was to Giscard, however, in practice it could be ruled out on the part of the PS, for a number of reasons.

Firstly, the two main previous attempts to construct such a Third Force during the Fifth Republic had shown that there were too many obstacles in the way. Both Defferre and Servan-Schreiber foundered on the rocks of party loyalties, personal jealousies, policy divisions and the seemingly irreversible movement towards bi-polarisation.

Secondly, opinion poll evidence has to be interpreted with caution and care. The same survey showed 23% of PS voters favoured a Union of the Left government while 30% favoured a PS only government, i.e. 53% did not express a preference for an accommodation with the Right. Furthermore, when options were restricted to relations with the PCF, 43% were still willing to negotiate some sort of programmatic agreement and a further 23% believed the two parties should at least enter into second ballot electoral arrangements. Only 22% wanted no agreement of any kind between the parties.

Thirdly, there was no reason to suppose that there was any significant support for such a development amongst PS members (as opposed to voters) or leaders. Certainly Michel Rocard, usually thought of as the leader of 'the Right' within the PS, gave no hint that he seriously entertained the idea. Furthermore, were he to have done so he would have split the Party and found himself in a minority.

Fourthly, and this is related to points two and three, such an alliance would have made little ideological sense. Though the PS may be to the right of the PCF, and the UDF to the left of the RPR (though more arguably so) there is little, other than a generally favourable attitude to Europe – and even then the Socialists embrace a large dissident minority – that the two share. A fundamental re-alignment seemed scarcely possible when the PS was committed to extending the interventionist powers of the State in social and economic affairs and the UDF broadly favoured the status quo.

Indeed, ironically, the Communists and the Gaullists, though arch enemies in many respects, have more in common with each other than do the PS and UDF; both are deeply suspicious of policies emanating from Brussels and are totally opposed to further European integration, both emphasise the need for economic nationalism and both stress the need for direct state intervention to re-stimulate industry.

2. Attempts to Unite the Centre-Left

The collapse of Defferre's campaign in June 1965 inevitably gave a boost to the creation of the more restricted Centre-Left coalition that many in the SFIO and Radical Party favoured. Discussions to this end began almost immediately and they led, in September, to two closely related events. On 9 September François Mitterrand, the leader of the small UDSR and also a prominent figure in the political clubs movement, announced his candidature for the Presidency of the Republic. The next day the SFIO, Radicals, UDSR and those political clubs who in 1964 had grouped themselves into the CIR announced that they would henceforth co-ordinate their activities through a new organisation, the *Fédération de la gauche démocrate et socialiste* (FGDS). The representation on the Executive Committee of the Federation was as follows: SFIO, 13; Radicals, 8; UDSR, 3; CIR, 6; others (mainly clubs), 9.[4] By the end of October each of the constituent units of the FGDS had formally given its support to Mitterrand's candidacy and so too had the PCF. In the election he was therefore the sole candidate of the Left.

How had he succeeded, and how had the FGDS been created, when both Defferre and his proposed Federation had failed? The basic reason was that, initially at least, both enterprises were less ambitious. Building on informal discussions, which had in fact taken place since 1962, the SFIO and the Radicals used Defferre's failure to establish a measure of unity which was both ideologically and organisationally more acceptable. The exclusion of the MRP meant the clerical question no longer arose. An arrangement could now more easily be sought with the PCF. Mitterrand, as the leader of only a small group, did not pose such a threat to entrenched party leaders.

Mitterrand attempted to use the relative success of his presidential campaign to consolidate the non-Communist Left. Elected president of the FGDS between the two election ballots in December 1965, he played a central part in advancing unity over the next two years. In May 1966 a 'Shadow Cabinet' was announced. This unprecedented move was designed to give the FGDS a wider respectability and legitimacy. In July 1966 a programme was issued by the FGDS which managed to steer clear of most of the traditional hostilities. It concentrated on the needs for greater economic growth and a more equitable distribution of resources. For the 1967 parliamentary elections, competition was virtually eliminated between the constituent units of the FGDS at the *first* ballot. After the elections a FGDS parliamentary group was constituted.

As ever, though, tensions were never far from the surface. Ideological differences between Socialists and Radicals had arisen over the 1966 programme and they became more acute in 1967 and 1968 when serious discussion began over making the FGDS a new political party. The doctrinal demands of the SFIO and Mitterrand's CIR (the latter were becoming more politicised and more socialist) resulted in the Radicals withdrawing from the discussions, although they remained as observers. When the FGDS signed a declaration of aims and policies with the PCF early in 1968 many Radicals were more alarmed than ever.

The FGDS was thus increasingly put under strain. Ideological tensions were exacerbated by other traditional rivalries. The various elements still basically viewed each other with suspicion and as competitors. They constantly disagreed over representation on the executive committee of the FGDS and the future of the proposed new party. Personalities clashed, with Mitterrand constantly being criticised for acting too independently. Factionalism within the parties themselves continued, which resulted in the FGDS becoming something of a political football.

Mitterrand's conduct during the events of May 1968 proved to be the breaking point. On 28 May, believing the regime to be on the point of collapse, he proposed that once the President had resigned, a provisional government should be formed under Mendès-France or himself. In the ensuing presidential elections he would be a candidate. On neither of these questions did he consult with the other leaders of the Federation. The regime of course survived, de Gaulle did not resign and the Gaullists in June gained the biggest parliamentary majority of any party in modern French history. Mitterrand's judgement had been disastrously wrong and his reputation was severely damaged. For many he now stood exposed as an untrustworthy opportunist.

Mitterrand's conduct and its consequences thus crystallised all the internal problems of the Federation. It had always been something of a Parisian phenomenon and even there the arrangement had been an uneasy one. In the provinces it had been viewed even more suspiciously. Indeed, it had given rise to considerable resentment when it had undermined long established local agreements or had attempted to throw together individuals and parties who had previously been antagonistic towards each other. Not surprisingly, in the light of all this, the Federation was virtually dead by the autumn of 1968, although the parliamentary group soldiered on into 1969.

Yet the FGDS had not been a complete failure. The parliamentary group had remained disciplined throughout. At the electoral level virtually all the non-Communist Left had been united in the 1967 and 1968 contests; only a few political clubs and the PSU (which preferred to retain its 'purity') remained outside. (The PSU is considered in greater detail in Chapter 6.) In addition, although the Federation had not been able to stem the decline in the electorate of the Centre-Left, the election of 1967 had shown that unity could provide some compensation by improving the votes/seats ratio. (The combined Radical/SFIO vote in 1962 was 20.4 per cent and in 1967 the FGDS vote was 19.0 per cent; in 1962 a total of 105 seats were gained and in 1967 there were 116. The improvement, it must be said, was also helped by greater co-operation with the PCF). The collapse of the Federation was thus never likely to be the end of attempts to consolidate the non-Communist Left.

The failure of Defferre's *grande fédération* and Mitterrand's *petite fédération* was followed by the even more modest moves to unite the non-Communist Left which got under way from 1969 in the reformed Socialist Party. As we have shown in Chapter 3, this enterprise, after an unpromising beginning, has borne fruit. The increasingly rejuvenated Party has extended its frontiers in a series of stages to embrace many of the former elements of the FGDS – Socialists themselves, the political clubs, a section of the Radicals (through both 'conversions' and the close working relationship with the MRG), and even much of the PSU. The grafting on of these elements has produced a party in which the lines of division still clearly show. But it has also created a more vigorous and confident non-Communist Left than seemed possible at the end of the 1960s. In the end the various components, owing much to Mitterrand's vigour and coalescing powers, have faced up to the unavoidable alternative posed by the dynamics of the Fifth Republic: unite or remain on the margins.

3. Attempts to Unite the Non-Communist Left and the PCF

The logic of political life in the Fifth Republic has increasingly meant that the non-Communist Left and the PCF must co-operate together if either is to enter government. As we have seen many changes have taken place within the parties concerned, which have permitted such co-operation to develop. But because the impetus to unity has been dictated by circumstances, rather than having naturally arisen from a meeting of similar views, tensions have never been far from the surface and the mutual distrust, built up over years of bitter struggle, has continued. At the centre of their relations there has remained a firm conviction on both sides that the other desires domination. As a result the whole unification process has been a tortuous one, with periods of open antagonism – 1958-62, 1968-70, 1974-5, and 1977-1981 – being interspersed with periods of relative harmony and co-operation.

Until 1974 it was the PCF which was the greater champion of unity. From deciding, in the early 1960s, that it wished to break out of its isolation it constantly took the initiative in seeking agreements: in 1962, it called on the SFIO to develop a joint programme and electoral strategy for the legislative elections; from 1963 it urged the SFIO to enter negotiations to draw up a 'common programme of the Left'; in 1965 it officially backed Mitterrand's campaign even though he refused to discuss his programme with it; during the events of 1968 it continually sought joint action by the Left as a whole; between 1970-2 it very much forced the pace behind the developments which led to the signing of the Common Programme of Government in June 1972.

The eagerness of the PCF stemmed from the fact that, unlike the non-Communist Left, it had no real alternatives. Its only way back into the mainstream of political life was via such agreements and this necessitated detaching the non-Communist Left from the lingering attractions of the Third Force. Such a strategy, even though it involved concessions, was believed to be quite safe since, by virtue of its electorate, membership, and organisational strength, the Party could expect to dominate any coalition which might be built. For the non-Communist Left however the situation was very different. It was politically divided, electorally in decline, and organisationally weak. As a consequence, fears of domination and penetration were very much to the fore and there was a general feeling that any progression towards unity should be only gradual. For most Socialist leaders in the 1960s, including Mollet, the development of any real unity was dependent, at a minimum, on an ideological liberalisation in the PCF and specific commitments to democratic norms and values. After Epinay, Mitterrand also sought such assurances, but he saw them as only being useful in a context of Socialist strength. As soon as he took over the leadership of the new PS in 1971 he set as his immediate task the rebuilding of the Party and he made it clear that a genuine dialogue and co-operation with the PCF could proceed only from the base of a strong and vigorous non-Communist Left. Because of this he was never apparently overly concerned with the much discussed question of whether the PCF *really* meant what it said when it declared its allegiance to democratic ways. For him the question became largely irrelevant if the Socialists were sufficiently strong to ensure that the Communists had no option but to act responsibly when they eventually entered government.

As for the chronological unfolding of what has been a very spasmodic process it will suffice to give a catalogue of only the major developments up to the 'watershed' of the signing of the Common Programme:

(1)   Shortly before the first ballot of the 1962 legislative elections Mollet, after previously ignoring PCF advances, advised supporters in those 'ten or twelve' constituencies where there was likely to be a straight choice between 'an unconditional follower of De Gaulle and an unconditional follower of Khruschev' to support the latter. Between the ballots he went further and said that, whilst an extra forty or so Communists in the Assembly would not significantly affect the PCF's overall position, another forty Gaullists might result in the Gaullist Party and their allies having an overall majority. This, in turn, might undermine parliamentary government itself. Accordingly, a limited number of local withdrawals between the SFIO and the PCF were advised. In the event rather more of these occurred than Mollet anticipated.

(2)   In 1965, as we have seen, the PCF endorsed Mitterrand's candidature.

(3)   In December 1966 a nationwide second ballot electoral agreement between the PCF and the FGDS was negotiated for the impending legislative elections. In addition they issued a *constat de convergence* which, though far from being a programme of government, entailed a commitment to measures such as the nationalisation of merchant banks and the arms industry.

(4)   In the March 1967 legislative elections the electoral agreement, which the PSU also joined, was highly successful. This was partly because of a greater willingness of non-Communist first ballot voters to support the PCF on the second ballot. It was also assisted by the PCF withdrawing their candidate in a few constituencies where they were actually second to the FGDS, but where, because of the narrowness of the difference between the two, the FGDS had a better chance of eventually winning. Overall the total Left vote slightly declined from 44.5 per cent to 43.6 per cent but the number of seats increased from 146 to 193.

(5)   In February 1968 the FGDS and PCF issued a joint declaration of common aims and policies. Though vague in many respects, and openly admitting differences in some areas, notably on nationalisations and foreign policy questions, it was a major step towards the development of a common Left-wing programme.[5]

(6)   The events of May 1968, followed by the Soviet invasion of Czechoslovakia in August, brought all the frailties of progress into the open. The reluctance of Mitterrand to co-ordinate tactics in May and

his clear determination to keep all his options open led the PCF to believe they were dispensable to his plans. Such suspicions were seemingly confirmed when Mitterrand proposed Mendès-France as a possible Prime Minister. This was not only because Mendès-France had associated himself with the *gauchistes* to whom the PCF – ever suspicious of spontaneity and workers activity they did not control – were bitterly opposed, but also because he had a long anti-Communist record. The result was that, although the PCF and FGDS managed to reach a second ballot agreement for the June elections, the Left campaign was not marked by the enthusiasm or the success of the 1967 contest.

(7) The divisions of 1968, followed by the disaster of the 1969 presidential election – when the Communists and Socialists both presented candidates and the Left found itself not represented on the second ballot – emphasised once again the necessity for Left-wing unity. Accordingly 1969-72 saw a process of picking up the pieces. By the end of 1969 the PCF and the Socialists were again talking, and in December 1969 they jointly announced that only 'the union of the Left' offered a real alternative to the governing coalition. Formal negotiations opened between the parties 'on the fundamental conditions of a political agreement to replace the present system by a new regime of economic and political democracy and to open the avenues of the passage to socialism. . .'6 In December 1970 the results of the discussion were published simultaneously in *L'Humanité* and *Bulletin Socialiste*. Though several divergences remained – including the issues of the alternation of power, NATO, European supranationality and foreign experiences of socialism – the parties reached agreement on a basic approach to the current problem confronting the country. Success for *Union de la Gauche* lists in the 1971 municipal elections, and the enlargement of the Socialists at Epinay, provided the final stepping stones to the signing, in June 1972, of the Common Programme of Government.7

The Programme was intended to set out what a joint PS and PCF government would do over a five-year period in government. To bring about the agreement concessions had to be made on both sides. Among the more controversial points in the negotiations were France's relations within the Atlantic Alliance and the EEC, the PCF's commitment to *alternance* and the number of projected nationalisations. (The PCF wanted 25 and the PS 7). As Bernard Brown has observed, when serious negotiations began at the end of April 1972 the two delegations had 'the arduous task of agreeing on language sufficiently precise to impress voters as a government program for the life of a parliament, and sufficiently vague to permit social democrats and Leninists to subscribe without abandoning their respective basic principles'.[8]

That agreement was reached is testimony to both a willingness to compromise and an ability to obfuscate. The Programme was divided into four parts. The first covered improvements in the 'quality of life' and included the promise of a regularly revised minimum wage plus many social, welfare and educational reforms. The second focussed on the management of the economy and had at its heart a proposal to completely nationalise certain key sectors of the economy, including banking and insurance companies still in private hands, and also nine major industrial companies. The third concerned political institutions and individual liberties and included amongst its promises the introduction of proportional representation for legislative elections and the abolition of the President's emergency powers article in the Constitution, Article 16. The fourth and final part was devoted to foreign affairs and defence and was as notable for what it did not propose as what it did; there was no plan to take France out of either the Atlantic Alliance or the EEC.

Specific commitments were, therefore, given. But difficult problem areas, such as *autogestion* (which the PS strongly supported and the PCF opposed) were resolved by a mixture of compromises and evasions. It was also left unclear what would happen once the Programme had been completed. For most Socialists it seemed to signify the culmination and fulfilment of their dreams. For the PCF, however, it clearly represented only the intermediary stage of advanced democracy that it had sketched out in its 1968 *Champigny Manifesto*.

The two signatories, who were soon joined by the MRG, were thus given abundant opportunities to interpret the Programme in different ways. The PCF was immediately to take a maximalist view while the PS and MRG were to have a more limited interpretation. Five years later, when the Programme had to be updated, differences were not so easily masked.

The signing of the Common Programme was followed by a two-year period in which, it may be said with the benefit of hindsight, Left-wing unity reached its zenith. The Left was naturally seen now as a much more viable alternative to the governing Majority and it quickly reaped considerable political dividends. In the 1973 legislative elections it gained its highest total vote since 1956, 45.8 per cent. In the following year, when Mitterrand was the sole candidate of the Left for the presidency he failed to win by a mere 0.7 per cent.

Events, however, were soon to show the delicacy of this unity. Indeed it had never been anything other than highly fragile. On the very day after the signing of the Common Programme, although this did not become public knowledge until 1975, Marchais had warned his Central Committee that there must be no illusions on the 'sincerity or firmness of the PS'; a strong PCF was the only guarantee that the Programme would be implemented and, therefore, in addition to the alliance with the Socialists, the Party must also pursue the development of its independent activity amongst the masses. He described some of the concessions in the Common Programme as 'essentially formal'.[9] At almost the same time, though he did not know of Marchais' remarks, Mitterrand publicly announced his intention of rebuilding a great Socialist party 'on the ground occupied by the PCF itself'. He estimated that the PS could hope, in time, to win three million of the PCF's five million voters.[10]

At the very height of their public cordiality the two main parties were thus concerned to dominate the Union. Their agreement was therefore always going to be delicate and subject to particular strain if the relative balance within the Union changed significantly. The first signs of such a change were apparent in the 1973 legislative elections. The PCF achieved a slightly higher vote than the UGSD (which united the PS and MRG) but the gap between the two was noticeably smaller than it had been between the PCF and FGDS in 1968 (0.6 per cent of the vote as against 3.5 per cent). Crucially, the UGSD appeared to have made inroads into what the PCF has always regarded as its special preserve – the working class. In 1974 there was further cause for Communist unease when Mitterrand in his presidential election campaign barely mentioned the Common Programme. Most disturbing of all, from the PCF's viewpoint, by-elections in the autumn of 1974, showed that the PS was not only becoming the largest party of the Left, in electoral terms, but was actually making gains at the Communist's expense.

The consequence of this PS advance was a marked cooling of relations between the two. By the autumn of 1974 the parties were beginning openly to appear more as competitors than allies. The PCF at its Extraordinary Twenty-First Congress, which had originally been called to launch the new appeal *'socialisme aux couleurs de la France'*, used the occasion to revive old criticisms of social democracy and to attack Mitterrand in particular. At the PS Congress at Pau in the following January, Mitterrand re-emphasised his 1972 remarks, that the PS must continue to expand in order to bring about a 'rebalancing' of the Left and to make itself the first party of France. He also stated, in a broadcast, 'The French Socialist Party is, itself, very democratic. I know this may be inconvenient. But, a democratic party represents an immense advantage and it would please me if Georges Marchais thought about that'.[11] The PCF rejoindered with a suggestion from the Politbureau that the PS Congress at Pau had seen a 'slipping to the Right'.

Such exchanges continued well into 1975, fuelled by continued PS successes in by-elections and public opinion polls: in the nineteen parliamentary by-elections held between the 1973 General Election and the end of 1976 the PCF, which contested them all, increased its vote in only five; the PS, which entered fifteen, improved on their 1973 result in every case. Other events too contributed to the decline in relations. The PS saw most of its old reservations about the PCF confirmed by the latter's support, guarded though it was, for the attempted 'Leninist' *coup d'état* of the Portuguese Communist Party. The PCF, for its part, viewed the entry into the PS, at the 1974 *Assises du Socialisme,* of *'autogestionnaires',* who had previously criticised the Common Programme, as a further sign that the Socialists regarded the 1972 agreement as being of but marginal importance. Some of the new entrants were leading CFDT figures and this, coupled with the Socialist's stated intention to extend its influence in industrial enterprises – thus challenging Communist dominance in that sphere – was taken as yet another indication that the PCF was under attack from its ally.

These quarrels did not seem to create any major electoral damage. In the departmental elections held in the spring of 1976 the Left, for the first time since the formation of the Fifth Republic, gained an absolute majority of votes cast on the first ballot, 56.4 per cent. Of these the PS obtained 26.5 per cent, the PCF 22.8 per cent, and other parties the remainder. These levels of support were subsequently confirmed in seven parliamentary by-elections held in November 1976 and in opinion polls. As the 1977 municipal elections approached the polemics began to cease, Left-wing unity again became the norm and all appeared to augur well for the Union. The local elections themselves saw the Left comfortably outpoll the parties of the Right (49.3 per cent as against 37.9 per cent) and make major gains throughout the country. A parliamentary election victory in 1978 seemed almost inevitable.

Yet the municipals were barely over before the parties in the Union were disputing how and to what extent the 1972 Common Programme should be updated in preparation for the 1978 contest. The PCF, which had made known its wish to update the Programme as early as March 1976, demanded major changes. The PS, which only agreed to talks in April 1977, insisted that any updating must be within 'certain limits'. A recipe for failure was present, although few observers at the time thought it would come to this. Electoralism and the desire for power seemed to have gone too far in the parties. Nonetheless, fail they did when the leaders of the PCF, the PS and the MRG, in the following September, were unable to reach agreement on the points which still divided the parties after many hours of work by a liaison group.

The formal grounds for the breakdown lay in policy differences. The most important of these were:

(1) Nationalisations. This was the dominant issue. The PCF insisted that the 1972 agreement implied nationalisation not only of parent companies but also of all subsidiaries where the holding exceeded 51 per cent. Their original estimate was that this added up to 1450 companies. The PS and the MRG totally refuted this interpretation of the original agreement. They also rejected PCF proposals for extending the number of major industries to be nationalised.

The formal arguments over nationalisations turned on a number of matters including compensation and whether control was possible without ownership, but a major reason why the PS was not prepared to concede too much was left largely unsaid in public; this was its concern that the PCF would use the provisions in the Common Programme for State industries to be run by management boards elected by the workforce, the government, and public organisations, to extend its influence throughout the public sector of the economy.

(2) The level of the minimum wage. The PCF wanted to fix this at 2400 francs per month and the PS at 2200 francs.

(3) The range of income between the highest and lowest paid. The PCF favoured a band of 5:1 and the PS a band of 7:1.

(4) The retention or not of the nuclear defence force. The PCF had recently announced that it favoured its retention though they insisted it should be directed towards the West as well as the East. The PS were unenthusiastic but Mitterrand (against the wishes of some of his followers) suggested they would be prepared to compromise by holding a referendum on the question.

(5) The composition of and distribution of posts within a Left-wing

government. The PCF wanted these to reflect the proportion of votes on the first ballot. The PS preferred that they be related to seats in Parliament. The difference reflected their own best positions since the PS always obtains a better votes/seats ratio. This is mainly because only about 65 per cent of PS voters transfer their votes to the PCF on the second ballot while around 90 per cent do so in the other direction.[12]

Most observers have inclined to the view that the PCF's stiffened demands were a pretext for a break they were determined to have. Even if the PS and the MRG had been more conciliatory (as the CERES faction wanted), agreement, it has been argued, would still not have been possible. The ambiguities of the Common Programme had not, after all, overly worried the PCF in 1972-3 when they were the major partner in the Union. Furthermore, it was now seen with hindsight, the PCF had probably been preparing the ground for the split since at least the spring of 1977; Marchais' embarrassingly expensive estimate of the cost of the Programme, made in May on the very eve of a television debate between Mitterrand and the Prime Minister Raymond Barre, now appeared to be more significant. Events after the breakdown also lend support to this view of the PCF's true intentions. There was virtually no sign that it hoped for reconciliation. Rather did it launch a fierce and unremitting attack against its erstwhile partners: the PS was content merely to 'manage the crisis' for capitalism; it was slipping once more to the Right; its essential social democratic reformism had once again shown itself; it, and Mitterrand in particular, wanted 'a blank cheque' in order to keep open all avenues. The bad grace with which the PCF acknowledged the Socialist's change in January 1978 on the minimum wage (they accepted the Communist's figure) seemed final proof.

Explanations for the PCF's about-turn have been many. They have ranged from an alleged change in the balance of power within the politbureau, between 'hardliners' and 'softliners' to the hand of Moscow once again making itself felt. The most plausible interpretation is, however, less dramatic and does not dismiss policy differences so completely. The PCF and the non-Communist Left have, as we have seen, long been locked in bitter struggle. Communists genuinely believe (for good historical reasons) that Social Democrats, including the 'advanced' PS, do not at heart want fundamental structural reforms. Marchais made this point in his 1972 Central Committee speech saying the PS embodied the tradition of 'reformist social democracy' and that 'the ideology that inspires the

Socialist party today is and remains absolutely reformist'. This message was reinforced in a book *L'Histoire du réformisme* published by the PCF in 1976, where it was argued that even when French Socialism has taken a 'Leftist' stance it has still been essentially reformist, has been tempted by overtures from the Right, and has been quite unwilling and incapable of transforming capitalism.[13]

A strong PCF role in a Left-wing government was therefore seen as a vital prerequisite in the building of socialism. Given all the dangers attendant upon the assumption of the Left to government and the pressures, which would undoubtedly be placed on such a government to be moderate and cautious, a supportive role was not acceptable to the PCF. This was a consistent theme of Party pronouncements from 1974, although at the time its significance was not fully appreciated. Constant statements that only a strong PCF would be a guarantee of real social change were viewed as simply traditional Communist rhetoric.

Until 1973-4 the electoral balance between the PCF and PS had guaranteed the Communists their central role. With the tilting to the PS this was no longer the case. By 1977 opinion polls were predicting that the PCF in 1978 would probably be restricted to its usual 20 per cent or so of the vote, while the PS might win as much as 30 per cent. It was in this situation that the PCF started talking more specifically about how it would not be sufficient for the Right to be defeated in 1978. There must be a *true* victory of the Left, which meant putting into effect all the reforms proposed in the Common Programme and ensuring that the working class and the PCF had their place in controlling the affairs of the country.[14] In other words, the PCF, having realised that it was not going to be an equal numerical partner in government, looked for alternative ways of ensuring its voice would be decisive and benefits would accrue to it. This involved trying to extract firm commitments from the PS in policy areas which had been left vague in 1972 or in which the passage of five years had outdated aspects of the Programme. It also involved trying to ensure that the PCF would be placed in key positions. Hence its attempts to distribute ministerial posts on the basis of votes and not seats, its position on nationalisations, which, some argue, might have paved the way for a *quid pro quo* by facilitating the extension of Communist influence in industry[15] and its attempts to try and persuade the PS to agree to divide the responsibility for the running of key ministries into two.[16]

When the PS and the MRG made it clear they were unwilling to give way on these points (and the PCF probably guessed in advance that they were hardly likely to), the whole exercise from the Communist viewpoint became no longer worthwhile. It had after all, as we saw in Chapter 4, paid a price for Left wing unity in the form of ideological 'concessions' and strategic agreements which had risked both its political identity and its internal unity. But while the Left as a whole had experienced a remarkable electoral growth as a result of the *Union de la Gauche,* within the Left it was the PS which had been the principal beneficiary. Indeed the more the PCF 'conceded' the more the PS seemed to prosper, not least within the Communist's own, much cherished, working class 'preserve'. This situation was in marked contrast to the two previous periods of Left wing unity – the Popular Front and the Liberation – when the PCF had greatly expanded its electorate. By the mid-1970s, for the first time since 1936, the Communists found themselves no longer the largest party of the Left. Naked self-preservation thus came to the fore, as PCF leaders themselves were later to come near to admitting. Writing in *L'Humanité* in April 1979, André Lajoinie, a member of the Politbureau, openly stated that the 'Union around a programme' had not facilitated PCF growth but, on the contrary, had worked for the sole benefit of the Socialists.[17]

The PCF's behaviour seems therefore to be explained by the fact that as a result of the *Union de la Gauche* it was experiencing a relative decline within the Left and this was not sufficiently compensated for by the prospect of participation in government. In a situation of general economic crisis affecting the whole Western world, the PCF were going to be the junior partner in a Socialist-led government. The senior partner had made it clear that its own hand would be firmly at the helm. If the Socialists balked at implementing aspects of the Programme, perhaps using the prevailing economic conditions as an excuse, the PCF's ability to exert pressure, short of bringing the government down, would be limited. With a Presidential dissolution of Parliament always looming in the background – presumably to be used at an advantageous moment for the Right – the many risks of participation, for uncertain benefits, appeared to be too great.

The breakdown of the September negotiations was followed by a major verbal assault on the PS by the PCF. The Socialists once again found themselves accused of having 'veered to the Right' and of being content to 'manage the crisis'. The PCF even refused to commit itself in advance to a second ballot electoral agreement, saying that it would do so only if it attained more than 21 per cent of the vote. In the event, a second ballot agreement was made the day after the first ballot, but it was not enough to make up for the bitterness of the previous six months. The Right was re-elected, although even then it seems to have done so only as a result of a late swing in public opinion.[18] The decisive electoral factor in explaining the Left's defeat was that the PS did not live up to the promise held out for it by opinion polls. It fell back to a position where it only narrowly led the PCF on the first ballot; 22.5 per cent of the vote to 20.5 per cent.

The electoral inquest which followed led to bitter recriminations with each of the parties denying any responsibility for what had happened. The exchanges continued up to the first ballot of the presidential elections in 1981 though there were abundant opportunities for renewed co-operation. The deepening economic crisis, the widespread unpopularity of the government's austerity policies and increasing antagonisms within the ruling coalition itself all contributed to a situation in which the Left appeared to have the opportunity for reaping considerable political advantage if it was united. Instead the polemics were almost unceasing. The PCF accused the PS of continuing its movement to the Right and of advocating policies little different from those of the government. In response the PS portrayed the PCF as having deliberately turned its back on power to safeguard narrow party interests. It was also accused of showing once again its Stalinist roots.

The deterioration in PS-PCF relations from September 1977 was associated, as we have shown, with internal debates within each of the parties as to their future strategy. In the PS, the internal differences which had been held in check until 1978 by the prospect of power came openly to the surface after the election disappointment. There was for some time no general agreement as to how the Party should proceed given that the PCF was apparently no longer interested, in prevailing conditions, in an election victory of the Left. In the PCF a clearer line emerged with the leadership turning attention, though not without internal opposition, to 'social struggles' and 'union at the base'. Though this was not, spokesmen emphasised, a rejection of *Union de la Gauche* it clearly implied a halt, for a while at least, to 'union at the summit'.

THE CONDITIONS OF UNITY

Even before the Left's victory in 1981 there was a clear potential for a

Left-wing victory at a national election. This was amply demonstrated before the 1978 defeat and it was subsequently confirmed by the 1979 departmental and European elections: in the first case the total Left vote was 55 per cent and in the second 47 per cent. (See Table 8.2 and Appendix 3 for details).

The problem of realising the potential was that, in national elections, when the government was at stake, the Left apparently had to present an image of unity at least as credible as that of the Right. The parties of the Left therefore needed to establish some degree of co-operation, tacit or explicit, if they were to achieve office.[19] In doing so, each party was of course aware that for each of them the objective was not only to obtain power, but also to dominate the other.

Left-wing unity was thus a delicate balance. Before the 1981 elections it appeared that the Left stood little chance of winning a national election unless the Socialists were the stronger party. Because of the static nature of the PCF vote – at around 20-2 per cent[20] – it was calculated that the combined PS/MRG vote would have to exceed that of the PCF by at least 8 per cent if the Left were to gain an overall parliamentary majority. Alternatively, at a presidential election, since no PCF candidate could hope to win, the Communists, or more precisely their electorate, would have to support the Socialist candidate on the second ballot. Either way the balance on the Left would swing in favour of the Socialists.

The PCF was reluctant to play the role of a 'supportive force' and it was for this reason that after 1977 it began to look for other ways to emphasise its strength. To avoid the possibility of being marginalised by the PS it took steps to remind supporters of its identity and it sought to reconfirm its traditional bases of support. This necessitated, PCF leaders concluded, the Party again becoming intransigent.

The logic of this situation seemed to suggest that the Left was doomed to continuing opposition, because the inflexible PCF put the PS in the position of either being seen to give way to the Communists – and thus running the risk of scaring those moderate supporters which the Left needed to secure an electoral majority – or standing firm and thus undermining the ability of the Left to present itself as a coherent, united and viable alternative government. But, as many Socialist leaders began to recognise in 1980, this analysis failed to take into account that the Left might not necessarily have to be *very* united for a Socialist to win the 1981 presidential elections. Disillusionment on the Right was such, and the desire for change was so widespread, that moderate voters might be attracted to a Socialist who was clearly

not a Communist 'hostage'. In that event only a minimum of Left-
wing unity – the transfer of votes on the second ballot – might be
necessary to put a Socialist in the Elysée. The Postscript shows this is
just what happened.

6 The Alternative Left

INTRODUCTION

Beyond the mainstream currents of the Left there exist may minor political groups which, in spite of their size, have made a considerable contribution to the development and impact of socialism in France. Most commonly they are referred to as the far-Left, the extreme-Left, or the ultra-Left, although other descriptions are sometimes heard. Touchard, for example, prefers 'independent Left'.[1] We shall employ the term 'alternative Left' which, to us, is strongly suggestive of the difficulty of placing the many different and continually changing groups in a single category, whilst simultaneously indicating that there is something common between them. That something is an unconventional approach to political activity which lays little emphasis on electoralism, but great stress on the development of philosophical ideas linked to critical agitation and direct action.

In order to facilitate our study of the alternative Left a two-fold distinction will be adopted. This more readily allows us to bring out the underlying differences between the two main branches of this Left. The PSU, which we consider in the first section, has been characterised by the diversity of its many constituent elements. At one time or another it has recruited seemingly from virtually the whole spectrum of the 'non-established' Left and has attracted many people who have been to all intents and purposes 'conventional' Left-wing figures, but who for various reasons have been critical of the established Left-wing parties. The Party has thus been ideologically ambiguous, a characteristic which has led it on different occasions to flirt with and even partially collaborate with the main parties of the Left. The second branch of the alternative Left, the *gauchistes,* are more distant than the PSU from the 'established' Left. They are also more ideologically distinct in that the various components of *gauchisme,* of which there are many, generally owe an allegiance to a particular revolutionary ideology; Trotskyism or Maoism in most cases.

THE PSU

The most prominent feature of the PSU throughout its twenty-year
history has been its constant internal divisions. Differences over
ideology, policy, and strategy have combined to produce a party
which has been subject to almost continual flux and change. The
Party is therefore best studied in the context of its historical development.

1. 1960-8

Even when it was first organised in 1960 the PSU was divided amongst
competing elements, each reflecting the influence of their diverse
political backgrounds. There were those who had their political
origins in the various Leftist, non-party associations, which had
sprung up since the Liberation. Many of these had banded together in
the mid-1950s to form the *Nouvelle Gauche* and later, in 1957, the
Union de la Gauche Socialiste (UGS). Amongst the personalities
involved in the UGS were Hubert Beuve-Méry (founder of *Le
Monde*), Claude Bourdet (founder of *Observateur*) and Maurice
Duverger (the political scientist). Others came from the SFIO.
Divisions in that Party, particularly over Algeria and the Fifth
Republic, had led to Edouard Depreux and others leaving in 1958.
Many of them had proceeded to participate in the foundation of the
Parti Socialiste Autonome (PSA), which was to be by far the largest
constituent element of the PSU. A third group came from the
Communist Party. Since 1956 factions had existed in the PCF, which
were virulently critical of the leadership's position following the
Soviet invasion of Hungary. The most prominent of these, numbering
a few hundred strong, was *Tribune du Communisme* which included
amongst its members Jean Poperen, Serge Mallet and François
Châtelet. In 1959 they were forced to leave the PCF.[2]
So in its very origins the PSU was made up of diverse ideological
traditions, cultures and temperaments. There was little agreement
amongst its members, who numbered around 10,000, as to what its
principal role should be. For some it should act as a bridge between
ancient and modern within the Left by questioning and criticising the
traditionalism of the main parties. For others it should be the
'conscience' of the Left, focussing on questions which the Socialists
and Communists tended to avoid facing, such as Algeria and the
appalling treatment of immigrants. For yet others it should

concentrate primarily on attempting to unify the many different
dissident strands of Left-wing opinion and hope that in the long term
this would help to bring about fundamental change in the Left as a
whole.

Figure 6.1   The genesis of the PSU, 1956-60

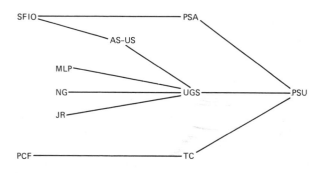

MLP	Mouvement de Libération du Peuple
NG	Nouvelle Gauche
JR	Jeune République
AS	Action Socialiste
US	Unité Socialiste
PSA	Parti Socialiste Autonome
UGS	Union de la Gauche Socialiste
TC	Tribune du Communisme

Opposition to the Algerian war served to maintain relative cohesion
until 1962. With the settlement of the war, the PSU found itself ever
more riddled with disputes and crises. It described itself as socialist
and revolutionary, but there was little agreement as to what this
actually meant in policy terms. There was a similar lack of consensus
on strategy. The Party committed itself to a re-grouping of the Left in
a 'Socialist Front', but whereas to some this meant co-operation with
the PCF, the SFIO and other groups, to others it necessitated a fundamental re-analysis of the nature of society and class relations in
industrialising France. Such disagreements reflected an increasing
factionalism, which at times left the Party virtually leaderless. As a
result it found itself increasingly reacting to events, rather than
initiating them.

The Party's attitude to the 'established' Left increasingly became
the main line of division. For the 1965 presidential elections a
compromise was attained between the 'integrationists' and the

'autonomists' through a decision to support Mitterrand's candidacy whilst emphasising the Party's own distinct positions, but that merely postponed the central question. The campaign itself, and the forging within it of the FGDS, sharpened the problem of direction even further by demonstrating to the 'integrationists' that the PSU's ambitions to influence the larger parties of the Left could only be achieved by working with them. Their views were further confirmed when four PSU candidates (including the Party's most celebrated member, the former prime minister Pierre Mendès-France)[3] were elected to parliament in 1967. They owed their success to support from the established Left; nationally the PSU's 115 candidates polled only two per cent of the vote.

Matters came to a head at the 1967 Congress when the supporters of a more autonomous line, led by Michel Rocard and Marc Heurgon, won 70 per cent of the votes. Within weeks, many of those who favoured integration into the wider Left had resigned or at least were ceasing to be active. Some, such as Jean Poperen, Pierre Bérégovoy and Robert Verdier, formed or participated in clubs which soon joined up with the FGDS, or later the PS.

In fact the 1967 Congress did not, as had been supposed, finally resolve the question in favour of the autonomists since Rocard, who now became National Secretary, and Heurgon, who assumed responsibility for the organisation of the Party within the decision-making Bureau differed in their long-term objectives. Whereas Rocard envisaged the ultimate participation of the PSU within the FGDS, though on better terms than at that time existed, Heurgon favoured a 'purist' autonomy and a reinforcement of the Party's revolutionary potential.[4] This difference of opinion was due to be discussed at the Party's National Council, but the 'events' of 1968 intervened to completely alter the scenario.

2. 1968-74

The PSU was as unprepared as the traditional parties for the social explosion of May 1968. But it was quicker to react and more suited to come to terms with and capitalise on the crisis. It supported the efforts of those most involved in the revolt and expressed sympathy for many of the demands made. Conventional solutions were rejected and the Party called for the creation of action committees and works councils.

The events temporarily injected new life into the Party. Its influence spread among the young *enragés* and close links were established with student and some worker organisations, notably the CFDT.[5] Around 6000 new members joined, most of whom were distinctly *gauchiste* in their sympathies, and this helped, along with the loss of about 2000 predominantly moderate members, to push the Party towards the 'autonomist' Left. In the June elections the four seats gained in 1968 were lost (partly because support was not given this time by the mainstream Left), but the PSU could still point to the fact that it almost trebled its number of candidates and doubled its votes. (Though this meant the votes *per candidate* fell back.)

So it was in a mood of optimism that the Party succeeded, at its Sixth Congress in March 1969, in adopting its first outline programme. Entitled the *17 thèses du PSU* the document defined the position of the Party in relation to the 'bourgeois state', its institutions and the *courante socialiste*.[6] Its policies centred on the need for a more equitable, less bureaucratised society in which the democratic, decentralised and participatory principles of *autogestion* would be introduced. The strategy to bring this about was vague and was left to a call for an 'alliance with the forces of May'. This was in the expectation of another social upheaval which, many believed, would pave the way for a successful revolutionary transformation.

The *17 thèses* allowed Rocard, who had been its main author, to assume a more prominent role in the Party. This was resented by many and such feelings were exacerbated when he ran a relatively successful presidential campaign in 1969 and was then, in the same year, victorious in a parliamentary by-election against the former prime minister, Couve de Murville, in Yvelines. This increasing and much criticised public visibility of Rocard was one of the reasons why many on the left fringes of the Party eventually resigned, in many cases to join up with Trotskyist or Maoist groups. These departures heralded a period of stagnation and continual unrest in the PSU. It was only in areas of 'traditional' influence, where the Party was often led by local notables and where it had gained access to municipal councils, that it remained sheltered from decline. The most important of these areas were Finistère, Côtes-du-Nord, the Ardennes, and Grenoble.

The departure of many of the *gauchistes* after 1969 did not resolve the continual debate over the role of the PSU in the political system. In a further attempt to resolve the problem, and also to attract new support, a series of documents were published, which defined the Party's relations with the rest of the Left. They culminated in 1973 in the production of the PSU's first complete manifesto, finished in time for the 1973 legislative elections. For Rocard, this was manifestly a re-arguard action for he had already decided, with many of his associates, to seek entry into the new Socialist Party. The 1974 presidential elections provided the opportunity and Rocard, having previously resigned his position as National Secretary, became one of the economic advisers to François Mitterrand. With some 1500 of the PSU's 10,000 members he formally joined the PS later in the year at the *Assises du Socialisme.*

The rallying of Rocard and his supporters to the 'established' Left had two main consequences for the PSU. Firstly, as had happened previously, the departures resulted in the emergence of a new leadership based on 'autonomist' perspectives, with Victor Leduc and Michel Mousel taking over the main functions in the National Secretariat. Secondly, although the damage of the departures was relatively slight in numerical terms, those who left included the so-called 'colonels' of Rocard; Borella in Nancy, Brana in Bordeaux, and le Foll in Saint-Brieuc. These were influential local *notables* and it was mainly in their areas that the PSU had achieved municipal representation.

3. 1974-80

From 1974 it became increasingly difficult for the PSU to carve out an independent strategy for itself within a political environment that was monopolised by the unitary strategy of the major Left wing parties. Indeed, it could do little more than support the Communist criticisms of Socialist moderation and uphold the Socialist arguments against the Stalinist tendencies of the Communists. This dilemma, not surprisingly, created further tensions within the Party and the debates at the Tenth Congress, held in January 1977, showed only too clearly that the problem of strategic direction remained as central as ever.

At the Congress the leadership sought confirmation of the dual strategy it was in the process of developing. On the one hand it wanted electoral agreements with the established parties of the Left. This had helped the Party in the 1976 departmental elections and it was hoped it could be repeated in the 1977 municipal elections. On the other hand it wished to gear this aspect of its strategy to creating links with trade unions and forging broader associations with developing social forces such as the ecologists, the women's movement, and the soldiers committees in the armed forces.

The proposals were acceptable to the majority, but were contested by a vociferous minority, much of it made up of the Trotskyist

Alliance Marxiste Révolutionnaire which had joined the Party *en bloc* in 1975. They favoured stronger ties with the revolutionary Left, in particular the *Ligue Communiste Révolutionnaire* (LCR), and after their defeat at the Congress they broke away to form the *Comités Communistes pour l'Autogestion,* with a small band who had left the LCR.

As a direct consequence of the support given at the Congress for the strategy of the leadership, the *Front Autogestionnaire* (FA) was formed later in the year. This was a confederal organisation within which the PSU formed the largest single bloc, contributing two-thirds of the 8000 membership. The other groups affiliated to the FA were the *Mouvement pour une Alternative Non-violent* – whose 1000 members were already sympathetic to the PSU – and the *Mouvement pour la Libération des Femmes.* Local environmentalist groups and some regionalist associations also joined.

The FA presented 218 candidates at the 1978 legislative elections, 60 per cent of whom were members of the PSU. In two seats it benefitted from the PCF desisting in its favour before the first ballot, but overall its results were disappointing. On a national basis it gained just over one per cent of the vote, losing about 25 per cent of the PSU's 1973 vote. It achieved over 3 per cent in only 40 constituencies. The existence of ecologist candidates fighting independently of the FA undoubtedly affected its overall result.

But, though the election results were disappointing, the rupture between the major parties of the Left, which increased in intensity after the election defeat, appeared to open up new possibilities for the PSU. It certainly was taken as vindicating many of the reservations it had expressed on the Common Programme and offered the chance of a new impetus to its calls for a *'véritable unité populaire'* built from the base. Since the elections the Party has therefore sought to capitalise on the friction between the two main parties by re-emphasising its claim to be 'the third component' of the Left and by re-asserting that the Left can only be truly re-juvenated by a meaningful agreement between *'les forces autogestionnaires'* and *'la gauche traditionnelle'.* To substantiate and strengthen its position the Party has courted Left-wing sympathisers who may be tempted to join this 'third component': 'dissident' members of CERES, disillusioned members of the PS who joined the Socialists with Rocard, and members of the PCF who are dissatisfied with the return of their Party to Stalinist practices. The events of 1981 may undermine this attempted courtship but the Party could now be in an advantageous position to capitalise on any disillusionment with the performance of the established Left in office.

Despite the incessant debates over its role, and the many schisms it has experienced, the position of the PSU within the French political system has changed little since its foundation. It remains in essence a small party on the fringes of the established Left, anxious to influence the mainstream but unsure as to how close it should get to the main parties. Some of its ideas and former members have filtered through into the established Left and this has made it more influential than its numerical weight would suggest, but it has made no progress in its prime aim of significantly altering the balance of power within the Left.

GAUCHISME

The term *'gauchisme'* is commonly used in France to bracket together the many small revolutionary groups which have proliferated, or in some cases have been given new life, since the mid to late 1960s. Their development in the 1960s was a result of the interaction of a number of factors: a rapidly expanding university population which was faced with an authoritarian educational system and was provided with in-adequate facilities; an entrenched conservative political regime backed by equally conservative social elites; a powerless opposition Left; an apparently sclerotic Communist Party, which from 1964 began to purge some of its 'dissident' youth; and an increasingly heterogeneous and fractured international Communist world.[7] To these factors some observers have added a broader cultural dimension which, they argue, also facilitated and encouraged the radicalisation process that led to the 'events' of May 1968 and the emergence of the *gauchiste* phenomenon. For example, Henri Arvon has made much of the supposed malaise amongst the nation's younger generations and has described *gauchisme* as essentially a spontaneous product of contemporary society.[8] In a similar vein Alain Touraine has seen much of the attraction of *gauchisme* in its ability to offer the seeds of future forms of political activity which will rely less on bureaucratised and heavily structured forms of protest.[9]

Though spontaneity may be a guiding principle of *gauchisme,* however, many of the *gauchiste* groups themselves are highly organised. A few are even, in effect, well-structured political parties. The numerically largest and most significant of these groups, and the ones we now turn to, owe allegiance to Trotskyism and Maoism. Other strains do exist, but only on the margins. Into this category falls anarchism, which can trace its French roots back into the nineteenth century and which, as elsewhere, comes in a number of forms. The main differences between the anarchist groups are the extent to which they regard some sort of structure as being necessary to co-ordinate activities, the degree to which they are Marxist flavoured, and the willingness with which *in practice* they are prepared to use violent action.

1. Trotskyism

As in most Western countries the Trotskyist current in France is highly fractured. A number of groups and factions exist, and departures and schisms, which do little to help the cohesion of the movement, are frequent occurrences. The bases of the fragmentation between specific organisations is often difficult for the outsider to detect, it being in most cases a complicated mixture of differing ideas over ideological purity, strategical necessity, and tactical advantage. The two largest groups are *Lutte Ouvrière* (LO) and the *Ligue Communiste Révolutionnaire* (LCR).

LO is the successor of *Voix Ouvrière,* a Trotskyist organisation which owed its *raison d'être* to its break in 1940 with the Fourth International and which was banned, along with many other extreme Left groups, in the wake of the 1968 'events'. Probably best known through its leader, Arlette Laguiller, LO avidly seeks, even more determinedly than most other far Left groups, a firm working-class base. To this end it is particularly active in the workplace and amongst trade unions. Since its foundation LO has had some limited success in building up its support; during the 1970s its membership increased from around 3000 to 5000 and it established itself electorally as the strongest Trotskyist force. In the 1978 elections it put forward 470 candidates – of all French parties only the PCF exceeded this – and averaged 1.7 per cent of the vote. Thirty-two of its candidates gained over 3 per cent.

The LCR has been known under different names. It first emerged in 1966 when, following schisms and purges in the PCF's student movement (the UEC), the *Jeunesse Communiste Révolutionnaire* was formed. It became prominent during the May upheavals, not least because of the astute direction given to it by its leader Alain Krivine, but, like *Voix Ouvrière,* was banned in June because of its revolutionary convictions. Determined to carry on the Trotskyist permanent revolution it re-emerged as the *Ligue Communiste.* In 1973 the *Ligue* was banned, on this occasion following violent clashes in the streets with the extreme Right, and so the name was changed again – to the LCR.

Whereas the LO has slightly increased its support since 1968, the LCR has declined. The strategy outlined by Krivine in 1971 – of expanding and infiltrating from 'the periphery to the centre' – in other words from the existing student base to the workers, via the trade union movement – has met with little success. Not only is membership still predominantly 'intellectual' but total numbers have actually fallen – from around 8000 in the early 1970s to about 6000 by the end of the 1970s. Moreover, on the electoral level, the LCR has been overtaken by the LO. In 1978 the LCR contested the legislative elections with two small 'non-aligned' far Left groups – the *Organisation Communiste des Travailleurs* and the *Comités Communistes pour l'Autogestion* – under the banner *'Pour le socialisme, le pouvoir aux travailleurs'*. The 187 LCR candidates gained a total of only 0.33 per cent of the vote. Individually they averaged only 500 votes, as opposed to 1000 for the LO. Not one LCR candidate polled more than 3 per cent.

Occasionally the values which Trotskyists share – the most important of which is perhaps their deep distaste for reformist leftism and orthodox communism – draws them together. For example, in the 1979 European elections the LCR and LO formed a common front, *Pour les Etats – Unis Socialistes d'Europe* (it polled 3.07 per cent). For the most part, however, they keep apart, exchanging polemics, ensuring that an already small current is weakened still further.

2. Maoism

The teachings of Mao, the Sino-Soviet split, and the cultural revolution in China combined in the 1960s to provide would-be *gauchistes* with a new focus for revolutionary activity. A model of behaviour was offered which was apparently untainted by Stalinism, which incarnated a total rejection of materialism and bourgeois values, and which provided an ideological framework with which to complement traditional Marxism-Leninism.

Like Trotskyism, Maoism in France has been weakened by internal divisions. The first significant Maoist group emerged in 1966. Like the LCR the *Union des Jeunesses Communistes Marxistes-Léninistes* (UJCML) was formed as a result of the upheaval in the UEC in the mid-1960s. Based on the *École Normale Supérieure,* where most of its leaders were or had been students of Louis Althusser, the philosopher, it vociferously argued the centrality of class and ideological struggle, totally rejected any dialogue with non-Communists, attacked Trotskyists for being 'bourgeois' and not sufficiently in touch with the workers, and adopted for itself the slogan *'servir le peuple'*. It was dissolved by the government in June 1968.

A second Maoist group, the *Parti Communiste Marxiste-Léniniste de France* (PCMLF), was formed in 1967 by a small number of militants, who had left the PCF and who joined up with a few ex-PSU members. It became prominent in the 'events' of May and it too was banned by the government in June for its pains, but unlike most others, which either disappeared or re-formed themselves, the PCMLF continued to operate, though on a semi-clandestine basis.

In traditional *gauchiste* style the PCMLF did not remain united for long. Some of its members became critical of the Leninist structure and sought a more libertarian association. To this end they linked up with some of the anarchistic elements, which emerged during the heady days of May, and some former members of the UJCML to form the *Gauche Prolétarienne*. For a short time at the end of the 1960s this organisation made much of the running on the far Left. Essentially an urban guerrilla group it engaged in minor acts of industrial sabotage, disrupted university activities, and 'liberated' goods from a few large stores which it then re-distributed amongst the poor. By these 'direct' means it hoped to focus attention on the iniquities of capitalism. Its ambitions were short-lived though; in 1970 it was dissolved by the government and most of its leaders were arrested. Subsequent efforts to keep it going under different names came to little.

In 1974 another schism occurred in the PCMLF. After criticising the leadership for espousing official Chinese policy too completely a group broke away and established the *Parti Communiste Révolution-naire (Marxist Léniniste)*. In 1981 the PCR can probably count around 1500 activists, as opposed to about 4000 for the PCMLF.

Maoist groups have thus been formed and transformed. As with the Trotskyists mutual co-operation tends to be restricted to major occasions. Interestingly, and somewhat surprisingly, such an occasion was the 1978 elections when the PCMLF and the PCR came together to put forward 124 candidates under the slogan *Union Ouvrière et Paysanne pour la Démocratie Prolétarienne*. They achieved a total of only 0.1 per cent, but their poll was of course incidental to their main purpose, which was to use the elections to expose the 'bourgeois illusion of democracy' and to make heard 'the voice of the proletarian revolution'.

THE IMPACT OF THE ALTERNATIVE LEFT

Although it has remained numerically weak and has functioned outside the main currents of political activity, the alternative Left has played an important role in French politics during the Fifth Republic. Its influence has been felt in a number of ways. Firstly, some of its ideas and campaigns – on *autogestion,* women's rights, exploitation of immigrant workers, and environmental questions – have seeped through into the debates within the mainstream Left, albeit in diluted forms. Secondly, many of its members and ex-members are active within the established Left. For current members this is mainly through the trade union movement; for many ex-members it is in the PS or the PCF, which they have joined often because of a frustration with being constantly on the fringes of the political struggle. Thirdly, and somewhat ironically, the electoral impact of the alternative Left has also been important. For the PSU electoral participation has of course always been an aspect of its political strategy, but, as it has become increasingly clear that the 'revolutionary potential' of May 1968 is not likely to be repeated in the foreseeable future, other groups, particularly the Trotskyists, have also turned towards electoral involvement, if only for its publicity advantages. The vote for the alternative Left has always been small, but it has sometimes been enough to influence the outcome of an election by deflecting votes away from one or other of the main Left-wing parties. So, in 1978, with 953,000 votes, the alternative Left won 3.33 per cent of the vote, almost the same percentage as in 1973 when, with far fewer candidates, it gained 3.29 per cent. (An important reason for this relative decline is that in 1978 votes appear to have been lost to *Ecologie '78* whose 199 candidates totalled 2.1 per cent of the vote). In the 1981 presidential elections their vote was crucial. Laguiller (LO) gained 2.3 per cent and Bouchardeau (PSU) 1.1 per cent. Both candidates recommended their supporters to vote for Mitterrand on the second ballot and his winning margin was about half of their combined vote. This hardly, however, benefited the far Left in the subsequent legislative elections – a total of around 500 candidates gained only 1.3 per cent of the vote.

As most conventional channels of communication are closed to the alternative Left outside election periods, considerable effort is devoted to publishing and distributing newspapers, reviews, and leaflets. Amongst the regular weekly newspapers are *Tribune Socialiste* of the PSU, *Lutte Ouvrière* of the LO, *Rouge* of the LCR, and *L'Humanité Rouge* of the PCMLF. Their circulation figures are around 8000, 7000, 5000 and 5000 respectively. The most successful alternative Left newspaper however is not attached to any political party at all, though its editor was for a short time a Maoist. This is *Libération* which has a circulation of about 60,000. It draws much of its strength from its support for a wide range of minority rights, its consistently high editorial standard, and its often revealing investigative journalism.

A point worth making about the alternative Left in France is that it has been associated with a surprising lack of political violence compared to its counterparts in West Germany and Italy. The small band of anarchists apart, the Maoists have been most prepared to use violent political action, but their activities have fallen well short of the urban guerrilla tactics of the *Rote Armee Faktion* or the *Brigate Rossi*. The reasons for this are not easy to discern, but it may be as much a consequence of more effective policing as contrasting strategies or differences in the political and social environments. When violence has occurred it has not been systematic and it has been mostly directed at the extreme Right groups rather than at the State and its institutions.

The accession of the 'established parties' to office in 1981 clearly marks a significant change of perspective for the alternative Left. If the government is seen to be over-cautious a platform could well be provided for resurgent radicalism. The PSU, the closest of all the parties of the alternative Left to the established Left, is likely to reap most benefit from such an eventuality. Another possible ray of light for the alternative Left lies in its popularity amongst the younger generations. According to one poll in 1979 (which it must be said was rather vague) it is 'considered favourably' by a majority of French youth.[10] Moreover, in the 1978 elections it received the support of 12 per cent of the 18-29 age group. Popularity for radicalism tends however to become muted as people age and so youthful support can hardly be seen as a long-term guarantor of growth. On the whole it is necessary to conclude that the stagnation of the 1970s seems likely to continue.

By the same token, the important political roles it has played will doubtless be continued. From a cynical, functional perspective it is serving French society well by channelling revolutionary fervour and much political frustration into relatively harmless dead-ends. More positively, by questioning existing habits and attitudes and displaying a limited political strength it is continually influencing the political environment, within which Left-wing politics as a whole operate.

Part III The Influence of the Left

7 The Left in the Political System

Until 1981, the Left had not held national office for nearly a quarter of a century. Although there were occasions when its return to power seemed possible, particularly in the 1970s, potential was not translated into reality. Every national election held after the Fifth Republic was established in 1958 was lost; in all, six parliamentary elections and three presidentials. As a result, the coalition of Right-Centre forces which emerged after 1958 to support General de Gaulle's presidency enjoyed an occupancy in office, the longevity of which, amongst other major governments of the democratic world, was surpassed only by the Right-dominated coalitions of Italy and Japan.

Moreover, it may be argued, the Left had not actually exercised power, as opposed to having *occupied office* for an even longer period. After the Communist Party was dismissed from office in 1947, there had been no occasion when a Left-dominated government, supported by a majority in parliament, had been able to introduce and implement its own legislative programme. It is true that the Socialists were in and out of office until 1959, but they were always dependent for support on parties to their right and, as a consequence, were continually forced to moderate their policies.

The post-war years, which have seen the Left out of government for the most part, and until 1981 in government only under conditions of restraint, reflect the long-term historical experience of the Left in France. For despite the country's insurrectionary and revolutionary heritage there have been few occasions since the Revolution of 1789 when the Left has unambiguously held the reins of government. The only clear examples are the short-lived Republican government of 1848, the Republican governments of 1879 to 1885, the Radical-led administration of 1902-5, the Popular Front of 1936-7 and, finally, the tripartite governments of 1944-7. Probably only two of these, in terms of the proclaimed intentions of the participants, could be said to have achieved their main objectives: those of 1879-85 and of 1902-1905. Two must be regarded as having ultimately failed: those of

1848 and of 1936-7. All eventually broke up in discord.

The Left's tale of woe could be extended even further if use is made of a distinction that used to be drawn by the Socialist leader, Léon Blum, between the *exercise* of power and the *conquest* of power. For whilst there have been periods, though not too many, when the former has pertained, it is questionable whether the latter, in a truly meaningful sense, has ever applied at all. Certainly it has not come near to doing so since the end of the Radical-led reforming ministry of 1902-5.

Yet, despite this apparently modest and depressing record, the influence of the Left on the political, social and economic life of France has been considerable. Many ideas and policies which it has championed have become firmly embodied in the structures, practices, laws, and culture of the nation. In some cases this has been a result of the specific achievements of the few Left governments; for example, the establishment of the Republic and the increasing secularisation of the state and education system in the first half of the Third Republic. In other cases the influence has been more indirect as the Centre and Right have adopted measures, in part at least, to stave off threats to their electoral position from the Left. The extension of welfare benefits and attempts to liberalise society by successive governments of the Fifth Republic are examples of this. Whether in office or not the Left has thus continuously contributed to a process whereby the centre of political gravity has gradually moved to the Left. Positions which had formerly been opposed by the Right – such as the introduction of universal suffrage, the protection of collective bargaining rights, or the nationalisation of key industries – have become its line of defence against ever-increasing demands for reform. If the Left has normally been denied office, it is clear that it has rarely been short of influence.

In addition to these long-term influences, direct and indirect, there are also specific ways in which the Left has been central to contemporary French politics.

Firstly, until 1981 it presented the only realistic alternative to the ruling Majority coalition. As party politics in the Fifth Republic have polarised into two large blocs, so the various shifting permutations of Centrist forces, which were so familiar during the Fourth Republic, have come to be no longer viable. The 1978 legislative elections illustrate the point; whilst there was confusion on the first ballot, with an average ten candidates per seat, on the second there was a straight fight between Left and Right in 409 of the 423 constituencies still at stake. This made the elections the most polarised of recent times.

Secondly, the significance of the opposition coming to power in France was greater than in most other major democratic countries. In the USA, Germany, Sweden, Britain and elsewhere (Italy is the most obvious exception) there is a broad consensus amongst competing élites on most major policy areas. There are different emphases, which are not without significance, but when governments change hands there is only occasionally a fundamental switch in direction on central issues. Election campaigns in these countries, allowing for the politician's liberal use of rhetoric, are normally matters of emphases and personalities. There are rarely basic conflicts on the more important questions of the day or fundamental clashes of ideology. In France this is not the case. If it is not quite a *choix de societé* that has been offered, the Left undeniably has proposed a programme of major social and economic reforms. Even if, in government, they now moderate some of their policies – as radical oppositions tend to do – there can be little doubt that far reaching changes will still be enacted. In addition, and over and above specific policy alternatives, the assumption to power of the Left could have led to serious institutional difficulties, quite possibly resulting in a major crisis. This is because the system, if it is to continue functioning in its evolved manner, with an initiating President and a largely compliant Parliament, is highly dependent on the two bodies sharing a similar ideological perspective. Indeed the Right in the 1960s and 1970s successfully used the fragility of the institutional balance to bolster its electoral position by intimating that it would be impossible for the Left to achieve such a combination of political strength. The Left itself seemed for a long time to be almost taken in by the persuasiveness of this argument and always had difficulty explaining it away, particularly in relation to legislative elections. In the 1981 presidential elections, however, Mitterrand went on to the offensive and turned the argument on its head by promising a dissolution of Parliament if he won. After his victory he used the Right's argument against it and this helped to achieve the Socialist landslide in the ensuing parliamentary elections.

Thirdly, the contemporary Left has derived importance from the fact that despite its long absence from government it has nonetheless directly exercised power and influence in many areas of public life. Sidney Tarrow has written 'The problem for the French Left lies in the relative impermeability of the French state to any political influence that falls short of total policy control'.[1] Whilst this is broadly true the case should not be overstated. Areas where its presence has been and is strongly felt include the following:

(1) At all levels of public enterprise, the state administration, and the

educational system members and sympathisers of the Left-wing parties, especially the Socialists are to be found. Their numbers are difficult to quantify, and conservative mores have dominated the upper echelons of most 'establishment' structures, but even at the highest levels there has been a Left-wing presence. As Suleiman has observed in his study of French élites 'Many of the respondents pointed to the fact that many of their colleagues are members of the Socialist Party and play important and active roles within this party'.[2]

(2)   Pressure groups and voluntary associations of many different kinds are sympathetic to Left-wing ideas and in some cases are closely allied with and are even 'fronts' for the parties of the Left. So, Left-wing sympathisers are active in the likes of student organisations, environmentalist lobbies, women's groups, regional movements, (notably in Brittany), and lay Catholic associations.

(3)   The Left is well represented in many of the semi-autonomous, advisory, consultative, and decision-making agencies and institutions that are attached to the official organs of the state. For example, Left-wing figures from both the political parties and the trade unions have made their voice heard – though, it must be said, with only a marginal effect – in the regional planning machinery; the Left has penetrated certain 'para-municipal' agencies, such as at Rennes where Socialists have 'colonised' the *Habitation à Loyers Moderés,* which is a sort of local housing body; even some of the *Maisons de la Culture,* such as at Grenoble and Caen, are governed by the Left.

In the next two chapters we consider the influence of the Left in two important political and social spheres in some detail. The account of the Left in local government draws attention to the increasing presence of the Left in the town halls and points to some of the policy implications of this. The chapter on trade unions emphasises the strong Left-wing influence amongst organised labour. The various factors which have restricted the ability of the unions to effect the direction of public policy is also a central theme of the chapter.

Such Left-wing influence as we have briefly described here, and explore further in Chapters 8 and 9, will considerably facilitate the implementation of many of the Left's policies now it is in government. This is particularly the case in the important areas of decentralisation to the regions and industrial reform.

8 The Left at Local Level

1. THE IMPORTANCE OF LOCAL GOVERNMENT

Although France is a highly centralised country, considerable importance still attaches to the layers of government below the national level. There are three of these: regional, departmental and municipal. Regional government is the weakest. Its role is essentially advisory, principally in the area of economic development, and this is reflected in the fact that the 22 regional councils (*conseils régionaux*) are not directly elected but are made up of the deputies and senators of the region plus nominees from the municipal and departmental councils. The *départements,* of which there are 96, have rather more influence. They are required to provide some limited services – notably on roads, school buildings, and social security – and they have their own directly elected departmental councils (*conseils généraux*). The councils work, however, under tight central guidelines and on a limited budget. The main importance probably lies in the role they play as mediating agents between central and local interests. It is the municipal councils – which are based on France's 36,000 communes – which have the greatest *potential* for directly exercising power and influence. Matters for which they have at least some responsibility include planning, housing, public transport, social welfare, and educational facilities. In practice the power municipalities *actually* exercise is closely related to size and in this they vary enormously; over 11,000 have less than 200 inhabitants, over 32,000 have less than 2000, whilst the larger cities have hundreds of thousands. Clearly the smaller communes have not the population, and therefore also not the resources, to provide the services expected by modern society. As a consequence they are very heavily dependent on the state and work under the close guidance of its various local representatives, in particular the prefect and his staff. In the larger towns however councils and their mayors (who are key political figures, unlike in Britain) can, and often do, provide a strong countervailing force to the national government. They may do this both directly – through the decision-making powers within their

formal spheres of competence – and indirectly – through the various
forms of political influence they can bring to bear.

Apart from its policy-making potentiality local government is also
important for other reasons.

Firstly, it can aid and can hinder national political developments.
For example, one of the reasons the FGDS proved to be so fragile in
the 1960s was that it was opposed by many local Socialist councillors,
who were comfortably ensconsed in municipal Third Force coalitions
with centrists and independents of one kind or another. More
recently, there is no doubt that the success of many jointly run Left-
wing councils in the 1970s greatly contributed to the national development and success of the *dynamique de la gauche.*

Secondly, local politics provide a valuable outlet for political
activity. This has been especially important for the Left given its
exclusion from office at national level until 1981.

Thirdly, local politics serve as a recruiting ground for the political
parties and a base for national political ambitions. Most parliamentary candidates hold a local elective post and those who become
deputies retain them. This *cumul des mandats,* as it is known,
strengthens a politician's ties with his local constituency. For the
municipality the situation is advantageous too because to have a
deputy amongst their number – usually he will be mayor – will more
readily allow local needs to be pressed with the prefect, the representatives of the field services of the central ministries, or even influential
figures in Paris. A study of candidates in the 1978 elections has shown
that a majority in all parties, apart from the Radicals, held at least one
local office.[1] The figures for the Left were: 65.3 per cent for the PS,
63.2 per cent for the PCF, and 51.5 per cent for the MRG. Of the
three the PS had the greatest number of *'collectionneurs'* with 16.7 per
cent of their candidates sitting on local, departmental and regional
councils. Of those elected, the proportions for each party were even
higher, as Table 8.1 shows.

Table 8.1   Cumulated posts of deputies of the Left

	PS	PCF	MRG
Number of deputies elected in 1978	103	82	10
Number of deputies who are mayors	61	43	7
Number of deputies who are not mayors, but who are members of departmental councils	24	18	2

A difference within the Left, not apparent from the figures quoted in Table 8.1, is that although the PCF does, like the PS and MRG, permit accumulation of elected posts it does not usually allow it for those who hold important Party functions. This is a trait which is reflected throughout the Party structure and it means at the local level that Communist mayors are usually not, and sometimes never have been, key figures in the organisational apparatus of the Party. The situation is quite different in the PS where mayors are usually the most influential local figure in the Party. Moreover, virtually all PS national leaders are mayors. For example, Mitterrand, until his election, at Château-Chinon in the Nièvre, Defferre at Marseilles, Mauroy at Lille, Rocard at Conflans-Saint-Honorine in Yvelinnes, and Chevènement is acting mayor at Belfort. Michel Crépeau, the leader of the MRG, is mayor of La Rochelle.

2. THE STRENGTH OF THE LEFT AT LOCAL LEVEL

Because most of its electorate is found in urban areas, the main strength of the Left at local level lies in the larger urban municipalities, rather than in the rurally-biased regional councils and departmental councils. Nonetheless, there is still a very strong presence at regional and departmental level. By 1980 the Left controlled 9 of the 22 regional councils, 8 of which were Socialist and one of which – Picardy – was Communist. In the 96 departmental councils a steady advance throughout the 1970s saw the Left with almost half of the seats after the 1979 elections: 1,879 out of 3,710. (See Table 8.2).

Following these elections the PS found themselves presiding over 28 departmental councils, the MRG over 8, and the PCF over 5. (The Communists' low figure is a consequence of their under-representation in the councils themselves and the reluctance of other parties to support their candidates when presidents are voted into office).

At municipal level, where elections take place every six years, the Left made major advances in 1977. It is now firmly entrenched, particularly in the large towns. In over two thirds of the largest towns – those with more than 30,000 inhabitants – there is a Left-wing mayor (see Table 8.3): 165 out of 221 if the 10 'Centre-left' (who are mainly ex-Socialists and ex-Radicals) are added to the 72 PCF, 81 PS, and 2 MRG.

The Influence of the Left

Table 8.2   Departmental elections 1973-9

	1973		1976		1979		
	% vote	seats	% vote	seats	% vote	seats	Total seats in 1979
PCF	22.7	205 (+74)	22.8	249 (+75)	22.4	244 (+41)	493
PS	21.9	423	26.6	520 (+194)	26.9	544 (+156)	1064
MRG	1.9	68	2.4	84 (-7)	1.8	78 (-6)	162
Extreme Left	1.0	9 (-15)	0.8	8 (-14)	0.85	2 (-7)	10
Other Left	6.4	174	4.0	90 (-180)	3.1	60 (-114)	150

Departmental councils are elected on the basis of one member per *canton*. In 1979 there were 3710 cantons. One half of the canton are elected every three years, therefore in each year there are around 1850 seats to be filled. The figures in brackets indicate the gains and losses as compared with six years previously. Because of the changes in the SFIO and Radical Party after 1967, accurate figures for 1973 for the PS, the MRG and 'other left' (many of whom are dissident Socialists) cannot be calculated.

Table 8.3   Socialist and Communist mayors elected in main towns in March 1977[2]

Size of town	Number of towns	Socialists/MRG	Communists	Total Socialists, MRG and Communists
6000-9000	403	108	81	189
9000-30,000	605	193	156	349
More than 30,000	221	83(+40)	72(+22)	155(+56*)
Total	1229	384	309	693

*The apparent disparity here is explained by the fact that 6 councils were lost from those won in the previous elections in 1971.

The march of the Left into the *mairies* in 1977 marked a spectacular broadening out from the traditional strongholds of the North, the South, and the Paris 'red belt'. Progress was made in all areas with many important towns gained; for example Saint-Etienne, Le Mans, Pessac, Montpellier, Macon and Chartres. Some of the most notable successes were in the heartland of traditional conservatism and catholicism in the West and East, where municipalities which had voted for Giscard in 1974 and would vote for the Majority in 1978 were carried along with the *dynamique de la gauche*. Amongst them were Nantes, Rennes, Brest, Cherbourg, Saint-Mâlo, and Poitiers.

The 1977 elections thus saw a sea of red spread over municipal government, particularly in the large towns. A new and, on the whole, much younger generation of Left-wing politicians was given the opportunity to show its political paces and to demonstrate that the rhetoric of the Left can be translated into acceptable practice.

3. LOCAL PARTNERSHIP

The prevailing tendency in local authorities before 1971 was the existence of rather entrenched local *notables* who rarely attached great significance to partisan political activity. The PCF was in some respects an exception to this, but outside of its traditional areas of influence in the 'red belt' around Paris and the Pas-de-Calais it was rarely well represented at local level. The Socialists usually sought and maintained advantageous alliances with either Radicals or Centrists. In some areas this strategy helped it to create powerful bastions and fiefs – of which Lille and Marseilles were the largest – from which Communists were strictly excluded.

During the 1960s this pattern of Communist isolationism and Socialist opportunism began to break down and a movement towards greater Left-wing co-operation at the local level began to develop. This was mainly a result of the national movement to unity that we have already examined, but it was also stimulated by specifically local pressures. Firstly, the PCF increasingly made it clear that they no longer saw municipal government as a forum in which to reinforce their revolutionary activities, but rather as an opportunity to demonstrate their commitment to democratic institutions and their ability to manage affairs constructively and efficiently. Since their traditional isolationism had contributed to their gross under-representation in the town halls (they still led only three per cent of all councils after 1971), local alliances now became a necessity. Secondly, the withering of the political centre made Third Force alliances increasingly less attractive to the Socialists, even if in some areas their opposition to Communism remained implacable. Thirdly, the changes in the local electoral system in 1964 strongly encouraged joint-lists in

the large towns. (The system is described in Chapter 5). Fourthly, and
finally, there were important changes in the local personnel in both the
Socialist and Communist parties from the late 1960s. We have already
noted in Chapter 3 the replacement of a majority of local Socialist
politicians in the formative years of the PS after 1969. From about the
same time, similar – though by no means as wholesale – changes also
began to take place in the PCF, as the generation most steeped in the
Stalinist heritage of the Party was joined by new and often more
accommodating figures. This replacement of local élites in both
parties greatly facilitated the development of freer and less rigid
bargaining processes since the negotiators themselves were now less
hidebound by the antagonisms of the past.

A number of factors have thus contributed to the creation of a
united Left strategy at local level. The process has been gradual, and
in the Socialist Party not without resistance, but it has been continuous and ever-evolving. It is most obviously seen in the increasing
presentation of joint Left lists in the larger towns. In the 1965
elections, when local Socialist organisations were given a free hand on
their tactics by the national Party, there were joint lists in 60 of the 159
largest towns (38 per cent). In 1971 the new PS leadership officially
favoured, though it did not insist on, joint lists and 124 were presented
in the 193 largest towns (64 per cent). In 1977 the process was taken a
stage further when PS candidates were forbidden to be part of Third
Force lists. This was a crucial step because, despite the large number
of joint-Left lists that had been presented in 1971, around two-thirds
of the 41 largest towns which the Socialists had won were based on
Third Force coalitions of one kind or another. The leadership in 1977
did not actually go so far as to try and enforce joint lists, but its Third
Force directive still had the effect, almost inevitably, of producing
desertions from the Party and in some cases defections to the
Majority. In the event a single list was presented in 204 of the 221
largest towns (92 per cent). This was four more than the Majority
itself could manage. In all there were joint lists in just over 50 per cent
of French communes in 1977, compared with around 25 per cent in
1971.

These developments have contributed to and reflected the 'nationalisation' and politicisation of local politics in France, which has
been apparent in all recent elections. In particular, since the signature
of the Common Programme the Socialists and the Communists have
consciously translated national debates to the local level. Their
objectives have been to capture and establish local power bases which

can facilitate their national strategies. The PCF, who have in the past been grossly under-represented at local level, have operated what has been called an 'insertionist' strategy in order to achieve a stronger position in the town halls. This has been based on their alliances with the Socialists on the one hand and 'a solid platform of social and political reforms and cultural activities' on the other.[3] The Socialists have acted in a similar way, but have been additionally motivated by the Party's ideas on decentralisation and more associative politics, which centre around a concern to augment the significance of the non-central tiers of authority.

But the development of Left-wing unity at the grass roots has not been without its problems. There have been two aspects to this.

(a) *The constitution of electoral lists.* The PCF because of its disciplined organisation can more readily insist that the strategy decided upon at national level is implemented at the base. The PS, because it is much more loosely organised, cannot do so. The national Socialist leadership can discipline flagrant deviations from its strategic priorities but it is less able than the Communists to rely on the co-operation of its local leaders. It is principally because some local Socialist leaders have not been prepared to accept pressure from the national leadership that local electoral unity, though well advanced, has not been wholly complete.

Because they are based on single member constituencies cantonal elections have seen few electoral difficulties between the major parties of the Left. In 1979, despite the considerable acrimony at national level, there were few places where the second placed candidate of the Left refused to withdraw after the first ballot.

Municipal elections have however been a source of tension. This has arisen from the desirability of presenting joint-lists of candidates on the first ballot in the large towns, and the provision for the merging of lists between ballots in the smaller towns. In 1977, despite a national agreement between the PCF, PS and MRG to try and run joint-lists wherever possible, local bargaining met with many obstacles. These reflected many factors. Amongst them were: long standing local rivalries of both personal and ideological kinds; differing perceptions by the local parties of their power and influence; lingering Socialist hankerings for the Third Force alternative (despite resignations and exclusions of many such advocates since 1971); the internal struggle for power between factions of the Socialist Party; beliefs that one or other of the parties was being over-demanding in the composition of the list;[4] and, in the PS – and above all at Marseilles – a firm conviction that they could win by themselves and should not give their traditional enemies a foothold. Where the PSU, who were anxious not to miss out on the popularity of the Left, and various 'independent' Leftists (including ex-Gaullists) had also to be accommodated, bargaining problems were exacerbated even further.

(b) *Management of the Municipalities.* Following so soon after the victories in the 1977 municipal elections the rupture between the signatories of the Common Programme quickly led to local difficulties. Yet the situation has been much less clear cut than at national level and in most cases local alliances have continued without too many ramifications from the national dispute. In this way the *Union de la Gauche* has continued in most Left-led municipalities despite its suspension (until 1981) at the summit.

In those cases where there have been disputes it is difficult to detect any overall consistent pattern. Many disagreements have been over relatively trivial matters, though this has often been masked by a vociferous exchange of polemics between local leaders. So, for example, at Saint-Chamond (Loire) much heat was generated in December 1977 over the refusal of the Socialist mayor to allow the PCF to hold a press conference in the town hall. In a neighbouring Loire municipality, Roanne, also in December 1977, the PCF refused to support a PS plan to establish a committee to create employment, arguing that the Socialist proposal was hypocritical following its attitude in the negotiations to update the Common Programme. At Belfort, in 1979, the Communists refused their support for the creation of a pedestrian precinct proposed by the Socialist majority. In general such comparatively minor disputes have not fundamentally disturbed the management of the council and the parties have co-operated on the more important questions. For example, at Belfort the pedstrian precinct disagreement did not prevent the two parties from uniting to support the strike at the Alsthom plant in the town until its successful conclusion.[5]

In some municipalities disputes have gone further. In most of these cases they have not resulted in a formal rupture but rumblings of discontent have been clearly apparent on many issues; above all, the decision-making processes of the council and the nature and extent of consultation granted to the minority partner in the alliance. Exchanges have sometimes been bitter. At Rennes, for example, in early 1980, the Socialist mayor denounced the *'démagogie partisane'* of the Communist councillors. They, in their turn, protested against '*la campagne haineuse et hystérique*' launched by the PS against the PCF. For all that the Communists still voted the municipal budget, doing so on the grounds that, to vote against it would have meant their removal from posts of responsibility on the council and this would represent a defeat for workers' interests.

In only a few councils have relations deteriorated to the extent that an open breakdown has occurred. One of these has been at Angers, where in the autumn of 1979 Communists were relieved of their municipal responsibilities – i.e. deprived of their posts as *adjoints* (deputy mayor) and the tasks which go with them – after they failed to support the urban transport policy of the Socialist led council. Another example has been at Brest where Communists were deprived of their official posts after refusing to vote the municipal budget.[6]

The varied pattern of disputes is further illustrated by the fact that even in those instances where there have been major differences within the local alliances the 'dissident' minority has not always been deprived of its portfolios as *adjoints*. So, in one of the earliest disputes, at Reims in November 1977, the Socialist minority voted against the supplementary budget proposed by the newly-elected Communist mayor after initially accepting it in committee. (A supplementary budget was necessary because the Left was not in office when the main budget was passed). The Communists did not seek however to exclude the Socialists from their executive positions. Similarly, the abstention of Communists on the municipal budget vote at Conflans-Saint-Honorine in 1980 did not result in them being deprived of their responsibilities by the mayor, Michel Rocard.[7]

The general picture that emerges from these various examples of disunity within Left-wing councils is of the individual parties sometimes finding it necessary to publicly express their reservations and dissatisfactions with their partner. In a few cases this has even led to the minority party voting against its ally on crucial issues. It is clear, though, that the formal reason for such disagreements – and they have covered just about every area of local authority responsibilities – is largely a pretext for what is essentially a competition for power. This competition demands that the parties establish their identity. It also often means that they want greater control over the local distribution of patronage. Both of these factors are closely tied to a desire at least to maintain and, if possible, improve relative positions at the next elections. In some places it is also apparent that a local party, particularly the PCF, has wished to make a gesture of opposition in order to complement the national campaign of harassment against the former ally. Certainly, it is not coincidental that de-stabilisation has been most frequent in councils where Communists have been the minority partner (even bearing in mind that they are in a minority position on most Left councils).

Looking at the overall picture (in mid-1981) difficulties such as we have noted should not be exaggerated. Two things would appear to signify a complete breakdown in a local alliance: a vote against the municipal budget by the minority partner and the withdrawal of the posts of *adjoints* from the minority by the majority. There have been very few examples of either of these. Most of the municipal, and indeed departmental, councils have withstood the collapse at the national level of *Union de la Gauche* and have succeeded in co-operating reasonably well, given the essentially mutually competitive situation in which they exist.

4. POLICY IMPLICATIONS

It is difficult to comment, other than in a general manner, on the public policy implications of the Left in office at local level. This is because there are so many factors operating which combine to produce different outcomes between municipalities. The varying composition of councils is the most important of these factors. The prevailing tendency up to 1977, even in the larger towns, was for the Left to hold local office either via a Third Force or Centre-Left coalition (in the cases of the PS and MRG), or alternatively through one party having a majority in its own right. It is only since 1977 that joint Left lists have been the dominant pattern. Moreover these lists display a considerable range in their political complexions. Some are led and dominated by the PCF, some by the PS (which of course is itself highly heterogeneous), some by the MRG, whilst many are also liberally sprinkled with groups and individuals of yet different hues. As a result, although all these councils were elected on the basis of a locally negotiated municipal contract drawn up within the general guidelines of the Common Programme, there were considerable variations in the specifics and priorities of their programmes, and these have continued to be apparent since the victorious lists assumed office.

On the whole, Communist-headed municipalities have, as in Italy, succeeded in establishing a reputation, amongst impartial observers at least, for being honest, often innovative, and generally well run. They differ in two main respects from non-Communist authorities:

1) *Spending.* Their overall *per capita* level of spending is only slightly higher than the average but their priorities are different. A significantly greater proportion of resources are devoted to educational and social programmes and less to maintenance functions such as roads, repairs, lighting, and street cleaning.

2) *Financing of Projects.* PCF municipalities tend to levy higher local taxes, to charge lower rates for use of services, and to use less of their revenue for self-financing investment.[8]

Interestingly, Communist authorities, though lacking many of the informal contacts with officialdom enjoyed by the parties of the former governing Majority, have not been unduly discriminated against on the vital matter of securing state grants and loans. There are a number of reasons for this, the most important of which is that PCF mayors and councillors usually dampen their political partisanship when in office. In most cases they attempt to conform to what Kesselman has identified as the two principal characteristics of French local government: the tendency to emphasise administrative capacity and the search for communal consensus.[9]

Three generalisations can be made about Socialist-led authorities. Firstly, likely the PCF, a major aim is to use local government to project a favourable image of the Party and to do this it is thought to be necessary to be seen managing affairs calmly, efficiently, and with as little fuss as possible. The example of Marseilles, which Defferre has dominated since the end of the war, has shown that a reputation for sensible and forward-looking policies is likely to produce political dividends. Secondly, a greater priority is given to educational and social policies and public services than it is in councils headed by parties of the Centre and the Right, but spending is not as proportionately high as it is in PCF-led municipalities.[10] Thirdly, and this is to be expected from a more heterogeneous and loosely-structured Party, there appears to be a much greater variation in specific priorities between PS-led councils than between PCF-led councils.[11] The range of issues identified by PS mayors and councillors as constituting their achievements and objectives is enormously varied. The traditional and expected concerns with housing, transport, educational facilities, urban renewal etc., still remain, but they have been supplemented by a wide variety of community, cultural, and environmental interests (some of which have been attacked by the Communists as 'bourgeois'). Amongst specific accomplishments proudly mentioned to us by Socialist mayors, in early 1980, were the provision of municipal taxi and bicycle services, the creation of pedestrian-only areas in town centres, making facilities available for young people (including, in Rocard's municipality, helping to set up cafés managed by the young themselves) and waste-disposal schemes. Interestingly, one of the most innovative of all authorities, is at La Rochelle where the mayor and leader of the MRG, Michel Crépeau, has consistently championed environmentalism since his election in 1971. Amongst his projects has been a major waste re-cycling scheme which now makes a profit for the town.

The tendency of the French until 1981 to support the Left at local elections in greater numbers than it was prepared to do when the government of the day was at stake provided greatly increased opportunities from the early 1970s for the Left to show that it could govern in relative harmony and through realistic policies. On the whole it has taken those opportunities and has demonstrated that an extension of public services is compatible with sound and efficient management. We will now consider whether or not this situation is likely to continue.

5. PROSPECTS

The emphasis by the Left on sound management in local government helped to dilute some of the distrust and antagonism that was apparent at national level from the autumn of 1977. Even though there have been some local disputes, tactical requirements, often assisted by astute and flexible politicians, have managed on the whole to create local co-operation. Underlying this a joint meeting of the Communist and Socialist associations of local councillors in February 1980 agreed a statement, which affirmed their commitment to preserve and improve their collaboration and to respect the agreements they made in 1977.[12] (The Communists are represented in the *Association nationale des élus communistes et républicaines, ANECR,* and the Socialists in the *Fédération nationale des élus socialistes et républicaines, FNESR.*)

Continued co-operation will depend on a number of factors. Writing in the early 1970s Jerome Milch said of the PCF, 'The party's approach to local government is closely tied to its national strategy; if conditions dictate a more rigid and militant attitude on the national level, municipal policy will not long remain at variance.'[13] As if to confirm this, Marcel Rosette, the president of the ANECR, in an interview with *L'Humanité* on the very day of the meeting with the FNESR, queried the commitment of Socialist councillors to policy agreements, alleged their position was moving further and further to the Right, and claimed that their principal interest was to weaken the PCF's influence.[14] This was of course, by mid-1980, ritual rhetoric from a national PCF figure, but it clearly indicated that there are circumstances – continued electoral decline for example – in which the central apparatus of the PCF might try to dismantle local unity. The evidence of the post-1978 *contestation* suggests that such a ploy would meet fierce resistance – not least because the much valued Communist gains have been achieved principally because of the *Union* – but ultimately it would doubtless succeed. In addition to such doubts about the Communists' long term intentions, it is possible to envisage circumstances in which the Socialists might also seriously have to reconsider their strategy. Flexibility has traditionally been one of their main characteristics at local level and there have already been a few cases where local parties have unofficially continued or have re-forged relationships with non-Left wing parties or *notables*. Disillusionment and anger at the national intransigence of the PCF has often been the cause of this. For the present, however, the national events of 1981 would appear to point to a period of enhanced co-operation at the local level. Certainly the Left-wing councils will need to maintain their cohesion if the radical reforms for a major strengthening and democratisation of regional government, which the new government proposes to introduce by 1983, are to be successfully implemented.

In conclusion it is apparent that Left-wing politics at the local level are far from merely a series of reflections of the state of play in Paris. A by-product of this has been that the Left in the regions, the departments and the municipalities has been able to contribute greatly to the credibility of the Left in the country at large.

9 The Trade Unions and the Left

INTRODUCTION

An overall assessment of the political impact of trade unionism in France would have to conclude that it has not been as great as might have been expected in a country where the politicians of the Left have usually failed to offer coherent, let alone united, leadership. There has been no question of unionism providing, in the absence of regular governments of the Left, a vigorous alternative avenue for 'progressive' social change. Indeed, far from that, trade unions have not even been able to act as a buttress to the party political Left in the way that they do in Britain, Sweden, West Germany and elsewhere. They have been internally weak and their relationships with the political parties that ostensibly represent the working-class movement have always been enigmatic. Both the *ouvrièrisme* of the PCF and the class rhetoric of the Socialists have testified to the need of the parties for close co-operation with the trades unions. Inevitably, unions in their turn have frequently sought the support and the backing of the principal Left-wing parties. But there have been so many different motives, cross-cutting pressures, and sources of dissension on both sides, that clear and consistent relationships between the parties and the union movement *as a whole* have never been possible. In much the same way as the parties, the main trade unions have usually found it difficult to agree on anything other than immediate tactics. The ideological perspectives of the individual unions have clashed sharply, with the consequence that they have perceived their *political* roles in quite different ways. The few periods when they have co-operated with one another have coincided with the periods of unity and strength of the party political Left: during the Popular Front, the immediate post-Liberation years, and the era of the *Union de la Gauche*. As a result, the unions have been quite unable to act either as a catalyst for party political unity or as a substitute for party political disunity.

We shall now examine in detail the two principal reasons for this relative political ineffectuality: numerical weakness and persisting internal divisions.

NUMERICAL WEAKNESS

Trade unions in France have never succeeded in attracting the density of support amongst the workforce given to unions in most similar industrialised countries. Apart from three peak periods – immediately after the 1914-18 war, during the Popular Front, and after the Liberation – they have represented usually between only 20-25 per cent of the workforce.[1] At the present time (1981) this adds up to a total, at the maximum, of about 4.5 million members.

Various explanations have been advanced for this low membership. One of the most frequently heard stresses the supposed individualistic nature of French political culture. Because of the structure of the French family, the hierarchical and competitive nature of the educational system, and other factors, the French are considered to be wary of most forms of collective action. The low membership of trade unions is therefore seen as part of the general phenomenon whereby pressure groups and political parties of all persuasions have traditionally found it difficult to attract members. This explanation is valuable, but not wholly satisfactory. For one thing it is vague and somewhat impressionistic. For another it verges on the tautological, since the suggestion is often that the French *must* be individualistic, *because* they do not join organisations.

Other explanations must, then, be considered. The economic structure, with its historically small-scale, often family-dominated units has undoubtedly been a major handicap. Concentration of industry into large enterprises has proceeded rapidly since the Second World War, but in the formative years of union development it was highly dispersed and this strongly militated against organisational effectiveness and the development of workers' solidarity. At the same time it hindered union recognition, in that employers were often able to be totally uncompromising, refusing even to allow unions into their factories, let alone negotiate with them. Until relatively recently victimisation against union members, the establishment of company unions, the hiring of blacklegs and refusals to implement agreements were all common practices used by employers to keep unionism at bay. Indeed it is only since 1968 that unions have been officially allowed to recruit openly within firms and hold meetings within working time. (Though unofficial 'dissuasion' is still far from unknown.) There is still no provision, as in Britain, for union dues to be automatically deducted from wages and salaries.

The state has also played an intimidating role, especially in •the crucial early years. Although, as far back as 1791, in the *Loi le Chapelier,* all employers' and workers' associations had been forbidden, in practice combined economic action on the part of employers was tolerated during the nineteenth century. The consequence was that anti-collectivism, which was frequently justified in Rousseaunian notions of the general will, became little more than a naked act of capitalist self-interest. Even after strikes were legalised in 1864, and trade unions themselves in 1884, politicians, concerned with the socialist menace, retained a guarded suspicion and were not unwilling, when necessary, to employ measures which deprived unions of much of their effectiveness. In the highly explosive strike wave of 1906-10 for example, the full weight of the state was marshalled to smash union influence and break the strikes. This reflected a view, which many amongst the ruling élite still firmly held until well after the Second World War, that unions were almost subversive organisations, all the more so when they deigned to articulate and struggle for demands. The way in which many concessions, won by unions in the heat of industrial action, have later not been enforced by the state, or their effect has been whittled down, may well have contributed to a disillusionment amongst workers with the effectiveness of unions.

But the trade union movement itself must also take its share of the blame for its inability to attract a mass membership. As we shall see in a moment, unions have, for the most part, been divided in their ideologies, strategies and policies. They have given the impression of being as much concerned to compete amongst themselves as to further the aims of their members via the presentation of a common front. Such antagonisms, which have periodically been exacerbated by unrepresentative union leaderships, have, it may be assumed, deterred many would-be members.

It is interesting to note, in the context of these comments about possible disillusionment with unionism, the findings of a survey published in 1979. It showed that trade unionism in itself is not unpopular but that a distinct gap exists between perceived usefulness of being a member of a union and perceived effectiveness of unions in defending members' interests. Eighty per cent of salaried workers stated that they believed it was useful for salaried workers to be members of a union. (Although only 33 per cent said they themselves were – which itself is 8 per cent higher than Ministry of Labour figures.) At the same time, however, only 13 per cent said they had complete confidence in the actions of unions to defend their interests, while a further 44 per cent said they had some confidence. Thirty-six per cent had little or no confidence and seven per cent expressed no opinion.[2] Of course, surveys should always be interpreted with caution, but there is the clear suggestion here of much less than whole-hearted commitment. This may be true to some extent in other countries, Britain certainly, but there popular scepticism can usually be overcome by traditions, built up over the years, of joining a union as a matter of course. In France there are few areas of economic activity where such traditions exist.

PERSISTING DIVISIONS

Unions began to be properly organised from the mid-1870s and splits appeared very quickly. On the one hand there were trade federations, which were unions in the proper sense. In 1895 they federated to form the *Confédération Générale du Travail* (CGT), through which they asserted the primacy of economic, as opposed to political, struggle. *Bourses du Travail,* on the other hand, were a curious mixture of labour exchanges, trade unions and working men's clubs. In 1892 they too federated into a national organisation and like the CGT, though in a more rigorous way, the *Fédération* developed a syndicalist philosophy based on economic action and political autonomy.

In a series of stages, in 1895, 1902 and 1906, the CGT and the *Fédération des Bourses* merged into an expanded CGT. Their similar outlooks had drawn them together, as had the increasing realisation that concessions and improvements in working conditions were more likely to be won by a united organisation that was efficient and effective, than by isolated and uncoordinated action. As they placed their relations on firmer ground, revolutionary syndicalism came increasingly to dominate the union. As much a mood and way of thinking as a plan of action, revolutionary syndicalism was never a clearly defined doctrine. It brought together a number of ideas and sentiments, some of which sat uneasily together: a complete hostility to the bourgeois state; the dream of a federated society in which economic units would be the basis of community organisation; a belief in the centrality of the class war and a complete hostility to all forms of ameliorative reformism; a faith that only through economic action – in particular the use of the general strike – could workers liberate themselves; and, finally, a resistance to all forms of co-operation with political forces, socialists included.

The success of revolutionary syndicalism stemmed from a number of factors: the anarchist/federalist tradition coming down from Proudhon, Fourier, Blanqui and others; the hostility of employers to conventional trade unionism; the decentralised and small-scale economy in which craftsmanship and independence were still valued; and the class antagonisms which had built up during the century and which had resulted, especially amongst politically-conscious sections of the working class in Paris, in a firm determination that no further opportunity should be given to bourgeois politicians to betray those who had given them power. These all provided fertile ground for a movement which paraded slogans such as 'the free worker in the free workshop' and 'the workshop will replace the government'.

Revolutionary syndicalism was always a minority strain, however, both amongst the workforce and the union movement. In 1906, out of about seven million industrial workers, only 800,000 were unionised and of these no more than 200,000 belonged to the CGT. Trade unions represented therefore only a small section of the workforce and the CGT but a part of that section. This facilitated the rise to power in union ranks of 'unrepresentative' minorities. The electoral arrangements for the central organs of the CGT also helped, because affiliated unions had equal voting strengths. This meant the moderate unions, who had most members, were under-franchised.

So, from 1902 until the outbreak of war, the CGT was neither disposed nor able to carry through the reformist and gradualist campaigns, based on negotiations and the threat of slowly escalating sanctions, that were becoming the hallmarks of trade unionism in most other European countries. But as Ridley remarks 'The whole idea of the general strike, the emancipation of the proletariat and the inauguration of a new society, is the type of dream theory that compensates for ineffectuality in the world of everyday affairs'.[3] Despite its fervour and apparent strength revolutionary syndicalism had not succeeded in uniting the trade union movement, nor had it truly penetrated the workers' consciousness. Stearns summarises its effect in this way: 'It answered, at best, the enthusiasm of the moment. . . . It could not radicalise immediate goals and probably had only limited success in shaping ultimate hopes'.[4] For this reason and also because the economic structure from which it had sprung was changing, revolutionary syndicalism began to decline as the war approached and with the declaration of war it virtually collapsed.

Revolutionary syndicalism may have died as a major force, but its influence continues to be felt. The famous assertion contained in the 1906 Charter of Amiens, when the CGT declared itself to be independent of 'parties and sects', still has a powerful appeal and is seen in the formal political autonomy to which all major unions have persistently clung. Even when the relationships between unions and parties have in practice been close – and the post-Second World War domination of the CGT by the Communists is the most obvious example – independence has still been proclaimed.

From 1914 the CGT's position largely paralleled that of the SFIO, in that general support was given to the government but voices of dissension were increasingly heard as the war dragged on. By 1918 fierce rivalries existed and the seeds of a split were sown. Divisions were exacerbated and came to the surface when the union leadership hesitated in its attitude to a series of strikes in 1919-20. Léon Jouhaux, the General Secretary, was severely criticised by the two principal minority elements in the union. One of these was made up of those who remained sympathetic to pre-war syndicalist aims. The other drew support from the Russian revolution and, after the division in the SFIO in 1920, from the newly established French Communist Party.

Arising from these developing tensions, and with the addition of a third element, there were from the early 1920s three main strands of industrial unionism competing for attention. In time, each was to establish itself and two are still, though in a greatly modified form, the dominating voices of unionism in the present day.

(1) *Communist*. At the 1921 Congress of the CGT at Lille a split corresponding to that of the SFIO at Tours occurred. On this occasion, however, the roles were reversed and the pro-Comintern faction, which was grouped around the two dissenting currents noted above, found itself in the minority. A principal reason for this was that Comintern's demand for Communist penetration of trade unions was so obviously at variance with the now enshrined tradition of union independence. Following its defeat the minority withdrew and in 1922 established the Communist inspired *Confédération Générale du Travail Unitaire* (CGTU).

Despite the vote at Lille the CGTU initially took with it over half the CGT's membership: 500,000 to 373,400.[5] But as Communist control of the CGTU became more apparent events took a similar turn to those in the political parties. The syndicalist element withdrew to leave a 'purer' but much smaller organisation. By 1935 the CGTU counted only around 200,000 members, whereas the CGT had three times that figure. But this in no way diminished the Communist ambition to dominate French trade unionism, and in a series of manoeuvres between 1936 and 1946 significant progress was made in that direction. In 1936 the CGT and CGTU merged and then, facilitated by the mood of Left wing co-operation which was fostered by the Popular Front and the Resistance, the Communists proceeded to penetrate the now expanded CGT from the inside. Although their efforts were interrupted between 1939 and 1943, when they were excluded from the union because of the international situation and the attitude of the PCF, the takeover was completed during and immediately after the Liberation. Capitalising on the administrative disorganisation which had resulted from the banning of unions by the Vichy Regime, an explosion in trade union membership which exceeded even that of the Popular Front period, and post-Resistance popularity, the Communists controlled 80 per cent of the vote at the CGT's first post-war Congress in April 1946. Since then they have dominated the decision-making organs of what has continued to be the largest trade union. They have used that dominance to pursue policies and strategies which, on the whole, have fitted in with the requirements of the PCF.

(2) *Democratic Socialists.* From its quick recovery after the 1922 split until the late 1930s, when it began to fall under Communist influence, the CGT, in political terms, was dominated by a democratic socialist view of the world. It was strongly influenced, too, by the spirit of Amiens which, despite the passing of the revolutionary syndicalist phase, continued to loom large: the Confederation was careful to maintain its distance from political parties.

The 1946 takeover by the Communists inevitably created strains within the CGT and the encouragement given to the strike movement that developed in 1947, which soon had clear political overtones, proved too much for those leaders who were steeped in a tradition of moderation and non-partisanship. They resigned in December 1947 and in the following April founded the *Confédération Générale du Travail-Force Ouvrière* (CGT-FO; later commonly referred to simply as the FO). As befits an organisation whose establishment was assisted by the SFIO and (it later became known) American trade union and CIA funds, it soon settled down and has subsequently practised a policy of stiff anti-Communism and cautious social reformism.

(3) *Christian Democratic.* In 1919 various Catholic trade unions amalgamated to form the *Confédération Française des Travailleurs Chrétiens* (CFTC). Initially its influence on economic and political life was limited. There were a number of reasons for this. Firstly, its membership was relatively small: it numbered only around 150,000 at the time of its formation. Secondly, it represented less militant sections of the workforce than the other two main unions. Although it did have some industrial strength, notably amongst textile workers and railwaymen, its main support was drawn from lower middle-class occupations, with women members being unusually prominent. Thirdly, its confessional base induced a distaste for most forms of direct action. Strongly influenced by its paternalistic, social Catholic origins, it encouraged co-operation between *capital* and *travail* and recoiled from the language of class conflict. Finally, each of these three factors encouraged the secular unions to dismiss it with a suspicion which bordered on contempt.

After the war the CFTC became more influential. Its membership increased, to surpass that of the FO, and it developed more vigorous, even socialist, perspectives. From the early 1950s it developed a particular interest in 'democratic planning'. (This has emerged as an important element in contemporary socialist thinking in France.) It also became less confessional, a process which was seen in its increasingly uneasy relationship with its party counterpart, the MRP. These developments led to more co-operation with other unions, in particular the FO, but also the 'white-collar' union the *Confédération Générale des Cadres* (CGC), and the main teachers' union the *Fédération de l'Education Nationale*. (The FEN also derived from the schism in the CGT; the teachers had insisted on their autonomy.)

Each of these processes – secularisation, increasing socialism, co-operation with other unions – contributed to a process which led to the CFTC abandoning its clerical trappings at an Extraordinary Congress held in November 1964. It renamed itself the *Confédération Française Démocratique du Travail* (CFDT) and from thereon began to develop an increasingly close, though still not openly avowed, relationship with the SFIO. The determined confessionalists for their part, who had still numbered as many as one third at the 1964 Congress, declined in influence. They retained in the 'new' CFTC only about eight per cent of their pre-1964 following.[6]

With the foundation of the CFDT the present structure of trade

unionism was set. There are three major confederations: the CGT, the
FO and the CFDT. They share a broad sympathy for the Left but, as
will be shown below, differ in many important respects.

IDEOLOGY AND STRATEGY

The trade unions were as surprised as the political parties by the
'events' of May 1968. The benefits of post-war prosperity, from which
the working class had benefitted (though not as much as the *professions liberales* or *cadres*), seemed to be called into question, and the
unions were unsure and divided as to how they should react. Political
indecision coupled with the re-emergence of anarcho-syndicalist sentiments made the spreading strike movement seem like impending
revolution to many trade union leaders. Ten million workers went on
strike, 150 million working days were lost, and hundreds of factories
were occupied. Yet the unions themselves had but a marginal role in
bringing the situation about, the impetus being largely spontaneous.
The difficulty which the union leadership had in coming to terms with
the upheaval was most clearly seen in the confusion of the CGT. Ever
distrustful of spontaneity it went to great lengths to try and bring the
situation under its control, but at the same time it did not want to be
seen as a reactionary force dampening workers' demands. Its way out
was to negotiate, in the Grenelle agreements, a package of social and
economic reforms with government and employers. Yet, to their
astonishment, union leaders found these rejected by the workers –
Georges Séguy, the General Secretary of the CGT, even found himself
booed when he proposed their acceptance to the workers occupying
the Renault factory at Boulogne-Billancourt.

The unions inevitably were shaken by the experience of May 1968
and this fed through into subsequent policy and strategy. The CFDT
was the most affected. Having been already sympathetic to some of
the 'new' ideas which were expressed during the 'events' –
decentralisation, profit sharing, workers on management boards etc. –
it found its predispositions reinforced by an influx of support from
many of those who had been most active in May. Its 1970 Congress
saw it refer, for the first time, to *'la lutte des classes'* and to its
membership of the 'socialist family'. Three pillars of this new
socialism were listed: collectivisation of the means of production and
exchange, democratic planning, and *autogestion*. These last two,
which have since been further developed, have sharply marked off the

CFDT from the CGT and the FO. In its own words, its ideological framework is not only socialist but is a *'socialisme autogestionnaire'*. (Briefly, this means that economic decisions, whenever and wherever possible, should be taken at plant level by management boards supervised by elected works councils.) The overall direction of the economy should be guided by a system of democratic national planning in which the aims should be a more prosperous, more egalitarian and more socially just society.

The CGT has also been infected by such ideas but much less so and much less willingly. *Autogestion* began to appear as part of its language from the mid-1970s and the virtues of decentralisation were also discovered, but on the whole its vision of the socialist future remains, at heart, that of a society characterised by centralised political and economic control. The CGT's vision of the pathway to socialism has also remained traditional and Communist inspired. CGT Communist leaders still defer, though not explicitly and not without some confusion as to its implications, to the classic Leninist model, whereby the union is the mass organisation of the working class and the Party is the 'superior' directing vanguard. Since the early 1960s this 'dual strategy' of Communism has seen a clearer division of labour than formerly existed between the PCF and CGT, with the latter now concentrating more than it did (though still by no means exclusively) on strictly trade union matters. It is intended that by focussing in this way on economic and social issues the CGT will be in a better position to expose the contradictions of capitalism, to mobilise the working class when that is necessary and gain specific advantages for its members.

The FO was also affected by May 1968 and its repercussions, but in a rather different and less direct way. It has become even less socialist, less partisan and more moderate. This is partly because after 1968 it lost many of its radical and committed Socialist elements. In addition, the general allegiance which FO leaders felt for the old SFIO has not been transferred to the new PS. They are suspicious of the new currents which have entered the reconstituted Party and also dislike the links between the PS and the PCF. The FO now makes a great virtue of its non-politicisation. It frequently criticises the CGT ('and the Communist Party – which is the same thing'[7]) and the CFDT (which has become a *'parti syndical'*[8]) for meddling too much in politics. They are accused of stepping outside their proper role of defending the economic interests of their members. 'Complete liberty' and 'complete independence', the central themes of the image the FO projects, in its case match up to the truth. It concentrates its energies on bargaining with employers and the state. In so doing it pursues a cautious and reformist line, by which it is much less likely than the CGT and the CFDT to resort to direct action and much more likely to co-operate with business and the administration.

The three principal industrial trade unions, therefore, are guided by contrasting ideological perspectives. This inevitably gives a sharp edge to the competition which exists between them for influence and membership and makes joint action difficult to mount. Since 1966 there have been a number of agreements between unions, notably 'unity in action' pacts between the CGT and CFDT, but they have been on a restricted list of trade union grievances and have had a very limited effect. The measure of the difficulties in forging co-operation was no more clearly seen than in 1979; the CGT, CFDT and FO could not even reach a general agreement when widespread and militant disturbances occurred, following an announcement by the government that it proposed to reduce the labour force in the steel industry by one quarter.

Much of the antagonism between the unions stems from the differing extents to which they wish to emphasise political, in addition to economic, strategies. As we have seen, the FO defines its role in a restrictive way and prefers to leave party politics aside. Not only is it suspicious of the individual parties of the Left, but it has always been reserved in its attitude to the *Union de la Gauche* and it even refused openly to support Mitterrand in the 1974 presidential election. Almost at the other extreme the CGT, conditioned by its close relationship with the PCF, does not disguise its belief that social struggle has a political as well as an economic side. Union officials and militants are ever prepared to try and use the workplace and industrial disputes to mobilise the workforce and raise their political and class consciousness.[9] The CFDT's position lies somewhere between that of the 'non-political' FO and the 'politicised' CGT. Article 1 of its Statutes categorically states that '[the CFDT] must distinguish its responsibilities from those of political groups and it must maintain an independence of action in relation to the State, the parties and the Church'. This a-politicism has been reinforced by the continuing influence of the syndicalist spirit and also by important policy differences with the political parties. (It is especially irritated by what it sees as the excessive reliance by the PCF and PS on 'statism'). At the same time the CFDT has recognised the importance of 'political action in the social struggle'. It has therefore sought a balance between, on the one hand, exercising a general political influence and, on the other, not becoming too closely involved in specific party activities. In the period leading up to 1978 legislative elections this led it to support the *Union de la Gauche,* but not to become too closely identified with any of its constituent units. (Following the breakdown between the parties in September 1977 the CFDT put forward its own proposals on nationalisations, which, falling between the PS and PCF positions, were seen by many observers as a possible basis for compromise.) In an attempt to resolve its dilemma – of wishing to avoid being seen as a political annex, whilst at the same time exerting a political role – the CFDT has periodically proposed, since 1974, a broadened and reconstituted *Union de la Gauche,* which will bring together not only all the parties of the Left but also the *forces autogestionnaires.* This *Union des Forces Populaires* is conceived as 'the union of all the forces of the Left which will establish, on the basis of class, a convergence of their strategies, in order to permit them to bring together the conditions for the passage to socialism'.[10] The project has made no headway.

The politicisation of union strategies inevitably creates problems when the political hopes and expectations are unfulfilled. Having supported the *Union de la Gauche* and reinforced it themselves through 'united action', the defeat of the Left in the 1978 legislative elections inevitably led in both the CFDT and CGT to recriminations and to some reconsideration of their political sympathies. Prior to and at both the 40th Congress of the CGT in November 1978 and the 38th Congress of the CFDT in May 1979, the *dynamique unitaire* was called into question and demands were made for less political involvement and more autonomous union activity. In the CGT, despite soothing statements from leaders, and well leaked (too well?) information that Séguy and others have battled within the PCF for more union autonomy, it seems unlikely that the protests will bring about any significant change in strategy. The links with the PCF are too close. The more flexible CFDT, however, which since the 1978 elections has declared its intention to be 'more syndicalist and less political', can be expected to pursue a more circumspect political strategy in the future.

SIZE AND COMPOSITION

Exact figures on the size of the membership of individual unions are not available. This is because the unions themselves, when they give figures at all, are inclined to overestimate their strength, by including in their totals many who have not paid their membership dues and many who are retired and who are not, therefore, full members. Bearing this in mind the CGT probably *really* numbers no more than two million fully paid-up members, the CFDT around one million, the FO about 700,000, the Fédération de l'Education Nationale (FEN) just under 500,000, and the CFTC at best 200,000.

Another way of looking at relative union strengths is through the elections to bodies on which they are formally represented. The most useful of these are the *comités d'entreprise* (works committees) and, since 1979, the *conseils de prud'hommes* (industrial tribunals). The conclusions drawn from these elections can only be tentative, since non-union members, but not all of the workforce, can vote. Nonetheless, they do serve as a useful indication of the general standing of the individual unions.

In recent years, in the elections to the *comités d'entreprises* (or *'élections professionnelles* as they are officially known), there has been a general decline in the support for the CGT and a slight rise in support for the other unions. The figures in Table 9.1 are an amalgam of different voting colleges, but even in the college most favourable to the CGT, which is made up principally of working-class and middle-class categories, the CGT's vote has declined; from 51.5 per cent in 1967 to 43.5 per cent in 1977.[11]

Table 9.1   Elections professionnelles

	1967 (%)	1977 (%)
CGT	45.0	37.4
CFDT	17.7	20.2
FO	7.5	9.0
CGC	3.9	5.4
CFTC	2.1	3.0
Others and non-union candidates	23.8	25.0

In the 1979 elections to the *conseils de prud'hommes* (in which a much larger proportion of the working population was entitled to vote than in the *élections professionnelles*), the results were rather better for the CGT, as Table 9.2 shows. But the other unions also gained, the FO most of all. This was because the campaign and voting system was organised along union lines and the more moderate and less political unions benefitted most from the votes of non-unionists.

Table 9.2   Elections to the Conseils de Prud'hommes 1979
(Electoral College for Salaried Employees and Workers)
Total Number of Eligible Voters: 12,179,431
Abstentions: 4,467,955 (36.7%)
Votes: 7,443,378 (61.1%)

	Industry %	Commerce %	Agriculture %	Diverse %	Total workers and employees %	Middle management (encadrement) %	Overall total %
CGT	50.2	42.4	31.0	35.3	45.5	16.8	42.5
CFDT	22.4	23.4	33.8	26.9	23.7	18.0	23.1
FO	15.7	19.7	23.0	22.2	17.9	14.0	17.5
CFTC	5.8	7.5	7.5	10.8	7.0	6.8	7.0
CGC	1.8	1.7	0.4	0.8	1.6	36.0	5.0
Others	4.1	5.3	4.2	4.0	4.3	8.3	4.7

Note   Large parts of the public sector, including education, did not participate in the elections. On past trends these would be likely to favour the
FEN and the FO.

For an explanation of the role and history of the Conseil de Prud'hommes see *Le Monde*, 5 Dec. 1979.

In terms of particular areas of strength, the largest union, the CGT,
is naturally the most wide-ranging, with influence in virtually all
industrial and public sectors. Its greatest areas of support are
amongst the industrial working class, notably in iron and steel,
mining, building, electricity and public transport. The CFDT, though
not itself without influence in some areas of heavy industry, tends
rather more towards light industry and tertiary sector occupations.
(This is reflected in the fact that it has a higher proportion of women
members than the CGT – almost 50 per cent as opposed to the CGT's
one-third). The FO draws most of its support from the non-industrial
sector: banking and insurance, commerce, the civil service, and public
transport.

STRUCTURE AND ORGANISATION

Along with the other factors we have considered, the organisational
structure of the trade unions has also played its part in contributing to
their relative weakness. The CGT, CFDT and FO are all confederations and are, therefore, decentralised and subject to many divisions.

The institutional arrangements within the three main unions, while varying in details, are broadly similar. If we concentrate on the CGT, it can be seen from Figure 9.1 that power at the national level is theoretically exercised by four main bodies: the Congress, which meets every three years; the *Comité confédéral national* which meets about every six months; the *Commission exécutive* which meets every month; and the *Bureau confédéral* which meets at least once a week. As in most similar organisations the bodies which meet the most frequently, though nominally working within policies decided by the larger and more representatives bodies, in practice exercise much more power than the formal structure would suggest. This is especially the case in the CGT, where the centralising influence of the strong Communist presence in all directing organs (see below) is a powerful force.

Figure 9.1   Organisational structure of the CGT

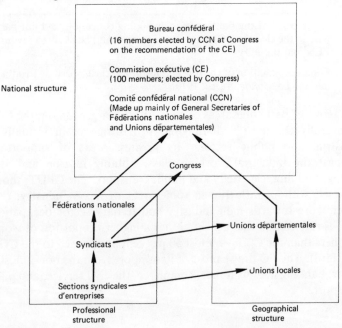

The unions are organised along both professional and geographical lines. The professional structure brings together workers in individual industries (as opposed to trades). The basic unit is the *syndicat* (which is comparable to the branch in Britain) and they are part of a *fédération* – of metal workers, miners, dockers etc. The geographical structure unites the *syndicats* within each confederation at local and departmental level. The main role of these *unions* is to try and co-ordinate activity and to act as a publicity agent for the confederation.

The most important consequence of this fractured structure is that united action, by even one confederation, let alone the union movement as a whole, is difficult to organise. On the one hand the confederations are dependent on the support of their constituent units. On the other hand the ideological divisions within particular industries – between the CGT, CFDT, and FO – means that more than one union is normally seeking to represent the same occupational groups. A common labour front, therefore, whether on demands, strategy or tactics, is usually not possible.

Even where a particular union is dominant (in relation to the others) in an industry or firm, its ability to act decisively in pursuing its objectives is still likely to be limited. For one thing all unions are poorly financed. This means they can afford few full time officers, with the result that co-ordination of activities at lower levels is often poor. Limited finance also puts restrictions on the sanctions that can be brought into play, because strike payments, where they are made, are minimal. (It is partly for this reason that go-slows, work-to-rules, short-term 'demonstration' strikes, are usually preferred to long protracted disputes.)

Another organisational limitation is that the industrial unions have poor control over their members. Loyalty to the union counts for little in itself and as a consequence union leaderships can never be sure in advance what the response will be if they call for industrial action. All they can be sure of is that attempts to pursue protracted national disputes – as opposed to short token protests – will probably be unsuccessful. Even below the national level, where union officials and militants are more closely in touch with the grass roots, strikes (which, incidentally, usually precede negotiations rather than follow them) are frequently initiated, not through the union organisation, but 'spontaneously' emerge and often spread from individual plants. Union officials almost invariably respond to such militancy by giving their official support, but this may not add up to very much in practice and it certainly does not mean that the union organisation automatically gains control of the situation.

RELATIONSHIPS BETWEEN THE POLITICAL PARTIES AND THE UNIONS

1. The Socialists

The emergence of the PS at the Congress of Epinay in 1971 had a significant effect in changing the nature of the relationship between

French Socialists and the trade union movement. Until 1971, as a result of a decision taken by the Conseil National of the SFIO in December 1957, Socialists were not allowed to join the CGT. This was because of its links with the PCF and its critical attitude to the Socialists. (It had severely attacked Mollet's 1956-7 government). This incompatibility rule was rejected by the new PS in the interests of trade union pluralism. The new Party committed itself to accepting the independent role of the unions and the primary role of political parties. But it also declared that 'it is the combination of political, syndical and democratic possibilities that will create the conditions for a change from one regime to another... .[12] The Party now obliges its members to join a trade union but it avoids expressing a preference and simply says they should 'belong to the trade union of their profession'.

The Epinay Congress also decided that it was important for the new Party to become influential in industry by setting up what were called *'sections d'entreprises'*. These factory branches of the PS were to remain distinct from the syndical organisations though inevitably the members of the *'sections d'entreprises'* would be trade unionists. In 1980 there were over 1300 of these *sections* in various industries including shipbuilding, electronics, chemicals and those areas which the Left wants to bring into public ownership, for example, insurance companies and banking. Whether the existence of the *sections* has furthered PS influence, or has merely reinforced it where it already existed, is unclear. What is not in doubt is that their existence has created problems for the Party. On the one hand, it has led to some tension with the CFDT who have seen the *sections* as an intrusion into their domain. On the other hand, it has contributed to Communist fears – in both the CGT and the PCF – that the PS is intent on becoming the dominant influence within the Left, including those working-class areas which the Communists regard as their special preserve.

Since 1971 the PS has increased its support amongst all trade unionists. It was claimed at the Party Congress at Grenoble in 1973 that 7 per cent of the CGT were PS members, 9.6 per cent of the FO, 18.3 per cent of the CFDT and 23.8 per cent of the FEN. Since then, and particularly since October 1974 when an influx of CFDT members boosted the Socialist Party's membership at the *Assises du Socialisme,* the PS has furthered its presence still more in the trade union movement.[13] As Tables 9.3 and 9.4 clearly show its influence is deep not only in the CFDT but also in the CGT, over one quarter of its members voting Socialist in the 1978 elections. It may also be assumed that a majority of FEN members and probably also FO vote for the PS.

The Socialist Party's influence within the union movement should not, of course, be exaggerated, given the Communist domination of the CGT and the 'non-political' preferences of the other unions. But nor should its importance be too readily discounted. The leaders of the three most prominent non-Communist unions are all members of the PS: Edmond Maire, CFDT; André Henry, FEN; André Bergeron, FO. It has become noticeable that even within the CGT the group *Pour l'Union,* animated by the prominent Socialist Pierre Joxe, has developed some influence. Two PS members are on the *Bureau confédèral* of the CGT, seven are on the 100-member *Commission Exécutive,* and they, along with other socialist activists, have been prominent in the internal criticisms that have been made of the CGT's leadership since March 1978. In the CFDT both the CERES and Rocard factions are influential, while Mauroy sympathisers are to be found in the FEN. Thus, as François Gault remarks: 'One cannot strictly speaking talk of the PS and the *syndicats;* one has to say the PS and the CGT, the PS and the CFDT....(etc.)'.[14]

2. The Communists

The relationship between the PCF and the CGT is, as we have seen, extremely close. Though the union has always insisted on its independence from the PCF it has in practice, for the most part, attempted to act as a classic 'transmission belt' for the Party. The claimed independence is little more than a formal organisational one.

Table 9.3   Voting intentions of CFDT and CGT members on the first ballot in the 1978 legislative elections

	CFDT (%)	CGT (%)
Communist Party	6 (23)	47 (63)
PSU and Extreme Left	6 (11)	4 (2)
Socialist Party	54 (36)	31 (28)
Left Wing Radicals	3	3
Ecologist Movement	7	2
Centrists	3 (15)	— (1)
Republican Party	11	3
Gaullist Party	1 (10)	2 (10)
No Response	9	8

Table 9.4   Confidence of CFDT and CGT members in the Parties of the Left

	CFDT (%)	CGT (%)
Socialist Party		
Great or some confidence	77	76
Little or no confidence	20	21
No opinion	3	3
Communist Party		
Great or some confidence	42	71
Little or no confidence	50	23
No opinion	8	6

Table 9.5   How CFDT and CGT members place themselves on the Left-Right scale

	CFDT (%)	CGT (%)
Extreme Left	6	5
Left	13	41
Centre-Left	48	37
Centre	21	9
Centre-Right	7	2
Right	2	1
Extreme Right	1	1
No opinion	2	4

Source of all three tables: Louis Harris poll, *Le Matin,* 27 and 28 Oct. 1977. The survey also contains a great deal of information on the background of CFDT and CGT members and their opinions on particular issues.
The figures in brackets in Table 9.3 are those from a post electoral survey by SOFRES on how people actually did vote. The discrepancies are doubtless explained by a combination of genuine changes between October 1977 and March 1978, and also the many problems and inaccuracies associated with sample surveys.

The overlap in personnel between the Party and the union is seen at all levels, from the lowest to the highest. In the factories the PCF cells and the CGT sections work very closely together. Georges Lavau goes so far as to say, 'The leaders of the Party cells and the leaders of the CGT sections are completely interchangeable: the two organisations operate in total harmony'.[15] At the intermediary CGT levels, every one of the secretaries of the *Unions départementales* is a Communist as are ninety per cent of the leaders of the *Fédérations*.[16] At the national Congresses of the CGT and the PCF the pattern of overlap is repeated. Thus at the 1979 PCF Congress it was officially reported that 1325 of the 1992 delegates had union responsibilities. Of these 1080 were active in the CGT, 21 in the CFDT, 171 in the FEN, and the remainder in specialised groups.[17] There was a similar situation at the 1978 Fortieth Congress of the CGT, with PCF members probably numbering around 75 per cent. When the candidates were declared for the *Commission Execution* – 127 for 100 places – the great majority were Communists; about 60 were subsequently elected.[18] In the highest executive organs there is also great mutual representation. Two members of the *Bureau Confédéral* of the CGT, General Secretary Georges Seguy and Henri Krasucki, have long sat on the Politbureau of the PCF and in 1979 they were joined by another leading CGT official, René le Guen (Secretary of *l'Union générale des ingénieurs cadres et techniciens CGT*). Two other *Bureau Confédéral* members, René Lomet and Michel Warcholak, are on the Central Committee of the PCF. On the *Bureau Confédéral* itself, eight of the sixteen members elected at the Fortieth Congress were also members of the PCF. Since the *Bureau* is elected by the Communist dominated *Comité confédéral national,* it is clear that PCF representation at this highest level is kept within bounds, and other 'sensibilities' are tolerated, for political and public relations purposes.

As Table 9.3 shows this Communist domination of the CGT's structure is not reflected in the electoral allegiance of the Union's members. Between one third and one half do not support the PCF. The presence of this substantial non-Communist element has not prevented the leadership, at crucial moments, from showing their Communist sympathies. This was especially so in the 1978 election campaign when Séguy departed from the traditional CGT practice of not explicitly recommending a PCF vote by playing a leading role in the Communist's campaign. He appeared at PCF rallies and, most brazenly of all, used the union's weekly magazine *La Vie ouvrière* (which is claimed to have a circulation of 250,000) to make his political preference clear. In his message to members in the edition immediately before the elections he did not, it is true, directly say 'Vote PCF', but he did, by supporting the Left whilst strongly attacking the PS, come as close as made little difference to advocating a Communist vote.[19] He was no less open in 1981.

Accusations and protests that the CGT is too partisan are denied by officials. The proof of its independence, it is claimed, is seen in its organisational autonomy and in its complete control over its own policies. Suggestions that the union ever takes orders from the PCF are dismissed as absurd. It is admitted that most of the CGT leaders do view the workers' interests as being more firmly represented in the PCF than in the PS but that, it is claimed, should not be taken as evidence of collusion. For it is not parties which are being compared with one another but each party with the CGT.

The extent to which the CGT is the privileged partner of the PCF is emphasised by the relationship which the Party maintains with other trade unions. There are areas of Communist influence, notably in the FEN, but on the whole exchanges are frosty. Suspicions run both ways. The unions and especially, of course, the FO are ever on their guard against possible Communist infiltration and ultimate Communist intentions. The PCF in its turn views the unions in a no less wary way. It suspects their social reformist and Socialist leanings, their more heterogeneous and less industrialised membership and, above all, *their* intentions of wanting to reduce Communist influence. As the CGT is more than twice as large as the CFDT and FO combined, more representative of the working class, and a firm ally, it is hardly surprising that it receives by far the most attention from the Party.

RELATIONS WITH GOVERNMENT AND EMPLOYERS

The various factors we have discussed above have each played their part in limiting the impact of trade unionism in its relations with government and employers. Organised labour has, for the most part, been neither flexible nor strong enough to persuade or coerce those it has sought to influence. The traditional resistance of the French state and French businessmen to threats to their authority has been reinforced and assisted by the low membership, the internal divisions, the ideological ridigity, the organisational fragility, and the Leftism of the union movement.

The weakness of unionism is most apparent in the limited and somewhat uncertain nature of collective bargaining procedures for determining wage levels and conditions of work. Although there has been a considerable extension in such bargaining since the mid-1950s, and more particularly since the 1968 crisis, it is still far from being established on a regular and institutionalised basis. Over and above the general factors we have already considered a number of specific reasons exist for this. Firstly, the state and private employers, despite a 'liberalisation' in recent years, continue to cling to many of their traditional attitudes and habits. Faced with a weak union movement they are by no means averse to by-passing unions, especially the CGT, when it is convenient and possible. Only in crisis conditions, such as occurred in 1968 or, to a lesser degree, over the steel closures in 1979, do they feel sufficiently threatened to have to directly react to whatever pressures unions can mount against them. The fact is that, compared with most similar countries, French unions have very little with which they can either threaten the authorities or alternatively offer them in the way of bargaining tools. The unions do not 'control' the working class and therefore they are not potential guarantors of social stability. Nor do they have much to provide in the form of professional expertise or privileged information about areas of social and economic activity. Because of their limited resources the unions normally are not even able to properly prepare themselves for those forums where they do meet with representatives of the state and business. Secondly, the unions themselves view many aspects of collective bargaining with suspicion. The CGT and CFDT in particular, who each in their way want to transform the economic system and not simply improve the position of the workers within it, usually take a very suspicious view of 'trade-off' negotiations with employers, or tripartite bargaining in which the state, directly or indirectly, make its presence felt. Collective agreements which could be seen as either integrating labour more fully into the capitalist system via, for example, productivity clauses, are regarded with particular reserve. The only serious attempts made under the Fifth Republic to establish a semi-formal process of tripartite bargaining and discussion – the *politique contractuelle* pioneered by the prime minister Chaban-Delmas between 1969 and 1972 – foundered in large part on union, and especially CGT, hostility. Thirdly, collective bargaining is hindered by the competition between the unions. In particular, the concern of the CGT to maintain its relative dominance exacerbates its already existing tendency to act as if it must be, and must be seen to be, highly aggressive and unconciliatory in its relations with employers. Toughness is part of the image it projects of being the only union which *really* defends the interests of the working class. In practice this often means a lack of pragmatism which, to non-communist eyes at least, is sometimes actually counter-productive to the interests of its members. (It was noticeable, for example, in 1979 that many CGT members accepted the redundancy terms offered in the contracting steel industry, which their own union had rejected but which the CFDT and FO had accepted).[20]

Lack of regular, institutionalised contact with the state and employers on a quasi-corporate basis could, of course, in some circumstances be a sign not only of the independence but also of the vigour and strength of a union movement. This is not the case in France. For the limited development of such procedures means that many crucial decisions affecting the wages and working conditions of the labour force are taken with only slight reference to the unions. Moreover, when collective bargaining does take place the role of the unions is still often limited. This is because national agreements – which are usually on an industry wide basis, though since the mid-1960s there has been a growth in multi-industry agreements – usually only set minimum conditions. These are then backed up by more specific arrangements, especially on wages, at regional, local, and plant levels. But it is precisely at the lower levels that the unions are often at their weakest and collective negotiations are most resisted by employers. (Despite legislation in 1968 giving a legal basis to trade union activities at the plant level or the individual firm.) The consequence is that the *real* – as opposed to minimum – wages and conditions of labour are frequently not determined as a result of negotiations between employers and unions but are either imposed by employers, or are a result of negotiations between employers and bodies such as plant committees or strike committees over which the unions have at best only tenuous control. It is doubtless in large part because of this weakness of unions as bargaining agents that disparities of income are so wide in France and that the lower income groups receive a smaller proportion of real disposable income than their counterparts in all other advanced industrial democratic countries.[21]

The collective bargaining pattern has been reflected in the minimal role unions have played in the more general policy development and decision-making processes of the political system. Unions, it is true, are represented on a whole range of official and semi-official bodies. These include boards of nationalised industries, arbitration bodies in the public sector, the national and regional economic councils, and the varied range of consultative and advisory agencies, which cluster around the social and economic ministries of most developed states. All the evidence suggests, however, that the influence exercised by the unions through these bodies has been marginal and that the governments of the Right have seen their usefulness primarily in public relations terms.

FUTURE DEVELOPMENTS

The trade union movement in France has traditionally exerted only a limited influence on the working conditions of the labour force and has had only a marginal impact on public policy. Though authorities in the 1960s and 1970s became increasingly prepared to listen to union representatives this was principally because it was considered to be more necessary to be seen to be doing so. On the whole it continued to be only when there was an apparent threat to social control, through widespread strike action, that the state and employers were prepared to make real concessions.

It is clear that with the Left now in office there will be a change in the relationship between the state and the trade union movement. Some senior union officials have actually been given posts in the new government and administration. Most notably André Henry has been appointed Minister of Leisure. The list of social measures which were announced soon after Mitterrand's election, following consultations with union leaders, also bears witness to the change in government-union relations that may be anticipated. Amongst the reforms were increases in the minimum wage, in pensions, and in family, disability and lodgings allowances. Increased consultation and co-operation with the unions, moreover, will not be important to the new political decision makers merely for reasons of sentiment, personal friendships or ideological affinity – though each of these will play a part. On the practical level a more important political and economic role for the unions will be necessary if the Socialists are to make real headway with their proposals to develop democratic and decentralised planning. Even within individual firms – especially in the publicly owned industries and those scheduled for nationalisation – the trade union movement may be called upon to help the political Left to implement and administer its projected policies.

It is too soon to predict the consequences of the new situation for the internal functioning of the trade unions. What is clear, however, is that such changes as may take place will be strongly conditioned by certain persisting features of the French trade union movement. In particular, the unions will doubtless continue formally to abide by their statutes which preclude any real overlap between union and overtly political activity.

Postscript: The Left and the Assumption of Power

THE PRESIDENTIAL PERSPECTIVE: THE SOCIALISTS

The Metz Congress of 1979, where Mitterrand, in alliance with CERES, retained control of the Party, did little to settle the personal and ideological differences which since the 1978 election defeat had made the PS look increasingly like the loosest of coalitions. When, in 1980, the Socialists began the process of selecting their presidential candidate the struggle for power was as sharp as ever.

The rivalry between the two principal potential candidates – Mitterrand and Rocard – was unendingly dwelt upon by the media. Not surprisingly this began to have a debilitating effect upon the Party and it suffered a decline in membership for the first time since its reconstitution in 1971. The internal struggle none the less persisted almost to the end of the year. There were two principal reasons for this.

Firstly, both candidates had reason to believe they could win the nomination. Mitterrand was strong within the organisation itself and, as the voting for the motions at the Metz Congress had shown, enjoyed considerable support within the federations (see Table 3.1). Rocard, on the other hand, though less popular in the federations, and in a less advantageous position to use the Party structure to help him in his campaign as a result of his minority position since Metz, could point to the many opinion polls which showed him enjoying wide public support.[1] This popularity appeared to be based not only amongst sections of Left-wing opinion but also in the moderate Right. His social-democratic image (which Chevènement called *la gauche americaine*) alienated the PCF, and was not very popular in areas of traditional Communist influence, but it clearly offered a measure of reassurance to those 'natural' Centrist and Right-wing voters whom the Left would need if it was ever to win a national election.

Secondly, Mitterrand consistently refused to give in to those in the Party who demanded that he take up the challenge of the presidential election by formally announcing his willingness to be a candidate. Having fought two previous campaigns he was resolved to postpone making known his decision for as long as possible. This was not only because of the pressures of campaigning itself but also, and more importantly, because it was in his interests to shield himself for as long as possible from the concentrated attacks of the Right, the PCF and internal Party rivals.

Finally, in November 1980, Mitterrand made it known that he intended to seek the nomination. Rocard, who had promised the Metz Congress that he would not stand if Mitterrand was resolved to do so, then withdrew his candidacy. Likewise, Chevènement, who had announced that he would be prepared to put himself forward rather than allow Rocard a free run, immediately gave Mitterrand his full support.

The Extraordinary Congress which had to be called under Party rules to choose formally the candidate and endorse his programme (which it was his privilege to draw up) was held in January at Créteil. With only one candidate it was naturally a formality and the mood was, in consequence, much more unified and relaxed than it had been at the divided Metz Congress. The results from the federations showed that Mitterrand received the support of 83.64 per cent of the Party's membership: a figure which was significantly greater than the joint Mitterrand-CERES vote at Metz, but which denoted that a minority continued to prefer an alternative candidate.[2]

Having thus been officially designated Mitterrand resigned from his official functions within the Party in order to place himself firmly within a presidential perspective. On his recommendation Lionel Jospin was unanimously elected the Party's new First Secretary by the *Comité Directeur*.

The close ally of the PS, the MRG, was divided over whether to present its own candidate in the presidential elections. Many of the Party's most prominent figures, including eight of its ten deputies, were opposed to an MRG candidate. They argued that the very nature of a presidential campaign would result in their candidate underperforming and this could put the very future of the Party in doubt: far better to back the PS nominee. Michel Crépeau, the MRG leader, argued almost the reverse case. In his view the Party ran a greater risk of contributing to its own gradual demise, and becoming little more than a barely distinguishable element within the PS, if it did not designate its own flag-bearer. An MRG candidate, in his view, was necessary in order to demonstrate that there was a third element within the Left: *'la gauche realiste'*. He acknowledged that the case for a separate candidate would be weakened were the PS to choose Rocard, but after Mitterrand had been chosen he pressed his candidacy and won a clear majority, by 771 votes to 157, at an Extraordinary Party Congress in February.

THE PRESIDENTIAL PERSPECTIVE: THE COMMUNISTS

That the PCF would present its own candidate in the presidential elections was a logical consequence of its calling into question the strategy of *Union de la Gauche*. But the post-September 1977 hard-line stance had created difficulties for the Party and these were still being experienced, and to some extent were even being exacerbated, as the elections began to loom.

A central difficulty was continuing internal disillusionment and dissatisfaction with the post-1977 strategy and, as a result, continuing opposition to the leadership. Moreover, the opposition was not restricted to those who had protested from 1978 onwards but was constantly supplemented by new voices of protest. Some of these voices brought different emphases to the nature of the opposition. For example, many critics of the leadership sought to build or maintain bridges with the other elements of the Left. This was most notably seen in the involvement of many active PCF members in the *Union dans les luttes* which was launched in December 1979 as an attempt to bring together, originally by signing a petition, sympathisers from all sections of left-wing opinion.[3] Another approach was seen in February 1981 when 60 PCF office-holders, or former office-holders, issued a manifesto in which they protested against the overly working-class and sectarian line of the Party. They claimed this prevented the PCF from playing its true role of *'animateur du mouvement de masse'*.

The leadership's reaction to such continued opposition was twofold. The first, which it might almost be thought was designed to fan the flames, was to deny that there had been any change of direction at all. Spokesmen constantly affirmed that the Communist course remained true not only to the Twenty-Third but also to the

Twenty-Second Congress. Secondly, an increasingly oppressive line was taken against opponents. At the lower levels this firmer stance was seen in the way many Party workers and local officials, amongst whom there was a certain malaise as a result of the post-1977 strategy, were replaced because they were considered to be ill-suited to carry out the work of the Party under the new conditions. Those who had joined in the 1968-77 period were particularly vulnerable and a considerable number were replaced by members who had entered since the breakdown of the programmatic alliance with the other parties of the Left. At the higher levels, also, individuals were removed from official posts and the principle of 'publicised' exclusions again began to be accepted. Some of the more prominent intellectuals, such as Jean Elleinstein, Jean Kéhayan and Etienne Balibar found themselves particular targets. In November 1980, for example, the Central Committee ratified the expulsion of Kéhayan at the request of the federal committee of the *Bouches du Rhône* for having published a book in which he attacked Marchais.[4]

Such a firm line from the leadership made it all the more difficult to mobilise Party support for the presidential campaign. In June 1980 the Central Committee announced that the Party's campaign had begun and that thenceforward all Party activity should be seen in that context. The announcement, however, met with considerable internal dissent, it being widely claimed that there had been no consultation with the rank and file and that none of the lower levels were being given any real opportunity for discussing who the candidate might be. Over and above this, the publication and promotion in September 1980 of a book, *L'Espoir au present*, by Marchais, gave rise to broader criticism because it had been published without consultation within the Party.[5] The consequence of all this was that there were difficulties in distributing the book, despite bold sales claims in *L'Humanité*. This was also the case with a new magazine, *Révolution*, which was launched in 1980 and which was aimed at the dwindling 'intellectual' membership.

Marchais was officially designated as the PCF presidential candidate at a National Conference in October 1980. This made his the first of the major candidatures to be announced and this early start was used by the PCF to leave the electorate in little doubt as to its intentions in the campaign. The main priority was not so much to win the presidency – it was realised that was impossible – but rather to consolidate the Party within the Left. This had two aspects. Firstly, Marchais should gain a good first ballot vote: according to

Politbureau member André Lajoinie anything less than 20 per cent would be unacceptable. Secondly, though this was not made explicit, many (and perhaps most) PCF leaders did not feel it to be in their interest for Mitterrand to win on the second ballot. Such an eventuality, particularly if it was achieved primarily on the basis of a large first ballot vote for the PS candidate, would further unbalance the Left to the disadvantage of the Communists and could also serve as a base for further Socialist growth.

THE PRESIDENTIAL CAMPAIGN

Although bitter polemics continued to be exchanged between the PS and the PCF throughout 1980 and up to the very night of the first ballot of the presidential elections in April 1981, public opinion polls, local elections and parliamentary elections all indicated that a candidate of the Left could win. In part this arose from the fact that despite the quarrelling between the parties themselves a desire for unity remained strong amongst voters of the Left. This was no more clearly seen than in seven parliamentary by-elections which were held at the end of 1980, two of which the PS won from the UDF and one of which the RPR won from the UDF. The transfer of votes to PS candidates on the second ballot by the Communists worked extremely well despite only half-hearted official PCF support. (There were no second ballot PCF candidates). Even in Aveyron, where the PCF leadership called for abstention on the second ballot – because the candidate of the Left belonged to the MRG – Communist voters largely ignored their Party's official recommendation.[6] In part too the Left had some cause for optimism in the unpopularity of certain government policies, in the antipathy which sections of the Right's electorate felt towards Giscard d'Estaing and the Gaullist leader Jacques Chirac, and in the feeling which many observers detected and which public opinion polls highlighted of a general desire for change. (One major survey conducted shortly before the elections showed a majority of the electorate believed that in seven years' time they would be better off under Mitterrand than under Giscard d'Estaing: in every social category Mitterrand obtained a more favourable response.[7]

Mitterrand's campaign, with which all sections of the Party were associated, was based on a strategy which was very similar to that which Rocard had proposed to the Metz Congress. He sought to strike a position which kept him firmly established as the main candidate of the Left but which also made him attractive (or at least not unreassuring) to Centrist and disillusioned Right-wing voters. This led him, as in 1974, to appeal to the electorate not as a party leader but as an alternative President who had the interests of the whole of the French people at heart: in other words he attempted to go beyond the more sectarian limits of parliamentary elections. Whilst reaffirming his socialist convictions and his adhesion to the fundamental principles of the Left, he glossed over those areas of the *Projet Socialiste* which were most likely to disturb moderate voters. He even made an attempt to put himself in the tradition of de Gaulle by criticising Giscard d'Estaing's foreign policy for not being sufficiently assertive and causing France to lose some of its grandeur; he also reminded the electorate that it was during and after the Liberation, when de Gaulle had been Prime Minister, that most nationalisations had taken place.

Calculating that the PCF would not risk withholding its support from him on the second ballot (because most Communist voters would support him anyway) Mitterrand's attempt to appeal beyond the Left's 'natural' constituency also led him to take a very firm line with the Communists. The question of whether Communists would participate in government would, he stated, depend on the outcome of the legislative elections that would follow his dissolution of the National Assembly. Even if conditions were then favourable to the entry of Communists into government their appointment would be conditional on the PCF ceasing to attack the PS and also on the Party modifying its attitude on such issues as Afghanistan, Poland, and the range and pace of social and economic reforms.

In common with the PS, the PCF was not content to simply retain its existing support – though that was its prime aim – but also wanted to reach a wider audience. In sharp contrast to the *ouverture* of Mitterrand, however, Marchais' appeal was within much narrower confines: he looked to the extreme Left and to left-wing Socialists, claiming that only the PCF was *really* committed to *fundamental* change. The themes developed by the PCF's General Secretary concentrated on such matters as the continuing reality of the class struggle, the bankruptcy of government economic policies, the inadequacies of Mitterrand's alternatives, and the iniquities of the EEC. More controversially he emphasised his Party's criticisms of the fact that so many immigrant families lived alongside 'native' French workers who themselves were suffering from increasing unemployment and a fall in living standards. Though this near-racism clearly enjoyed some support amongst the unskilled working class, who were ready to accept an easily identifiable scapegoat for their problems, it shocked many people both inside and outside the Party and brought forth trenchant accusations that the PCF was grasping for support in an almost wholly unprincipled manner.

To further the PCF claim that only it offered real and radical change for France attacks on the PS remained unrelenting. They added up to the charge that, if circumstances were favourable, the Socialists would not hesitate to govern with the Right and continue with the policies of the existing government. This assessment of PS inclinations was used as part of the justification for the demands, which were continually heard, that there should be PCF ministers if Mitterrand were elected. Only by there being Communists in government would wholesale social and economic reforms be guaranteed, though even then 'social struggles' would be a necessary complementing force. The spectre was thus raised, undoubtedly in large part to ensure Mitterrand would not be elected on the second ballot, of the PCF 'governing with the Socialists and struggling with the workers'. It might be said that an indirect and ironical effect of the PCF's continual attempts to present Mitterrand as untrustworthy, and its association of the PS with 'the other parties of the Right', was to confirm Mitterrand in his campaign strategy and to reinforce his standing amongst moderate voters.

The presidential campaign also provided an opportunity for the smaller parties of the Left to promote and receive publicity for their policies.

Of these parties the one which was most in the mainstream, the MRG, set itself the most ambitious task. Notwithstanding the fact that his candidature did not enjoy wholehearted Party support Crépeau optimistically hoped his vote would be large enough to persuade Mitterrand to adopt some of the ideas set out in the manifesto which the MRG had published in June 1980 – *l'Avenir en face*. The role of smaller parties, according to Crépeau, was to 'give the others a push' and the particular contribution of his candidacy was to offer 'the realistic and human dimension' that hitherto the Left had lacked. The problem with his candidacy, however, was that elections in the 1970s had shown that either there was no call for such a dimension or the electorate did not particularly associate it with the MRG whose ten deputies owed their seats in large part to first ballot electoral deals with the PS. Moreover, since Crépeau made it clear in the campaign that he was *'un allié et un partenaire'* of Mitterrand, and would support him on the second ballot, there was little incentive for electors to vote for him on the first ballot. Such incentive as there was was reduced even further – and this applied to the candidatures of Marchais and the two far-Left candidates too – when in the closing weeks of the campaign it came to be feared that Chirac could conceivably beat Mitterrand into third place. This *'effet Chirac'*, as it came to be known, was taken up by the Socialists and they urged all Left-wing voters, including Communists, to *'vote utile'*.

The ability of the far-Left parties to use the elections for publicity purposes was made more difficult than in previous elections by the introduction of a new rule which meant that for the first time each potential candidate had to be sponsored by 500 signatures drawn from the 491 deputies and the thousands of local mayors. This obligation was too much for the *Ligue Communiste Révolutionnaire* and the Maoists. Two parties of the alternative Left did manage to achieve the required number of sponsors, however. (It must be said that this was partly because they received some signatures from supporters of the main candidates who calculated that, in this way, they could damage the first ballot choices of their major opponents). The *Parti Socialiste Unifié* was represented by its National Secretary, Huguette Bouchardeau. Her campaign was based heavily on themes close to the feminist movement, though it also provided for a 'presidential contract' which was related to an appeal for a new type of relationship between the trade union movement and the parties of the Left. The other alternative Left candidate was Arlette Laguiller of the Trotskyist *Lutte Ouvrière*. Stating that she did not have a programme, but that she did have some ideas, her aim was to show that the Left could have a more radical, more working-class and more principled face than that offered by either Mitterrand or Marchais.

The trade unions participated in the campaign to varying degrees. Although, as we have seen in Chapter 9, the trade unions in France claim to be apolitical they do in fact have political perspectives. Not surprisingly the CGT was by far the·most partisan, its leadership coming out openly in December 1980 in support of Marchais. In Marseille, and then elsewhere, campaigns were quickly launched by local federations of the CGT which called into question this pro-PCF stance. It was more appropriate, 'dissenters' argued, that the union should not endorse any one candidate but should adopt a commitment to the Left as a whole.

The other unions, including the CFDT, the FO and the FEN, were much more circumspect. Privately the leading figures in these unions all leaned heavily towards Mitterrand but they refused to be drawn into making recommendations before the first ballot.

THE RESULTS OF THE PRESIDENTIAL ELECTION

Mitterrand believed that if he was to win the election it would be necessary for him to obtain a first ballot vote which was not too far below that of the outgoing President. This meant, he calculated, that he would have to obtain at least 25 per cent of the vote if the thrust of his campaign was to be maintained: in other words he would have to obtain the highest Socialist vote in the history of the Fifth Republic.

The results showed Mitterrand to have achieved his target: with 25.8 per cent of the vote he was only 2.5 per cent behind Giscard d'Estaing (see Appendix 2). Equally significantly the results showed an enormous, and in recent times unparalleled, disparity within the Left between the PS and the PCF. Whereas Mitterrand had obtained the *highest* Socialist vote since the Popular Front, Marchais, with 15.3 per cent, had obtained the *lowest*. A subsequent *Sofres* survey suggested there were four main reasons for the decline in the PCF vote: (a) the decision of some Communist voters to support Mitterrand for tactical reasons from the outset, fearing that there might not be a Left-wing candidate on the second ballot; (b) respect for the candidate who had in the past borne the colours of a united Left; (c) disapproval of the strategy and certain policies of the PCF; (d) a feeling that Marchais was not a good candidate.[8]

Overall, when the votes of the other Left-wing candidates were included, the Left gained 47.7 per cent. This compared with 49.3 per cent for the Right. The ecologist candidate, Brice Lalonde, gained the remaining 3.9 per cent.

Between the two ballots Mitterrand continued with the same strategy: balancing firmness, moderation, caution and the promise of stability on the one hand, with the prospect of reform on the other. Clearly he needed to mobilise the whole of the Left for the second ballot and also attract some support from the Right and from the ecologists if he was to win. The attitude of the defeated Left candidates and parties was therefore crucial. In the event all, with varying degrees of enthusiasm, came out and supported him. The PCF, who had clearly suffered a major reverse, felt they had no option. Though they had fallen well short of their first ballot target of

20 per cent they were well aware that a refusal to back Mitterrand could worsen their own situation even further since most of their voters would support him anyway. As a result the Central Committee, which met two days after the first ballot, gave Mitterrand their support without attaching any conditions. Thereafter, until the second round of voting, the Party leadership was uncharacteristically quiet, though they continued to claim, as they had done throughout the campaign, that they wanted to participate in any future government of the Left. To this the Socialist response remained unchanged: the composition of the government under Mitterrand would depend on the result of legislative elections and on the PCF modifying its attitude both to the PS and on various policy matters.

On the second ballot Mitterrand won by 51.7 per cent to Giscard d'Estaing's 48.2 per cent. For the first time in French history a Left-wing President was elected by universal suffrage. Within minutes there were scenes of spontaneous enthusiasm in the streets of all France's towns the like of which had not been seen since the Liberation.

In attempting to explain why Mitterrand won in 1981 it is important to bear in mind that the elections did not witness a massive swing to the Left. Since the 1973 legislative elections the Left had consistently polled 45-8 per cent in national elections and had, at times, performed even better in local elections and public opinion polls. Moreover surveys had long shown that a higher proportion of the electorate regarded itself as being of the Left than of the Right.[9] A great swing was therefore not needed.

In commenting upon the reasons for the defeat of the Left in 1978 the authors of a recent study asked themselves whether the Left could ever win an election.[10] They pointed to the clear increase in support for the Left since 1967 but nonetheless concluded on a pessimistic note. They argued that whilst electoral demography should condemn the Right to defeat (a younger population, increased urbanisation, increased number of working women, etc.) a number of factors inclined potential supporters of the Left ultimately to vote for parties of the Right. The primary factor, they concluded, was the desire of such voters to conserve their acquired or inherited possessions – the *effet patrimoine* as the authors call it.

What then were the factors which tipped the balance the other way in the 1981 presidential elections? Three inter-related factors appear to have been crucial.

(1) The first ballot votes for all the candidates of the Left went solidly to Mitterrand on the second ballot. According to a *Sofres* survey 92 per cent of PCF voters transferred in this way.[11]

(2) By contrast, the first ballot votes of the candidates of the Right were by no means as solid. According to the same survey, only 73 per cent of first ballot Chirac votes were subsequently transferred to Giscard d'Estaing, 16 per cent went to Mitterrand, and 11 per cent either abstained, spoiled their ballots or cannot be accounted for. Unquestionably major reasons for this 'indiscipline' were widespread antipathy towards Giscard and the less than wholehearted support Chirac gave him between the ballots. Equally certainly 'natural' supporters of the Right were more able to contemplate the possibility of a Mitterrand presidency as a result of his much stronger position *vis-à-vis* the PCF. Giscard's almost desperate accusations that Mitterrand in the Elysée would be the hostage of the Communists carried much less weight after the first ballot.

Mitterrand also benefited from the dispropriate split of the environmentalist vote in his direction: 53 per cent of Lalonde's supporters transferred to him, 26 per cent went to Giscard d'Estaing, and 21 per cent either abstained or kept their decision to themselves.

(3) There appears to have been a greater wish for change amongst the electorate than in previous elections. The *Sofres* poll showed that most people thought Mitterrand had won because of his wish to bring about major changes in French society. Conversely the main reason for Giscard d'Estaing's defeat was thought to be his insufficient efforts to combat unemployment.

THE LEGISLATIVE ELECTIONS

One of the first acts of the Mitterrand presidency was to sign a decree for the dissolution of the National Assembly. Legislative elections were then planned for 14 and 21 June – the earliest possible dates which would allow the parties of the Left, and especially the Socialists, to benefit from the momentum acquired by the presidential victory.

In a move which reflected his continuing concern to reassure the Left, whilst not unduly alarming the Right, Mitterrand appointed the essentially pragmatic and conciliatory Pierre Mauroy as Prime Minister. The balance of the interim government which he and Mitterrand subsequently chose was of the broad Left. The PCF was not given ministerial posts but the various currents of opinion within the PS were all represented. In addition posts were given to the MRG and – in a clear attempt to appeal to the Centre – Michel Jobert, who had been foreign minister under Pompidou and who had rallied to Mitterrand during the campaign, was appointed as one of the five Ministers of State. The government then proceeded to try and use the period up to the legislative elections to demonstrate that whilst its commitment to major reforms remained firm, it would not act irresponsibly.

It was clear throughout the short campaign that none of the parties of the Left intended to embrace any new themes beyond their support for the President and their desire to give him the means, in Parliament, for the enactment of his political programme. In contrast with the Right, where recriminations were openly visible, relative harmony prevailed on the Left. Policy statements and electoral agreements were quickly negotiated between the PS and the MRG and the PS and the PSU. (The MRG fielded 65 candidates, 14 of whom were not opposed by the PS on the first ballot. The PSU were the major component of an electoral grouping *Alternative 81* which put up 182 candidates. Huguette Bouchardeau was given an unopposed run on the first ballot by the PS but she was narrowly defeated by the Communist candidate.[12]) With greater difficulty an agreement was also made between the PS and the PCF. The two parties issued a joint declaration in which they listed areas of agreement (which were principally on social and economic matters), they affirmed their wish to confirm Mitterrand's victory by 'developing their co-operation', and they committed themselves to second ballot withdrawals. There was not, however, as the PCF had hoped, any commitment to Communist ministers. The PS made it clear that such an eventuality would not simply depend on the newly found moderation of the PCF but would necessitate an agreement between the two on *'problèmes de fond'*. This reflection of PS strength was further reflected in the campaign wherein the PCF played down their own policies and preferred often to present themselves under the banner *'pour la nouvelle majorité présidentielle'*. The Socialists identified themselves everywhere *'avec François Mitterrand'*.

On the first ballot (see Appendix 4) the PS with its MRG ally gained the highest vote in its history: 37 per cent. The PCF did not recover the ground it had lost on the first ballot of the presidential elections and with only 16.2 per cent of the vote was outdistanced by the PS/MRG by over 20 per cent. The Left as a whole gained over 55 per cent.[13]

The second ballot confirmed the victory of the Left but also, because the PS had been the leading party in so many constituencies on the first ballot, greatly magnified the Socialist/Communist imbalance. Overall, with 334 seats, the Left gained an overwhelming parliamentary majority. This was made up of 271 PS deputies, 14 MRG, 5 independent Left associated with the PS, and 44 PCF. Communist support was not therefore necessary for governmental stability.

CONCLUDING REMARKS

After the elections, and following delicate negotiations, the Communists joined the Socialists in office. However, they were given only four posts in the 44-member government and each was in a relatively insensitive area: Transport, Civil Service and Administrative Reforms, Health, and Vocational Training. Furthermore, as the price for being able to show their supporters in this way that they were part of the new majority, the PCF was forced to sign a declaration in which it made major concessions to the PS (see pp. 144-6 and Appendix 6).

After so many years in opposition, during which the parties of the Left grew accustomed to their role, the electoral developments of 1981 and the assumption of office clearly considerably alters many political perspectives. Though in government for the first time since 1947 the PCF has suffered a major reverse and doubtless faces a period of great internal debate about its future role, identity and direction. In the PS the occupancy of the Elysée and the Matignon means that awkward policy areas can no longer be fudged. In time, sections of the Party may well become dissatisfied with aspects of government policy. At the same time, there is likely to be considerable pressure placed upon the Party to bend to the will of the government. While this may be acceptable where tactical considerations are concerned, longer-term strategy will require, if internal harmony is genuinely to be sought, effective co-ordinating mechanisms to be established so that the government may remain responsive to its base and to its election manifesto. Whether, in such a heterogeneous party, internal harmony is *possible* is, of course, yet another question.

The Left enters government at a difficult time. International peace and *détente* is under threat, the social fabric of the industrialised world is endangered by recession, and the future of the European Community is very much in question. The Left has five years in which to make a credible start to implementing a socialist strategy. If it succeeds it will be seen as a model by many socialist and social-democratic parties in Europe and beyond. If, however, in France, with its rich socialist and revolutionary tradition, the government of the Left fails, the consequences could be no less far-reaching.

Appendixes

Appendix 1

PARLIAMENTARY ELECTIONS RESULTS (*ELECTIONS LEGISLATIVES*) IN THE FIFTH REPUBLIC, 1958-78

(% 1st ballot vote – metropolitan France only; National Assembly seats – metropolitan and overseas)

	Oct 1958 %	seats	Nov 1962 %	seats	March 1967 %	seats	June 1968 %	seats	March 1973 %	seats	March 1978 %	seats
Abstentions (% of electorate)	22.9		31.3		18.9		20.0		18.7		16.6	
Left												
Communists (PCF)	19.2	10	21.7	41	22.5	73	20.0	34	21.4	73	20.7	86
SFIO (Socialist Party pre-1969)	15.7	44	12.6	66								
Socialist/Radical alliances FGDS (1967-8); UGSD 1973; PS/MRG 1978					19.0	116	16.5	57	20.8	101	25.0	114
Radicals	8.3	32	7.8	39								
PSU, Extreme Left, Other Left			2.4	—	2.1	4	4.7	—	3.6	2	3.6	—
(Total Left)	(43.2)	(86)	(44.5)	(146)	(43.6)	(193)	(41.2)	(91)	(45.8)	(176)	(49.3)	(200)
Centre												
MRP	11.1	57	9.1)									
Independents	22.9	133	7.1)	55								
Opposition Centre (CD/PDM)					13.4	41	10.3	33				
Réformateurs (CD + Rad, 1973)									13.1	34		
Majorité												
CDP (Pro-*majorité* centrists, 1973)										(30		
UDF (*Giscardiens* + centre, 1978)											21.4	137
RI (*Giscardiens* pre-1978)			5.9	35	37.7	(44	44.7	(64	36.0	(55	22.5	150
Gaullists	19.5	199	31.9	233		(201		(296		(183		
Other *majorité*									0.7	5	2.0	3
(Total Majorité)			(37.8)	(268)	(37.7)	(245)	(44.7)	(360)	(36.7)	(273)	(45.9)	(290)
Other	3.3		8.6	13	5.4	8	3.5	3	4.4	7	4.8*	1

* includes 'Ecologists' — 2.1%

Source: J.R. Frears and J.-L. Parodi, *War Will Not Take Place* (C. Hurst, 1979) p.5.

Appendix 2

PRESIDENTIAL ELECTION RESULTS IN THE FIFTH REPUBLIC

	1965 *First ballot (% of vote)*	*Second ballot (% of vote)*
De Gaulle	43.7	54.5
Mitterrand (Joint Left)	32.2	45.5
Lecanuet	15.8	
Others	8.2	

	1969 *First ballot (% of vote)*	*Second ballot (% of vote)*
Pompidou	44.0	57.6
Poher	23.4	42.4
Duclos (PCF)	21.5	
Defferre (Socialist)	5.1	
Rocard (PSU)	3.7	
Others	2.4	

	1974 *First ballot (% of vote)*	*Second ballot (% of vote)*
Mitterrand (Joint Left)	43.4	49.3
Giscard d'Estaing	32.9	50.7
Chaban-Delmas	14.6	
Others	9.3	

	1981 *First ballot (% of vote)*	*Second ballot (% of vote)*
Giscard d'Estaing	28.3	48.2
Mitterrand	25.8	51.8
Chirac	18.0	
Marchais	15.3	
Lalonde (Ecologist)	3.9	
Laguiller (LO)	2.3	
Crépeau (MRG)	2.2	
Debré	1.7	
Garaud	1.3	
Bouchardeau	1.1	

Appendix 3

EUROPEAN ELECTION RESULTS 1979

	% votes cast	seats gained
Extreme Left	3.1	—
PCF	20.6	19
PS and MRG	23.8	22
RPR[1]	16.3	15
UDF and presidential majority[2]	27.5	25
Ecologists	4.4	—
Others	4.5	—

[1]Presented itself as the *Défense des intérêts de la France en Europe*.
[2]Presented itself as *Union pour la France en Europe*.

Appendix 4

PARLIAMENTARY ELECTION RESULTS, JUNE 1981

	% vote first ballot	seats gained
PS/MRG	37.5	285
PCF	16.2	44
Extreme Left	1.3	—
Other Left	0.7	5
RPR	20.8	88
UDF	19.2	62
Other Right	3.2	7
Ecologists	1.1	—

Appendix 5

THE BACKGROUND OF VOTERS IN MARCH 1978
(First Ballot. Minor diverse opposition excluded)

		PCF	Extreme Left	PS + MRG	UDF	RPR
Total	100	21	3	25	21	22
Sex						
Men		24	3	25	19	20
Women		19	2	25	22	24
Age						
18 to 24		28	9	25	17	15
25 to 34		26	5	24	18	17
35 to 49		19	3	25	20	24
50 to 64		20	1	24	22	23
65 +		15	—	25	27	28
Profession of Head of Family						
Farmers		9	1	17	33	31
Self-employed		14	—	23	25	26
Higher management, industrialists and Liberal professions		9	5	15	27	30
Middle management and clerical workers		18	6	29	14	20
Manual workers		36	4	27	16	14
Inactive, retired		17	—	26	25	26
Monthly Family Income						
Less than 2000 Francs		22	3	26	22	20
2001-3000 Francs		26	3	27	18	21
3001-5000 Francs		25	3	28	18	19
5001 Francs		16	4	20	23	24
Education						
Primary only		24	1	26	21	22
Secondary		15	4	21	22	27
Technical		27	5	26	14	21
Higher		10	9	19	26	20

Religion

Regular practicing Catholic	2	1	13	39	31
Occasional practicing Catholic	11	—	20	28	33
Non-practicing Catholic	24	3	30	17	20
No religion	49	6	29	4	6

Source: SOFRES post-election poll. *Le Nouvel Observateur,* 24 Apr. 1978.

Appendix 6

EXTRACTS FROM DECLARATION
MADE BY PS AND PCF, 23 JUNE 1981

Having met together, following the legislative elections, as they had previously arranged, the Socialist Party and the Communist Party welcome the choice made by the French people which on 21 June confirmed the vote of 10 May giving the presidential majority a large majority in the National Assembly.

Conditions have thus been created to put into effect the changes which the country expects. With the objective of establishing a common governmental platform, the two parties concentrated mainly in their discussions on the points which were left on the table following their last meeting.

Conscious of the obligations which the current situation dictates, the two parties declare themselves ready to put into practice the new policies which have been chosen by the people of France in electing François Mitterrand as President of the Republic. They will do this in the National Assembly in the context of the governing majority which has just been formed; they will do so in government in complete solidarity; they will do so in the local community and in the regions as well as at the place of work, while respecting the proper functions of these institutions and parties. While reaffirming the individual characteristics and fundamental positions of their respective parties, they will use the choice made by the country and other points of convergence which emanate from their discussions as the basis for their action.

The policy of change, which has already been started through the first measures of the government, will continue. Agreements will be kept. Change will continue as it has begun, on the basis of democratic decisions which have been supported by universal suffrage.

This change will consist in particular of new measures of social justice and an increase in the level of income of the underprivileged sectors which will be introduced in the coming months. It will be continued in stages, according to a rhythm of transformation which will take into account the effects of the current crisis, the fact that the French economy is open to external pressures, and the necessary balance of economic and financial factors.

In the same spirit, the two parties feel that, following discussions between the unions and the employers which have already begun, legislation must be prepared as soon as possible to reduce the length of the working week. Once the legal framework has been established, under the government's initiative, new sectoral discussions will follow which will fix the exact methods and timetable to enable the measures to be brought into effect within individual firms.

The two parties feel that the expansion of the public sector will constitute a guarantee as to the efficiency and democratisation of the planning process. They agree that the extension and the organisation of the public sector should take place, according to the propositions which were ratified on 10 May.

... the two parties consider it necessary ... that a recovery plan for the next two years be drawn up ... that policies reducing social inequality be established ... that freedom should be extended ... workers' rights developed ... and public life democratised.

Both parties will support France's international activity – while respecting her alliances – for peace and progressive disarmament with a view to the simultaneous dissolution of military blocs, while assuring the balance of forces in Europe and the world, and the security of each individual country. In this spirit, they favour the urgent opening of negotiations on the limitation and reduction of armaments in Europe. These negotiations must concentrate in particular upon the presence of Soviet SS20 missiles and the decision to install the American Pershing II systems.

Both parties will respect the right of self-determination and the sovereignty of nations, non-interference in internal affairs, and the right of each country to its own security. They give to these principles a universal value.

By virtue of these principles they affirm the right of the Afghan peoples to choose their own regime and government, and call for the withdrawal of Soviet troops from Afghanistan and the cessation of all foreign interference.

Taking into account the situation reached with the Camp David Agreements, they reaffirm the right of existence and the security of Israel and all the states of the region, at the same time as recognising the right of the Palestinian people to their own state [*patrie*].

Both parties will actively support French participation in the EEC, its institutions and its common policies, while respecting [France's] freedom of action and its legitimate interests. They will support common policies in the social field, in the defence of agriculture and threatened sectors, and for the strengthening of research and technologically advanced industries.

The two parties raised the evolution of the situation in Poland, and felt that the country and its people should lead themselves in time towards the process of economic, social and democratic renewal on which they have started.

They express, both on the economic and political level, their solidarity with the peoples of the Third World who, as in Nicaragua and Salvador, are struggling for national emancipation, their development, and their democratic and social liberation.

Notes and References

CHAPTER 1   WHAT IS THE LEFT?

1. F. Goguel, *La Politique des partis sous la IIIᵉ république* (Seuil, 1946).
2. D. Johnson, 'The Two Frances: The Historical Debate', in *West European Politics,* vol. I (1978) p.9.
3. The two studies also contain other survey evidence related to the Left-Right question. E. Deutsch *et al., Les Familles politiques* (Minuit, 1966); D. Butler and D. Stokes, *Political Change in Britain* (Macmillan, 1974).
4. R. Rémond, *The Right Wing in France* (University of Pennsylvania Press, 1966) p.23.
5. T. Zeldin, *France 1848-1945: Politics and Anger* (Oxford University Press, 1979) p.19.
6. A. Siegfried, *Tableau des partis en France* (Bernard Grasset, 1930) p.57.
7. D. Caute, *The Left in Europe* (Weidenfeld & Nicolson, 1966) p.26ff.
8. It is of course possible to break this down even further. For example, René Rémond has recently talked of there being four or five Left tendencies. See his essay 'Existe-t-il encore une gauche en France?', in La Nef *Où va la gauche* (Libraire Jules Tallandier, 1979).
9. G. Lefranc, *Les Gauches en France* (Payot, 1973). R. Rémond, op. cit.
10. J. Touchard, *La Gauche en France depuis 1900* (Seuil, 1977).
11. J. Defrasne, *La Gauche en France de 1789 à nos jours* (Presses Universitaires de France, 1975).
12. M. Rocard, speech given to the Socialist Congress at Nantes (18 June 1977). Verbatim Report.

CHAPTER 2 THE DEVELOPMENT OF THE MODERN POLITICAL PARTIES OF THE LEFT

1. G. Dupeux, *French Society 1789-1970* (Methuen, 1976) p.154.
2. There are a number of case studies on the early development of socialism. For a recent study see T. Judt, *Socialism in Provence 1871-1914* (Cambridge University Press, 1979).
3. R. Wohl, *French Communism in the Making 1914-1924* (Stanford University Press, 1966) p.14.
4. Jaurès himself was assassinated just before war was declared on Germany. Because he held strong pacifist convictions it has been suggested by some historians that his death may actually have averted a major division in the SFIO at this time.

5.   A. Kriegel, *The French Communists* (University of Chicago Press, 1972) p.191. For a detailed account of the Tours Congress and its background see her *Aux origines du communisme français (1914-1920)*, 2 vols. (Mouton, 1964).
6.   Obviously the exact dating of these phases is a matter of judgement. Most studies however take a very similar historical framework to the one outlined here. See, for example: J. Touchard, 'Introduction à l'idéologie du Parti Communiste Français', in F. Bon *et al.*, *Le Communisme en France* (Armand Colin, 1969); J. Fauvet, *Histoire du Parti Communiste Français*, 2nd ed. (Fayard, 1977); R. Tiersky, *French Communism 1920-1972* (Columbia University Press, 1974).
7.   Op cit., pp.192ff.
8.   A. Vassart and C. Vassart, 'The Moscow Origin of the French Popular Front' in Drachkovitch, M.M. and Lazitch, B. (eds), *The Comintern: Historical Highlights* (Praeger, 1966) p.235.
9.   Even today the Party still struggles in its interpretation of the events and attempts to demonstrate that far from there being a sudden turn the policy was based on the pre-1939 situation. For recent views see: 'Le "tournant" de 1939' *Recherches et débats: Supplément aux Cahiers d'histoire de l'Institut Maurice Thorez*, no.3 (1979). G. Willard, 'Sur la stratégie du PCF en 1939', *Cahiers d'histoire de l'Institut Maurice Thorez*, no.29-30 (1979) pp.49-52.
10. Figures quoted in A. Kriegel, op. cit. pp.33 and 20 respectively.
11. A full résumé of their argument is to be found in Léon Blum's speech to the Congress. The full text of the speech can be found in the booklet, *Léon Blum, Discours de Tours* (Parti Socialiste, n.d., probably 1978).
12. P. Williams, *Crisis and Compromise* (Longmans, 1964) p.89.

CHAPTER 3 THE SOCIALIST PARTY

1.   On the Club movement and their political loyalties see in particular G. Lavau and R. Cayrol, 'Les clubs devant l'action politique', *Revue Française de Science Politique (RFSP)*, (June 1965); F.L. Wilson, *The French Democratic Left 1963-69* (Stanford University Press, 1971) pp.77-107.
2.   For a detailed account of the CIR see D. Loschak, *La Convention des Institutions Républicaines* (Presses Universitaires de France, 1971).
3.   For a more detailed analysis of how they saw their role see M. Charzat *et al.*, *Le CERES: un combat pour le socialisme* (Calmann-Levy, 1975).
4.   A very useful account, which includes a review of different interpretations of the crisis, is B.E. Brown, The *Anatomy of a Revolt: Protest in Paris* (General Learning Corporation, 1974).
5.   A summary of divisions at the Congress can be found in D. Pickles, *The Government and Politics of France,* vol.I (Methuen, 1972) pp.381-2; also P. Guidoni, *Histoire du Nouveau Parti Socialiste* (Tema-Action, 1973) pp.79-86.
6.   The resolution adapted by the Congress is printed in C. Hurtig, *De la*

SFIO au Nouveau Parti Socialiste (Armand Colin, 1970) pp.85ff.

7. A. Savary, *Pour le Nouveau Parti Socialiste* (Seuil, 1970) p.37.

8. This was especially so at local level. According to one estimate 70 per cent of the secretaries of departmental federations were replaced and their average age fell by 20 years. Quoted in V. Wright and H. Machin, 'The French Socialist Party in 1973: Performance and Prospects', *Government and Opposition* (Spring, 1974) pp.127-8.

9. Delegates to the Congress reflected a membership of 70,000 for the PS and 10,000 for the CIR. This calculation of respective memberships was somewhat arbitrary.

10. For the full text of Mitterrand's speech at Epinay and for his other major public statements see his anthology, *Politique* (Fayard, 1977).

11. *Changer la vie: programme de gouvernement du parti socialiste* (Flammarion, 1972). For a discussion of the document see A. Jeanson and G. Fuchs, 'A propos du programme du PS', *Projet* (Apr. 1972).

12. There were negotiations in the spring of 1972 between the PS and the Centrists but they foundered, principally on the latter's refusal to have anything to do with the PCF. It should be said that the clear leftist strategy to which the PS now turned did produce some ripples of dissent within the Party. For example, Eric Hintermann, once closely associated with Defferre, left to form his own *Parti-Social-Démocrate*.

13. For an account of the *Assises* see Parti Socialiste, *Pour le Socialisme: le livre des Assises du Socialisme* (Stock, 1974).

14. Strictly speaking the 21 per cent includes a proportion gained by the Socialist's allies (see below and Appendix 1).

15. On the significance of the 'majority'/'minority' division and of the Pau Congress see R. Cayrol, 'Avenir du PS', *Projet* (Apr. 1975).

16. Speech to the Congress by Pierre Guidoni of CERES.

17. For a first hand account of the creation and development of the MRG see R. Fabre, *Quelques baies de Genièvre* (J.C. Lattès, 1976).

18. In 1980 it claimed around 20,000 members.

19. The MRG was very tempted to present its own list in the 1979 European elections. It eventually drew back from doing so for fear that it would not reach the 5 per cent threshold necessary for representation in the Parliament. In the 1981 presidentials its candidate gained 2.2 per cent.

20. For the full text of this and other Rocard statements and speeches see M. Rocard, *Parler Vrai* (Seuil, 1979).

21. It certainly seems to have been a contributory reason for the relatively poor 23.6 per cent gained by the joint PS/MRG list in the June 1979 European elections.

22. *Le Poing et la Rose* (Nov.-Dec. 1979).

23. For an account of a meeting in the 13th arrondissement in Paris see *Le Nouvel Observateur,* 14 Jan. 1980.

24. The initial agenda was set out in the Party paper *L'Unité*, no.381, May 1980.

25. For fuller details see R. Cayrol, 'La direction du Parti Socialiste', *RFSP* (Apr., 1978) pp.201-19.

26. Wright, for example, points out that in 1977 the Socialist mayors elected in such important towns as Nantes, Rennes, Angoulême, Poitiers,

Dreux, Chambéry and Castres were all under 40 years old. V. Wright, *The Government and Politics of France* (Hutchinson, 1978) p.156.

27. Party treasurer's Report to Congress 1979.
28. Ibid.
29. The cost of Mitterrand's campaign was 9 million francs as compared with 1.5 million in 1965. The PS itself was not directly financially involved since the campaign was organised and financed outside the Party. In 1981 his campaign cost nearly 19 million francs.
30. This figure, given to us by Party headquarters, is of Apr. 1980.
31. For a discussion on this see 'Les socialistes et le débat idéologique, Colloque de l'ISER' 22 May 1976. Reproduced in *La Nouvelle Revue Socialiste*, no. 26, (1977).
32. P. Bérégovoy, 'La stratégie socialiste du front de classe', *Le Monde*, 12-13 June 1977.
33. P. Bacot, 'Le Front de Classe', *RFSP* (Apr. 1978) p.293.
34. Quotes taken from the text adopted at the 1974 Assises du Socialisme, 'Pour le Socialisme'. Printed in *Le Poing et la Rose* (Sep. 1974).
35. *Projet Socialiste pour la France des années 80* (Club Socialiste du Livre, 1980).
36. For detailed discussions of *autogestion* from Socialist viewpoints see P. Rosanvallon, *L'Age de l'Autogestion* (Seuil, 1976); J-P Cot 'Autogestion and Modernity in France', in B. Brown (ed.), *Eurocommunism and Eurosocialism* (Cyrco Press, 1979).
37. C. Pierret and L. Praire, *Plan et Autogestion* (Flammarion, 1976) p.175.
38. *Projet Socialiste*, op. cit., pp.192-4.
39. This 'nationalistic' position of CERES has lost it many friends. For example, C. Pierret, a deputy from the Vosges, told us in conversation that it was his main reason for resigning from CERES. For a more detailed explanation of the CERES motion see the article by J.P. Chevènement in *Le Matin*, 5 Dec. 1977.
40. For a detailed account of how the PS believes that such changes can be achieved see its *Proposition de Résolution* to the *Commission de l'Agriculture*, Parlement Européen, 15 Jan. 1980 (presented in the name of E. Pisani and others).
41. See B. Criddle, 'The French Parti Socialiste' in W. Paterson and A. Thomas, *Social Democratic Parties in Western Europe* (Croom Helm, 1977) p.34.
42. Source: P. Hardouin, 'Sociologie du Parti Socialiste', *RFSP* (Apr., 1978) p.227.
43. Ibid., p.241.
44. For information on characteristics of the PS membership not discussed here, e.g. age structure and sex ratios, see P. Hardouin op. cit.; J.-F. Bizot, *Au Parti des Socialistes* (Grasset, 1975); documents issued by PS *Bureau National d'Adhésions*. For a detailed study of the leaderhip see P. Bacot, *Les Dirigeants du Parti Socialiste* (Presses Universitaires de Lyon, 1977). For the social background of deputies elected in 1978 see the table in *Le Matin: Le Dossier des Legislatives 1978,* p.68.
45. Survey conducted by IFOP, *Le Point*, 27 June 1977. Also published in Sondages: *L'Opinion en 1977 et 1978*. nos. 2 and 3 (1978).

46. A detailed analysis of changing regional support is to be found in G. le Gall, 'A gauche, toujours le reéquilibrage', *Revue Politique et Parlementaire,* (Mar.-Apr., 1978) p.33ff. From 1967-78, the Socialists, in percentage terms, advanced most in Lorraine, Alsace, Brittany, and Basse Normandie. The only significant decline was in Limousin, though in Nord Pas-de Calais, Aquitaine, Provence and other long standing areas of strength there was a virtual stagnation.
47. *Sofres* survey. *Le Nouvel Observateur,* 4-10 July 1981. For the *Sofres* survey of the presidential elections see *Le Nouvel Observateur,* 1-7 June 1981.

CHAPTER 4 THE COMMUNIST PARTY

1. Interview in *Le Nouvel Observateur,* 6 Sept. 1976.
2. *France Nouvelle,* 5 and 12 Dec. 1977.
3. It is not possible to examine here the question of whether there really is (or was) such a thing as Eurocommunism. From the enormous range of literature which has arisen out of the phenomenon the following are amongst the most useful: R.L. Tokès (ed.), *Eurocommunism and Detente* (Martin Robertson, 1978); B.E. Brown (ed.), *Eurocommunism and Eurosocialism: The Left Confronts Modernity* (Cyrco Press, 1979); P.F. della Torre *et al.* (eds.) *Eurocommunism: Myth or Reality?* (Penguin, 1979).
4. E. Adler *et al. L'URSS et nous* (Editions Sociales, 1978).
5. *Le Matin: Le Dossier des Legislatives 1978,* Institut Louis-Harris poll (Sep. 1977) p.32.
6. For Marchais' address see *L'Humanité,* 4 Feb. 1980.
7. See, for example, P. Fromonteil, '1920-1975: un parti révolutionnaire pour la démocratie et le socialisme', *Cahiers du Communisme,* Dec. 1975, pp.50-9.
8. 'Pour une démocratie avancée, pour une France socialiste!' (Champigny Manifesto), *Cahiers du Communisme,* Jan. 1969, p.134.
9. It is possible here to give only an outline of SMC and the PCF's economic policies. For a more detailed resumé see D. Bell. 'The Economic Policies of the French Communist Party'. Paper presented to the annual conference of the *Political Studies Association,* Apr. 1980. Of the many PCF sources the Champigny Manifesto is particularly important, because it marks the first full development of much of the Party's current economic analysis. For a more recent account from the PCF's viewpoint a useful summary is to be found in E. Fajon, *ABC des Communistes* (Editions Sociales, 1979), chs. 2-4.
10. Politbureau statement of 5 July 1978. It is printed in a useful compilation of PCF pronouncements on the EEC, *Les Communistes Francais et l'Europe: bulletin des Communistes Francais a l'Assemblée de la Communauté Européenne,* Jan. 1979.
11. For a more detailed discussion of the different strategies see H. Portelli 'La Voie nationale des PC francais et italien', *Projet,* no. 106, 1976.
12. *The Times,* 18 Nov. 1946.

13. P. Robrieux, 'Colloque de l'ISER', 24 April 1976, published in *La Nouvelle Revue Socialiste* (special edition), p.74.
14. *Changer de cap: programme pour une gouvernement démocratique d'union populaire* (Editions sociales, 1972); *Programme commun de gouvernement du Parti Communiste Francais et du Parti Socialiste* (Editions Sociales, 1972).
15. *Le Défi démocratique* (Grasset, 1973) p.128.
16. *Vivre libres!* published by *L'Humanité,* May 1975. See especially Part One, 'Les Libertés Individuelles et Collectives'.
17. *The Times,* 19 Nov. 1975.
18. *L'Humanité,* 16 Feb. 1966.
19. The list of infringements was produced in pamphlet form; 5 million were claimed to have been printed. It also appeared in *L'Humanité,* 21 Feb. 1980, and *L'Humanité-Dimanche,* 22 Feb. 1980.
20. This view of *rapporteurs* as 'political persuaders' is developed and illustrated by Denis Lacorne in his article 'Left Wing Unity at the Grass Roots: Picardy and Languedoc' in D. Blackmer and S. Tarrow, *Communism in Italy and France* (Princeton University Press, 1975) pp.315ff.
21. J. Elleinstein claimed in 1976 that there were 860 *permanents* employed by the Central Committee and the federations. *Le PC* (Grasset, 1976), p.90.
22. *Cahiers du Communisme,* June-July 1979, p.300.
23. *Le Monde,* 16 Mar. 1979.
24. Interview with G. Labica in O. Duhamel and E. Weber, *Changer le PC* (PUF, 1979) p.94.
25. L. Althusser, *Ce qui ne peut plus durer dans le PC* (Maspéro, 1978).
26. C. Ysmal, 'La crise du Parti communiste', *Projet*, Nov. 1978.
27. See, for example, *Le Monde,* 21-2 June 1978.
28. Only two years previously the PCF had published a booklet *Coexistence pacifique et lutte de classe en 1975.* This comprised the report of Jean Kanapa, the foreign policy spokesman to the Central Committee held on 14-15 Apr. 1975. In it he denounced 'the instrument of security' which, on the contrary was a menace to security. That this was so 'justifies more than ever our wish that France renounces its nuclear arm, as the Common Programme of the Left wants', p.38.
29. *Le Canard Enchaîné,* 12 Apr. 1978. Those reported as voting for the opening were Marchais, Laurent, Colpin; those voting against were Leroy, Plissonnier, Fiterman, Piquet.
30. *Les Statuts, du Parti Communiste Francais 1979,* Article 7.
31. P. Laurent, 'A propos du centralisme démocratique', *France Nouvelle,* 22 May 1978. See also his *Le PCF comme il est* (Editions Sociales, 1978).
32. The articles to provoke the most discussion, because they were amongst the first and because of the status and frankness of the authors were: J. Elleinstein, 'Du XXIIe congrès du PCF à l'échec de la gauche', *Le Monde,* 13, 14, 15 Apr. 1978; L. Althusser, 'Ce qui ne peut plus durer dans le parti communiste', *Le Monde,* 25, 26, 27, 28 Apr. 1978.
33. For the 'inside' version of these events, see H. Fiszbin *et al., Les Bouches s'ouvrent* (Grasset, 1980).

34. Gerald Sfez writing in *La Nouvelle Critique,* Oct. 1978. The Apr. 1978 edition was so critical the Politbureau attempted to prevent publication.
35. *La vie du parti,* Mar. 1979. Special edition for Twenty-third Congress.
36. *L'Humanité,* 13 Feb. 1979.
37. Ibid., 10 May 1979.
38. *Le Monde,* 16 Mar. 1979.
39. *L'Humanité,* 9 Mar. 1979 for the contributions of Spire and Rony. *L'Humanité,* 10 Mar. 1979 for the replies by Félix Damette (a Central Committee member) and Nicole Grynszpan.
40. Ibid., 14 May 1979.
41. See the report on local conferences in *Le Monde,* 25 Apr. 1979.
42. A. Kriegel, *The French Communists* (University of Chicago Press, 1972).
43. Figures of the independent *Centre d'Etudes des Supports de Publicité.* It should be said that these figures were falling rapidly in the late 1970s and by 1980 some estimates put the sales of *L'Humanité* at well less than 100,000 and those of *L'Humanité Dimanche* at around 250,000.
44. See, for example, *La Vie du Parti,* Mar. 1979.
45. *Le Monde,* 21 Oct. 1978. As is shown in Chapter 9 official estimates of this kind must be approached with caution and it is probable that the figure is somewhat lower.
46. *L'Humanité,* 14 May 1979.
47. A. Campana, *L'Argent secret* (Arthaud, 1976); J. Montaldo, *Les Finances du PCF* (Albin Michel, 1977).
48. Op. cit. Also, *Les Secrets de la banque soviètique en France* (Albin Michel, 1979).
49. *L'Humanité, 14 May 1979.*
50. *J. Elleinstein, op. cit., pp.90-1.*
51. *L'Humanité,* 14 May 1979.
52. J. Lagroye *et al., Les Militants politiques dans trois partis français* (Pedone, 1976) p.34.
53. *L'Humanité,* 28 Apr. 1979.
54. For a detailed breakdown of this and other characteristics of the delegates see *Cahiers du Communisme,* June-July 1979, pp.295-300.
55. For a complete regional analysis see J.R. Frears and J.L. Parodi, *War Will Not Take Place* (C. Hurst, 1979) p.74.
56. F. Bon, *Les Elections en France* (Seuil, 1978) p.144.
57. R. Tiersky, *French Communism 1920-1972* (Columbia University Press, 1974) p.7.
58. Of Annie Kriegel's many published works, see especially *The French Communists* op. cit; 'Communism in France' in T.J. Nossiter *et al., Imagination and Precision in the Social Sciences* (Faber & Faber, 1972).
59. G. Lavau, 'Le Parti Communiste dans le système politique français' in F. Bon *et al., Le Communisme en France* (Armand Colin, 1969) pp.7-81. For an 'updating' of his views on the subject see the interview with him in Duhamel, O. and Weber, E., op. cit.
60. For a socio-economic breakdown of voting in the presidential elections see the *Sofres* survey in *Le Nouvel Observateur,* 1-7 June 1981; for the parliamentary elections see *Le Nouvel Observateur,* 4-10 July 1981.

CHAPTER 5 THE LEFT IN THE FIFTH REPUBLIC: THE STRUGGLE FOR UNITY

1. J.J. Servan-Schreiber and M. Albert, *Ciel et terre, le manifeste radical* (Denoël, 1970).
2. Published in English as *Towards a New Democracy* (Collins, 1977). This quote pp.46-7.
3. *Le Nouvel Observateur,* 9 Apr. 1979.
4. *L'Année Politique,* 1965. The terms of the charter of the FGDS are also available here, pp.442-5.
5. The declaration can be found in *Le Monde,* 25-6 Feb. 1968.
6. 'Déclaration commune du parti communiste français et du parti socialiste', 18 Dec. 1969. Printed in *Cahiers du Communisme,* Jan. 1970.
7. *Programme Commun de Gouvernement du Parti Communiste et du Parti Socialiste* (Editions Sociales, 1972).
8. B.E. Brown, 'The Common Program in France' in B.E. Brown (ed.) *Eurocommunism and Eurosocialism: The Left Confronts Modernity* (Cyrco Press, 1979).
9. The speech is printed in E. Fajon, *L'Union est un combat* (Editions Sociales, 1975).
10. Speech to the Socialist International at Vienna, 28 June 1972. *Le Monde,* 30 June 1972.
11. *Le Monde,* 21 Jan. 1975.
12. This means the Left loses seats it would win if their second ballot was a Socialist and not a Communist. For an examination of its effects in 1978 see J.F. Frears and J.L. Parodi, *War Will Not Take Place* (Hurst, 1979) ch.6.
13. D. Blume *et al. Histoire du réformisme en France depuis, 1920,* 2 vols. (Editions Sociales, 1976).
14. See, for example, R. Clément, 'Un parti plus fort pour une véritable changement', *Cahiers du Communisme,* Apr. 1977, pp.38-45.
15. It was on this issue that the PCF campaigned most loudly before the September negotiations. See, A. Le Pors 'Nationaliser ou pas', *France Nouvelle,* 29 Aug. 1977.
16. Some commentators have suggested that the PS refusal to give way on this was the real sticking point for the PCF. See, for example, the interview with P. Robrieux, *Le Nouvel Observateur,* 30 Jan. 1978.
17. *L'Humanité,* 19 Apr. 1979.
18. *Le Nouvel Observateur,* 23-30 Apr. 1978.
19. In early 1980 Mitterrand floated the idea of a homogeneous Socialist government, but he added that this could be only on a temporary basis. Interview in *France-Soir,* 21 Feb. 1980.
20. The PCF has improved its image over the years, but it is still deeply distrusted by a wide section of the electorate. For example, in a SOFRES poll conducted in April 1979, 46 per cent of respondents said they would not vote for the PCF in any circumstances. This was much higher than any of the other major parties, the figures for which were: UDF 18%; RPR 25%; PS 11%; MRG 16%. *Le Nouvel Observateur,* 7 May 1979.

CHAPTER 6 THE ALTERNATIVE LEFT

1. J. Touchard, op. cit., p.310.
2. For a detailed account of this gestation period of the PSU see G. Nania, *Un Parti de la gauche; le PSU* (Lib. Gedalge, 1966).
3. Though a member of the PSU, and the PSA before it, Mendès-France never fully participated in the life of the Party.
4. Interview with M. Rocard, *Combat,* 28 June 1967.
5. The main student union, UNEF, was already led by a member of the PSU, Alain Sauvargeot.
6. The 17 theses are reproduced in M. Rocard, *Le PSU et l'avenir socialiste de la France* (Seuil, 1969).
7. Some of these factors are examined in greater detail in E. Sprinzak, 'France: The Radicalisation of the New Left', in M. Kolinsky and W.E. Paterson, *Social and Political Movements in Western Europe* (Croom Helm, 1976).
8. H. Arvon, *Le Gauchisme* (PUF, 1974).
9. See in particular A. Touraine *et al. Lutte étudiante* (Seuil, 1978) and *La prophétie anti-nucléaire* (Seuil, 1979). Also the more polemical A. Touraine, *L'Après socialisme* (Seuil, 1980).
10. Institut Louis Harris France poll for *Maintenant,* 19 Mar. 1979.

CHAPTER 7 THE LEFT IN THE POLITICAL SYSTEM

1. S. Tarrow, *Between Center and Periphery* (Yale University Press, 1977) p.257.
2. E. Suleiman, *Elites in French Society* (Princeton University Press, 1978) p.144.

CHAPTER 8 THE LEFT AT LOCAL LEVEL

1. G. Fabre-Rosane and A. Guede, 'Sociologies des candidates aux élections législatives de mars 1978', *RFSP,* vol. XXVII no. 5, Oct. 1978.
2. Source: V. Wright, *The Government and Politics of France* (Hutchinson, 1978) p.171. (Slightly adapted here.)
3. S. Tarrow, 'From Cold War to Historic Compromise: Approaches to French and Italian Radicalism', in S. Bialer (ed.), *Strategies and Impact of Contemporary Radicalism* (Praeger, 1977) p.298.
4. It is worth nothing that in the 17 large towns where no joint-list agreement was made the PS came out in front after the first ballot in 14.
5. Discussion with J.P. Chevènement, deputy and acting mayor for Belfort, Mar. 1980.
6. For an account of the dispute at Brest see *Riposte,* 9 Apr. 1980; *Le Monde,* 9 Apr. 1980. *Le Monde* carried a series of studies on Left-wing councils from 8-15 Apr. 1980.
7. In discussion with us in May 1980 Rocard said the question of

Communist exclusion had never even arisen. It must be appreciated however that had Rocard sought to remove the Communists he would have given ammunition to his opponents within the PS.

8. For further details on spending and financing see M.A. Schain, 'Communist Control of Municipal Councils, and Urban Political Change: A Reconsideration of Local Politics in France'. Paper presented to the *Annual Conference of the UK Political Studies Association,* Apr. 1979. The paper includes useful references to other studies.

9. M. Kesselman, *The Ambiguous Consensus: A Study of Local Government in France* (Knopf, 1967). For a more detailed explanation of why PCF municipalities do relatively well from the state see S. Tarrow, op. cit. pp.168-71.

10. This statement is partly based on the findings of a study undertaken by M.A. Schain. We are grateful to Mr Schain for providing us with this (as yet) unpublished information.

11. It must be said this view has not been statistically verified. It is largely based on unstructured discussions with local politicians and on overall impressions. It would be interesting to see a systematic and comparative study of policy outcomes of PS-led authorities since 1977.

12. Printed in *Le Monde,* 28 Feb. 1980.

13. J. Milch, 'The PCF and Local Government: Continuity and Change', in Blackmer and Tarrow, op. cit., p.342.

14. *L'Humanité,* 29 Feb. 1980. Such themes had been constant themes in the PCF's newsletter for its councillors, *L'Elu d'Aujourd'Hui* since the summer of 1978.

CHAPTER 9 THE TRADE UNIONS AND THE LEFT

1. As compared with France's partners in the EEC this is by far the lowest percentage. The next lowest is Germany with around 42 per cent. Britain has about 51 per cent and the highest is Belgium with about 78 per cent. Even in those areas where union membership is high by French standards, which is principally in the public sector and in large enterprises, percentages are still relatively low.

2. SOFRES survey of Oct. 1979, *L'Expansion,* 7-20 Dec. 1979. The findings of the survey were similar to those of a major survey into working-class attitudes carried out in 1969. Then 21% had great confidence, and 36% some confidence in the ability of unions to defend their interests, i.e. an exactly similar total of 57%. G. Adam *et al., L'Ouvrier français en 1970* (Fondation Nationale des Sciences Politiques, 1970) p.154.

3. F. Ridley, *Revolutionary Syndicalism in France* (Cambridge University Press, 1970) p.19.

4. P. Stearns, *Revolutionary Syndicalism and French Labour* (Rutgers University Press, 1971) p.102.

5. Most of the figures given in this historical section are taken from G. Lefranc, *Le Syndicalisme en France* (Presses Universitaires de France, 1975).

6. J.D. Reynaud, *Les Syndicats en France,* vol. 1 (Seuil, 1975) p.109.
7. FO pamphlet, *Votez Force Ouvrière,* Nov. 1979.
8. Statement of André Bergeron, General Secretary of FO, *Le Monde,* 11 Dec. 1979.
9. It may be said that action which is seen as *too* political is often the most ignored by the workforce. See P. Brechon, 'Syndicalisme et politique sur le terrain de l'entreprise: essai d'analyse de la situation francaise'. Paper presented to the *European Consortium for Political Research Workshop* (ECPR) on 'Trade Unions and the Political System', 1979. pp.13ff.
10. *Conseil National,* 24-26 Jan. 1974. Quoted in G. Lavau, 'The Changing Relations between Trade Unions and Working Class Parties in France', *Government and Opposition,* vol. 13, 1978.
11. For more detailed figures see *Le Matin,* 13 Dec. 1979; *L'Expansion,* 7-20 Dec. 1979.
12. Statutes of the PS, 1971.
13. See J.P. Oppenheim, 'La question du cumul des mandats politiques et syndicaux à la CFDT', *RFSP,* vol. 25, no. 2, 1975.
14. *Regards sur le PS,* no. 3 (Smafranc, 1977) p.65.
15. Op. cit. 1978, p.441.
16. D. Labbé, 'Les enjeux du 40ᵉ Congrès de la CGT'. Paper presented to the ECPR Workshop, op. cit.
17. *Cahiers du Communisme,* June-July 1979, p.296.
18. *Le Monde dossiers et documents: La CGT,* Dec. 1979.
19. See his message to members, *La Vie ouvrière,* 6-12 Mar. 1978.
20. More detailed examinations of the lack of corporatism and the reasons for it can be found in: *Rapport du comité d'étude pour la réforme de l'entreprise* (Sudreau Report), La Documentation Française 1975; M. Schain, 'Corporatism and Industrial Relations in France', paper presented to the *Annual Conference of the UK Political Studies Association,* Apr. 1980.
21. According to OECD figures. See *La Répartition des revenues dans les pays de l'OCDE* (OECD, 1976).

POSTSCRIPT: THE LEFT AND THE ASSUMPTION OF POWER

1. See J.L. Parodi and P. Perrineau, 'Les leaders socialistes devant l'opinion', *Projet,* 134, April 1979.
2. For the breakdown of Mitterrand's support by federation see *Le Poing et la Rose,* no. 91, Feb. 1981, p.6.
3. See *Le Monde,* 8 January 1980, in which appears the half-page advertisement which launched the campaign. By 30 January 1980 10,000 signatures had been collected; by early April this had grown to 160,000.
4. J. Kehayan, *Le Tabouret de Piotr* (Seuil, 1980).
5. G. Marchais, *L'Espoir au present* (Editions Sociales, 1980).
6. See *Le Monde,* 2 Dec. 1980, for results and comments.
7. 'Deux scenarios pour un septennat', *Sofres* poll conducted for *L'Expansion,* 20 March-2 April 1981.
8. *Sofres* poll, *Le Nouvel Observateur,* 1-7 June 1981.

9. In a survey carried out in March 1981 42 per cent of all respondents thought of themselves as being of the Left; 31 per cent as being of the Right; 20 per cent refused to classify themselves; and 7 per cent offered no opinion. *Le Nouvel Observateur*, 30 March-5 April 1981.
10. J. Capdevielle *et al., France de gauche: vote a droite* (FNSP, 1981).
11. *Sofres* poll, *Le Nouvel Observateur*, 1-7 June 1981.
12. For the attitude of the other alternative Left parties and groups in the legislative elections, see *Le Monde*, 10 June 1981.
13. We have already considered, in Chapters 3 and 4, some of the changes amongst the electorate which produced these results. See especially pp.90-3 and pp.140-5.

Select Bibliography

GENERAL

Dreyfus, F.G., *Histoire des gauches en France 1940-74* (Grasset, 1975).
Defrasne, J., *La Gauche en France de 1789 à nos jours* (PUF, 1975).
Duhamel, O., *La Gauche et la Vᵉ République* (PUF, 1980).
Johnson, R.W., *The Long March of the French Left* (Macmillan, 1981).
Lefranc, G., *Les Gauches en France 1789-1972* (Payot, 1973).
Touchard, J., *La Gauche en France depuis 1900* (Seuil, 1977).
Verdier, R., *PS-PC: une lutte pour l'entente* (Seghers, 1976).
Willard, C., *Socialisme et Communisme français* (A. Colin, 1978).

THE PARTIES OF THE LEFT IN THE MODERN PERIOD

1. The Socialists

Bacot, P., *Les Dirigeants du Parti Socialiste* (Presses Universitaires de Lyon, 1977).
Bizot, J.F. *et al., Au Parti des Socialistes* (Grasset, 1975).
Chevènement, J.P. *et al., Le CERES: un combat pour le Socialisme* (Calmann-Lévy, 1975).
Evin, K., *Michel Rocard ou l'art du possible* (J-C Simoën, 1979).
Giesbert, F.O., *François Mitterrand ou la tentation de l'histoire* (Seuil, 1977).
Guidoni, P., *L'Histoire du Nouveau Parti Socialiste* (Tema-Action, 1973).
Pfister, T., *Les Socialistes* (Albin Michel, 1977).
Simmons, H., *French Socialists in Search of a Role* (Ithaca, Cornell, 1970).

2. The Communists

Blackmer, D. and Tarrow, S., *Communism in Italy and France* (Princeton University Press, 1975).
Elleinstein, J., *Le PC* (Grasset, 1978).
Fauvet, J., *L'Histoire du Parti Communiste Français,* 2nd ed. (Fayard, 1977).
Harris, A. and de Sedouy, A., *Voyage à l'intérieur du Parti Communiste* (Seuil, 1974).
Kriegel, A., *The French Communists* (University of Chicago Press, 1972).
Laurens, A. and Pfister, T., *Les Nouveaux communistes aux portes du pouvoir* (Stock, 1977).
Molina, G. and Vargas, Y., *Dialogue à l'intérieur du Parti Communiste Français* (Maspéro, 1978).
Stiefbold, A.E., *The French Communist Party in Transition* (Praeger, 1977).
Tiersky, R., *French Communism 1920-1972* (Columbia University Press, 1974).
Weber, H. and Duhamel, O., *Changer le PC* (PUF, 1979).

3. The Alternative Left

Arvon, H., *Le Gauchisme* (PUF, 1974).
Biard, R., *Dictionnaire de l'extrème gauche* (Belfond, 1978).
Brown, B., *Protest in Paris: Anatomy of a Revolt* (General Learning Co., N.J., 1974).
Fišera, V-C., *Writings on the Wall* – May '68 (Alison and Busby, 1979).
Rocard, M. *et al., Le PSU et l'avenir socialiste de la France* (Seuil, 1969).
Touraine, A. *et al., Lutte étudiante* (Seuil, 1978).

TRADE UNIONS

Caire, G., *Les Syndicats ouvriers* (PUF, 1971).
Capdevielle, J. and Mouriaux, R., *Les Syndicats ouvriers en France* (A. Colin, 1973).
Lefranc, G., *Le Syndicalisme en France* (PUF, 1975).
Reynaud, J.D., *Les Syndicats en France,* 2 vols. (Seuil, 1975).

Index

Abelin, P., 460
Allemane, J., 24
Althusser, L., 117
Aragon, L., 95
Assises du Socialisme, 57, 171, 184, 228
Autogestion, 79–81, 220

Balibar, E., 239
Bérégovoy, P., 182
Bergeron, A., 229
Berlinguer, E., 110
Blanqui, A., 17, 24, 216
Bloc des Gauches, 13, 20
Bloc National, 22, 29
Bloc Ouvrier et Paysan, 30
Blum, L., 27, 36–7, 42, 48, 78
Borella, F., 184
Bouchardeau, H., 190, 243, 247
Bourdet, C., 180
Brana, P., 184
Brousse, P., 24
Brown, B. E., 168

Cartel des Gauches, 13, 148
Cartel des Non, 158
Centre d'Etudes de Recherches et d'Education Socialiste (CERES), 48, 53, 55–6, 59, 62, 70, 79, 83, 86, 173, 229
Chaban-Delmas, J., 233
Champigny Manifesto, 100, 109
Chevènement, J-P., 58, 64, 201, 237
Chirac, J., 150, 240, 243, 246
Clubs, 52–5, 163
Combes, E., 20
Common Programme, 57, 125, 170, 172, 208

Confédération Française Démocratique de Travail (CFDT): development, 215, 219–20; and the PCF, 215–18; and the PS, 57, 171, 227–9; and ideology/strategy, 220–1; organisation and membership, 223–7, 229; and relations with government, 232-4
Confédération Française des Travailleurs Chrétiens (CFTC), 229, 224
Confédération Générale du Travail (CGT): development, 215–18; and ideology/strategy, 221–2; and the PCF, 115–16, 131, 221, 229–31, 243; and the PS, 227–9; organisation and membership, 223–9, 232–4
Confédération Générale du Travail-Force Ouvrière (CGT-FO), *see Force Ouvrière*
Confédération Générale du Travail Unitaire (CGTU), 217–18
Convention des Institutions Républicaines (CIR), 52, 55
Crépeau, M., 201, 210, 237–8, 242–3

Daladier, E., 41
Dayan, G., 72
Defferre, G.: and 1965 Presidential Election, 51, 78, 157–9, 162; and 1969 Presidential Election, 54, 89; and Marseilles, 74, 209
Delors, J., 58
Depreux, E., 40
Dreyfus Affair, 5, 19-21
Duclos, J., 150
Duverger, M., 180

272

Ecologie '78, 190
Elleinstein, J., 95, 124, 239
Europe, PS attitude towards, 84–5
Eurocommunism, 96–7, 111, 119

Fabre, R., 59, 61
Fajon, E., 127
Faure, M., 59
Faure, P., 27, 36
*Fédération de l'Education
    Nationale* (FEN), 219, 224
*Fédération de la Gauche Démocrate
    et Socialiste* (FGDS), 52–4, 149,
    152, 162–5, 200
Fiszbin, H., 125
Fiterman, C., 122, 127, 128
Force Ouvrière (FO), 218, 221, 224–
    7
Fourier, C., 17, 216
Front Populaire, see Popular Front

Gambetta, L., 17
Garaudy, R., 117, 123
Gauchisme, 186–90
Gaulle, C. de, 40, 151, 241
Gaullism, 10, 39, 152
Gaullist Parties, 43, 49, 151–3
Giscard d'Estaing, V., 161, 240–1,
    245–6
Goguel, F., 5
Gramsci, A., 106
Gremetz, M., 122
Guèsde, J., 24, 26

Henry, A., 229, 235
Herzog, P., 122
Humanité, L', 29, 35, 131–4

Jacobinism, 9, 14
Jaurès, J., 25, 78
Jospin, L., 72, 145, 237
Jouhaux, L., 217
Joxe, P., 229
Juquin, P., 96

Kanapa, J., 96
Kéhayan, J., 239
Kriegel, A., 27, 30, 117, 129
Krivine, A., 187, 188

Laguiller, A., 187, 190, 243
Lajoinie, A., 122, 240
Laurent, P., 124
Lavau, G., 144
Lefranc, G., 13
Leroy, R., 123, 128
Libération, 191
Ligue Communiste Revolutionnaire
    (LCR), 187–8, 243
Lutte Ouvrière 185, 188, 191

May 1968, 8, 182, 220
Maire, E., 229
Marchais, G., 110, 119, 122–3; and
    Union de la Gauche, 127, 170;
    and dissent in PCF, 122, 125; and
    PCF Congresses, 119, 122, 127;
    and Eastern Europe, 109, 128;
    and Afghanistan, 95, 97; and
    1981 elections, 144, 145, 149,
    239–44
Mallet, S., 78, 180
Mauroy, P., 56, 62, 70, 85, 93, 246
Mayer, D., 37
Mendès-France, P., 42, 182
Millerand, A., 24
Mitterrand, F., 65, 81, 200–1;
    Presidential elections 1965, 52,
    54, 153, 162–3; Presidential
    elections 1974, 58, 184;
    Presidential elections 1981, 89,
    149, 236–7, 240–6; and FGDS,
    51, 59, 163–7; and *Union de la
    Gauche*, 165–78; and Congresses
    of PS, 54–5, 56–7, 62, 65, 69–72,
    236–7; as President, 246–8
*Mouvement de la Jeunesse
    Communiste de France* (MJCF),
    100
*Mouvement des Radicaux de
    Gauche* (MRG), 60, 81, 160, 165,
    169, 200, 237–8, 240, 242–3,
    247–8
Mouvement des Reformateurs, 160
Mouvement Républicain Populaire
    (MRP), 11, 33, 37, 152, 154, 219
Mollet, G., 37, 40, 49–54, 83, 228;
    and elections, 50, 159; and PCF,

50, 166; and Alliances, 50, 159, 166–7

Nancy (1970 by-election), 160
Nazi-Soviet Pact, 32–3, 101

Ouvrièrisme, 100, 212

Paris Commune, 22
Parti Communiste Français (PCF): general, 7, 10; and origins, 26, 29–35, 94; and Comintern, 27, 30, 36, 135; and organisation, 112–29; and membership, 31, 35, 118, 136–40; and elections, 32, 149–50, 171, 174, 200–3, 238–48; and electorate, 140–5; and alliances, 34, 96–7, 100, 102, 105–6, 119, 128–9, 138, 148, 153, 165–76, 203–8; and congresses, 29, 100, 108, 110, 116, 118–19, 122, 126–9, 170; and Eurocommunism, 96–7, 111, 119; and trades unions, 102, 115, 131, 217–18, 221, 223, 229–32; and finances, 133–6; and dissent, 117, 123–6, 211, 238–9; and Czechoslovakia, 98, 110, 156, 167; and press and propaganda, 129–33
Parti Communiste Marxiste-Léniniste de France (PCMLF), 188
Parti Radicale, see Radicals
Parti Socialiste (PS): general, 7; and origins, 55–7, 78; and organisation, 57, 59, 62–72, 77, 92–3; and membership, 57, 73, 85–9; and elections, 58, 73, 78, 149–50, 171, 174, 200–3, 236–8, 240–8; and electorate, 89–92; and alliances, 60, 65, 148, 153, 165–78, 203–8; and trades unions, 222–3, 227–9; and congresses: Epinay-sur-Seine, 56–7, 227–8; Grenoble, 58; Pau 58, 170; Nantes, 59, 89; Metz, 62, 63, 68–72, 236; Créteil, 65, 237; and finance, 75–7; and press,

74–5; *see also* Section Française de l'Internationale Ouvrière
Parti Socialiste Autonome (PSA), 40, 180
Parti Socialiste de France, 25
Parti Socialiste Francais, 25
Parti Socialiste Unifié (PSU), 57, 89, 180–6, 191, 206, 243, 247
Philip, A., 40
Pisani, E., 58, 160
Pompidou, G., 149–150, 247
Poperen, J., 78, 86, 180
Popular Front (1936), 31–2, 41, 48, 53, 212
Project Socialiste (1980), 63, 84–5
Proudhon, P-J., 17, 216

Radicals, 6, 10, 18–22, 40–2, 51, 59, 152, 154, 165
Ramadier, P., 34
Rémond, R., 11
Rocard, M., 14, 48, 57, 62, 69–70, 81, 162, 182–4, 201, 207, 236–7
Rony, J., 124

Savary, A., 55
Section Française de l'Internationale Ouvrière (SFIO): general, 6, 47–54, 82, 154; and origins, 22–6, 29, 35–40; and organisation, 54; and membership, 39, 85; and elections, 36, 38, 157; and alliances 37–8, 50, 51, 59, 148, 158–60, 167; and trades unions, 36, 217
Séguy, G., 132, 220, 223, 231
Servan-Schreiber, J-J., 59, 160–1
Siegfried, A., 12
Soulié, M., 160
Soviet Union, 34, 94–8, 108, 155–6

Third Force, 37, 159–61, 203
Thorez, M., 30, 34, 95, 103, 108, 119
Tiersky, R., 144
Touchard, J., 14–15

Tours, Congress of (1920), 26–9, 47, 217

Tripartism, 33, 37

Union des Clubs pour le Renouveau de la Gauche (UCRG), 53–5

Union pour la Démocratie Française (UDF), 161–2, 240

Union de la Gauche, 13, 60–1, 78–9, 105–6, 128–9, 138, 168, 174–5, 208, 212, 222–3

Union de la Gauche Socialiste et Démocrate (UGSD), 170

Vassart, A., 32

Viveret, P., 83

Waldeck Rochet, 103, 119

Williams, P., 37

Wohl, R., 25

Zeldin, T., 11